KV-545-322

The Spectacle of Democracy

Spanish Television, Nationalism, and Political Transition

Richard Maxwell

University of Minnesota Press
Minneapolis
London

UNIVERSITY OF PLYMOUTH

Item No. 900 276847-9

Date 3 0 AUG 1996 B

Class No. 384.5540946 MAX
Contl. No. 08166 235 70

LIBRARY SERVICES

Copyright 1995 by the Regents of the University of Minnesota

All rights reserved. No part of this publication may be reproduced, stored
in a retrieval system, or transmitted, in any form or by any means,
electronic, mechanical, photocopying, recording, or otherwise, without the
prior written permission of the publisher.

Published by the University of Minnesota Press
111 Third Avenue South, Suite 290, Minneapolis, MN 55401-2520
Printed in the United States of America on acid-free paper

Library of Congress Cataloging-in-Publication Data

Maxwell, Richard, 1957–
    The spectacle of democracy : Spanish television, nationalism, and
political transition / Richard Maxwell.
        p.   cm.
    Includes bibliographical references and index.
    ISBN 0-8166-2357-0 (hc: alk. paper)
    ISBN 0-8166-2358-9 (pbk.: alk. paper)
    1. Television broadcasting — Spain — History.   2. Television and
politics — Spain.   I. Title.
PN1992.3.S6M39   1994
384.55'4'0946 — dc20   94-18784

The University of Minnesota is an
equal-opportunity educator and employer.

90 0276847 9

WITHDRAWN
FROM
UNIVERSITY OF PLYMOUTH
LIBRARY SER

The Spectacle of Democracy

For my parents,
Ruth Lorraine Shannon and
William Tate Maxwell,
who met somewhere between
Loveland and Whynot

Contents

Abbreviations

ANIEL   Asociación Nacional de Industrias Electrónicas (Spanish Association of the Electronics Industry)

AP   Alianza Popular

CCRTV   Corporació Catalana de Ràdio i Televisió (Catalan Corporation of Radio and Television)

CEOE   Confederación Española de Organizaciones Empresariales (Spanish Confederation of Business Organizations)

CRTVG   Compañía de Radiotelevisión de Galicia (Galician Radio and Television Company)

EC   European Community

EITB   Euskal Irrati Telebista (Basque Radio and Television)

ERM   exchange rate mechanism

ETA   Euskadi ta Askatusuna (Euskadi and Liberty)

ETB   Euskal Telebista (Basque Television)

FORTA   Federación de Organizaciones de Radiotelevisiones Autonómicas (Federation of Autonomous Radio and Television Organizations)

LOC   Ley de Ordenación de las Comunicaciones (Regulatory Law of Communications)

LOT   Ley de Ordenación de las Telecomunicaciones (Regulatory Law of Telecommunications)

OECD   Organization for Economic Cooperation and Development

ONCE   Organización Nacional de Ciegos de España (Spanish National Organization of the Blind)

PCE   Partido Comunista Español (Spanish Communist Party)

PRISA   Promotores de Informaciones S.A.

PSOE   Partido Socialista Obrero Español (Spanish Socialist Workers Party)

RTVA   Radio y Televisión de Andalucía (Canal Sur) (Andalusian Radio and Television)

RTVE   Radiotelevisión Española (Spanish Radio and Television)

SER   La Sociedad Española de Radiodifusión

TVE   Televisión Española

TVG   Televisión de Galicia

UCD   Unión de Centro Democrático (Union of the Democratic Center)

UGT   Unión General de Trabajadores (General Union of Workers)

Acknowledgments

It is a pleasure to remember companions, colleagues, and friends whose lives crossed with mine in the space of this study; they made a difference. With Alda Blanco, I became a traveler; without her, I would not have begun a later journey that led me back to Madrid. Isabel Romero helped me gain access to the executive offices of government and, even more daunting, of the phone company. Among the dear friends who compensated for underfunded research support were César Bobis, Paca Aranjuelo, Mariano Eizaguirre, David and Maimen, Juan and Rosa, Karmentxu and Pili; in Bilbao were Jon and Begonia. Gratitude goes to my mentors in Spain, Miquel de Moragas for his help in Barcelona and, in Madrid, Enrique Bustamante. Roberta Astroff helped me long ago to reach Moragas, and I remember. Others who provided the interviews that contribute to part III of this book are acknowledged officially in the bibliography. In Spain, too many friends remain who deserve mention — I promise to make it up in *copas*.

There are some who keep a place in my heart (rentfree, as one of them always says) whom I must thank. Iris and Carlos Blanco will remain forever an intimate part of my life in Spain; they were perhaps my best teachers on that and other subjects. And from Curro, who did not survive, I learned the language.

My colleagues and graduate students at Northwestern University deserve many thanks for the stimulation that helped clarify the ideas expressed here. Victor Sampedro deserves special mention in this regard.

Finally, I want to thank my distant colleagues who read early drafts and contributed in immeasurable ways to this book: Tom Streeter and

John Fiske, who confronted me at the beginning; John Downing and Dan Schiller, who helped me at the end. Thanks especially to Dan, who read parts of the present book more than once and whose engaging criticisms forced me to sharpen my arguments. An emphatic acknowledgment of debt goes to Janaki Bakhle, my editor, who took this project seriously and offered the perfect mix of intelligence, wit, and unruly debate to make this a better book. Thanks are also due Laura Westlund, whose copyediting was impressively thorough and clarifying.

And to MV in sunglasses—you know who you are—thanks.

Preface

Who's Speaking?

My authorship of this book may be explained in two ways. One is personal, the other is professional. Unlike many American Hispanists, my introduction to Spain was far removed from an academic setting. I lived and worked as a laborer in Spain between 1977 and 1981. This gave me a particular purchase on the post-Franco period. I was strongly influenced by the social ferment that characterized the transition from dictatorship to democracy. Music, fashion, film, theater, spectacles, neighborhood festivals, coffeehouses, bars, meetings and demonstrations, poetry readings, visual arts, graffiti — all of these were sites of personal experiences; they were places in which I witnessed, and participated in, the popular war of words over the meaning of democratic culture. It is here that my knowledge of Spain's transition took root. I held a strong utopian belief in the power of the popular, in the strength of culture to make a difference.

But I also worked, sought work, was unemployed, and foreign. It was not an easy life, though friends and extended families of friends made life more than bearable. When things got tough my optimism may have been replaced with a more skeptical view, but I never became too disheartened or cynical. There was the attempted coup d'état of February 1981, preceded by the constant threat of fascist resurgence in the military. A couple of years before that, my best friend was arrested without reason and held for a month in a country where police were known to torture political activists and regional separatists. I encountered and protested the censorship of artists, theater groups, and journalists. I was drawn to the rise of nationalist politics in the regions, trying to understand as best I could what was going on during the first elections in the Basque Country. I was close to many workers and families of workers who suffered increasing impoverishment, but who showed an incredible sense of humor and optimism—often in telling contrast to union leaders. Friends, who like me were immigrant workers or professionals, though mostly Latin American, were constantly trying to make ends meet—planning, building, selling, whatever. The explosion of city life in Madrid could not hide the widening gap between the all-out commercialization of urban culture and the decline of living standards in the countryside. Finally, only the most self-centered were ignorant of the institutional abuse of women, who fought to organize in the neighborhoods, at party congresses, and within the Women's Institute in the Ministry of Culture. Of the too few years I lived in Spain, these are just some of the stories I cannot fully tell here, although bits and pieces will surface in chapters of this book.

I do want to tell one story. On May 2, 1978, I was dancing in my neighborhood in Madrid, celebrating the defeat of the French that had taken place during the previous century. A woman named Amor, who was born in Russia (actually by then the Soviet Union) and raised in Spain as a communist during the years of the fascist regime, was grilling some Spanish sausages in order to make *bocadillos*. She would sell these at a stand next to the arch at the center of the Plaza Dos de Mayo, the focal point of this yearly fiesta. The smell of the sausages triggered an attack of munchies so extreme that even with a full stomach I couldn't resist, but I was too frustrated by my poor use of the language to bring myself to ask. I was aware that what was holding me back was a nagging embarrassment that accompanies cultural incompetence—my Spanish was too fresh, too untried, not mine, I was shy. I tugged on the shirtsleeves of my companion and asked in English for someone to help me get some food. Infantile megalomania, primal need, and so on. But my friend would not help; everyone was tired of the dependence. I was getting angry because no one would translate for me. Amor was watching us, and she was getting even angrier than I. "Es imposible dejar de llevar el Yanqui por dentro," she said. Amor was looking at me. The condescending smile got to me. Of course I understood the words; I had been in Spain for more than six months. She was saying that I couldn't speak because I refused to give up the Yankee inside of me; she said it as if to imply that a kind of imperiousness I internalized denied me access to the culture (well, the food). I felt that accusation very strongly. I looked at her and said, in fluent Spanish, that I wanted a sausage. I realized that I was embarrassed not at my language deficiency but at my own complacency.

Maybe it's an exaggeration, but I felt as though my mental geography had changed that night. My physical presence did not seem to be enough to justify feeling like I was "in Spain." Amor was saying as much. I was really ashamed, though the level of my shame is, in truth, too personal to relate here (I was only just twenty-one). From that moment on I suffered a kind of identity mutilation. I tried to act in a different way; at every turn I tried to blow apart what I had been. What I was destroying, what I was producing, I really didn't understand or couldn't locate. What is a cultural identity? What are those characteristics that make one person Spanish and another not? What might happen to me if I continued being something defined in my mind as not being what I had been? But I lived there, I was not a tourist.

I was very happy when people began to remark how they weren't always sure where I was from. I began to hear side comments about how I was, of course, not Spanish, but not really American either. At one point that was difficult: fluency and style brought on some sort of mutation. I was beginning to become something I had not been. But Spanish, I could never achieve that—I was simply less American. And that would be all that I could ever be. It was expected. But it was enough so that the following May 2, Amor gave me little grief and a lot of *bocadillo*.

It still bothers me that people need some sort of credentials to be what they were not originally, or to justify an accent, a change in their vowel formation—even if we agree that there is no origin. Expatriates, I suppose, all get bothered by the same feeling. The question is how they get that way—or is it how they don't get another way? The loneliness of total immersion into another culture feels similar to what it must be like when an acrobat flies without a safety net. It is a kind of emotional risk you take alone, but making the leap changes you forever.

In 1985, 1986, and 1988 I flew back to Spain to conduct the academic research for this book. In graduate school I began to write about Spain, so the book could be said to be the product of a decade of academic work on Spanish culture, mass media, and broadcast policy. Even though I could add a few nonacademic years to that, the professional story of my authorship begins in 1983.

Like others with an interest in critical communication research, I had been influenced by cultural studies and poststructuralism. To understand the statecraft of the transition from dictatorship to democracy in Spain, I needed additional theoretical frameworks besides those offered by these approaches. A poststructuralist approach, with its emphasis on the family of meanings and the discursive practices in and around texts, obviously provided a model for "reading" press and government documents; it also helped to catch me in my own discursive strategies. Still, more obviously, poststructuralism could not address the problems of economic crisis that shaped the political horizon during the transition. And although British cultural studies emphasized the relevance of the state and provided insights into the intersection of economics and politics (especially in its Gramscian idiom), it did not offer a model for understanding a state in transition. In fact, when I began my academic research, few works theorized postdictatorship statecraft in relation to cultural or communication policy.

Since then, of course, much has been written on transitions to democracy, civil society, and the extension of the public sphere. This book is less a response to—or confrontation with—these last, and more of a contribution to that literature. I think Hispanists, perhaps only Hispanists, would agree that the subject of the Spanish transition in media and politics deserves its own book. A kind of caste system in European history and European media studies positions Spain on the margins— just go to any university history department and witness the geographical hierarchy in European studies. So instead of referencing its analysis of Spain against the nations privileged by academic canon or, more likely these days, the U.S. State Department, this book attempts to put democratic Spain, its transition, and its media, at the center. This is not to say that this book is without comparative rhetoric; frequent signposts help the reader who is not a specialist in Spanish politics or history.

In the end, I approached broadcast policy and the transitional state in Spain with an admixture of interpretive sociology, historiography, and a critical political economic perspective. Tying these academic approaches together, and giving emotional substance to the adventure of doing research on media and the transition, is my memory of living in Spain. Between the celebrations and the difficulties around me, I was challenged to think beyond my own very local experiences and to focus on the operations of state and economic power. This explains my choice of method and system of analysis: to study political economy, society, and history—the distant operations of power, structure, and change. The hard part was dealing with how this professional approach changed the way I had been thinking about what was near to me, the stories I remember of my life in Spain. I confess the writing shows more of this distance than I'd prefer.

Primary sources for this study were collected in the form of direct interviews and interviews drawn from newspaper accounts, and from other personal observations of developments in Spanish television culture. Secondary materials included published and unpublished research, newspaper reports, and other materials from television and radio programs. I have relied on history written by some of the best-known Spanish and

Anglo-American Hispanists, although I have also cited lesser-known writers who offered a pithy phrase or clarified a particular episode of the transition. Unless otherwise noted, I translated most of the Spanish material quoted in the book, and I assume responsibility for any awkwardness.

The historical account of broadcast reform during the transition period is composed from interviews, newspaper stories, recent reports, and my personal record of events. Interviews were conducted with industry personnel from the state TV and regional systems, officials from the central state and regional governments, academic specialists, and research specialists at the Center for Documentation and Communication at the Autonomous University of Barcelona. A full list of contributors can be found in the bibliography.

Of course, I've tried to analyze the firsthand testimonial information from newspaper accounts critically in relation to the commercial press's interest in the privatization of TV. Other data were provided by the Center for Sociological Investigation in Madrid and EGM, a television ratings firm.

Finally, a word on the format of the book. Apart from the general introduction, most of the chapters are very brief. This is intentional. The organization furnishes easier access to particular themes (as in part I), or to specific episodes of the transition (as in part II), or to distinct spatial dimensions of Spanish television (as in part III). Readers interested in a quick picture of Spanish TV before and after the political transition might want to start by looking at the beginnings of the introduction and conclusion for background information prior to reading specific chapters. However, I encourage readers to proceed linearly in order to grasp the dimension of social change embedded in the geography of Spanish television and in the rendering of maps accompanying the text.

Introduction
The Decline of National Mass Media?

Three areas of social transition in Spain mark out the parameters of this book: the democratization of political institutions, the decentralization of political authority, and the transformation of the national model of television. The most prominent area examined here is the third. This is a book about the decline of the territorial imperative of the media system that democratic Spain inherited from the fascist dictatorship — an imperative that developed from a nationalist, centralist, monocultural perspective. It is also about the genesis of a new territorial imperative of the media that replaced the old — one that is transnationalist, regionalist, and multicultural. Nevertheless, the book makes sense of this transformation of television in Spain by laying stress on the politics of the transition to democracy, i.e., on the processes of democratization and decentralization. The question is how much stress to put on these external processes.

Causality has always been a central concern in media studies. The question of causality in the case of Spanish media and the politics of transition can be asked simply: are the media decisive causes of the political transition to democracy? And, simply reversed: are the politics of transition decisive causes of the media transformation? The premise of this book tends to reject media causality, but, as academic books written by media specialists are prone to do, the argument may at times appear to have it both ways. Risking betrayal of the discipline, this book makes the following commitment: the social and media transitions are interdependent, yet democratization and decentralization are the weightier elements. Stated flatly, the media did not cause, or play a significant historical role in bringing about, the transition to democracy in Spain.

This is not meant to suggest that there were no episodes in which radio, TV, and the press played important parts in the processes of democratization and decentralization. Rather, proportion accorded to the episodic role is the issue. The media were, without a doubt, means of communicating, demonstrating, or evoking processes at the center of the transition; they were a crucial component, a transitional mechanism. But to contend that these episodic protagonisms caused social change is outright technological determinism, an approach to media history that does grave disservice to the people and processes at the heart of social change.

In matters of causality, then, the arguments of this book borrow the historiographical template from Raymond Williams's *Television: Technology and Cultural Form*. Basically, the general procedure emphasizes social transformation, while technology and cultural form are treated as outcomes of action taken by real people who make decisions under conditions generated by past and present social changes—changes they might or might not have directly contributed to. Social change, in this sense, might or might not be manifest in institutions and institutional power, but institutions are definitely sites of action for and against the forces of change.

In these terms, the Spanish television system made the transition from an apparatus of dictatorship to a forum of civil society because human intentions sought to make it so. These intentions were nonetheless disputed, compromised, and denied as well as encouraged and shaped by the intentions of others. Responsible for these intentional actions were individuals, organizations of civil society and official politics, and the institutional imperatives of the state, local authorities, and capitalist businesses. These were the general relationships that shaped the larger social transformation, the transition from dictatorship to democracy in Spain.

National mass media can be defined as the ensemble of institutions of mass communication that have a definite territorial purview matching technically, or aligned with politically, the administrative space of the modern nation. This book focuses exclusively on television for two reasons: it was the most highly centralized of all mass media in Spain, and it was the medium most closely tied to the national project of the Francoist state. In both technical and political terms, Spanish television was organized like the authoritarian state it served: it spoke from the center in one language about one nation ruled by one state.

The transition to democracy in Spain radically changed this relation of television to the state and the nation, to language and governance. Out of the struggles and reforms of the transition arose three key media policies that established a new institutional framework for television in Spain. These are the Statute of Radio and Television (1980 RTVE Statute), the Third Channel Law (1983–84), and the private TV law (1988). Each of these policy events and each of the institutional transformations connected to them contributed to the decline of the national mass media system created during and after the Spanish civil war (1936–39).

In what sense did the national television system decline? Basically, new radio and television institutions emerged from the regions of Spain, while commercial media promoters fought for a stake in private radio and television at local and national scales. The impact of these infranational forces was significant. They weakened the internal boundaries of the national television of the national state; yet at the same time they made feasible the greater presence of supranational forces. This book demonstrates how decentralization and privatization had the effect of extending the transnational phenomenon in Spanish media. In the end, the model of national mass media was no longer viable; the media of small-nation nationalism and the forces of transnationalism signaled this decline.

It is an obvious overstatement, however, to suggest that the national television system of Spain has lost its prominence. Certainly, the political region of the nation-state is still present, and powerful, as is the attendant electronic region of radio and television. What this book argues is that the territorial dominance of a strictly national mass media system is diminishing; that the decline of national mass media was an outcome, indeed a goal, of democratization in Spain; and that the "deterritorialized" national media system gave rise to new political and electronic regions.

The boundaries of these new regions can be located at both the infranational scale (i.e., inside the nation) and at the supranational scale (i.e., linked to processes beyond the nation). This book analyzes the preferences for democracy in Spain (individual, group, and institutional) that led to general changes in the television industry and to the decline of the national model. As part II of this book stresses, such preferences were, with few exceptions, the only available ways for political actors to see, and explain, the social transformations that caused the political crisis and transition; this is manifest, moreover, in the discourse of TV reform. As such, these preferences are at once identified as contending political ideologies and as screens that filter the view of distant economic causes. While preferences for democracy appear to give reason, and definition, to political action—the transition in close-up, as it were—political ideology and action are analyzed within a much wider field of global economics.

As a result of this approach, the book engages a number of crucial issues in contemporary international media theory. Before discussing these theoretical issues, it will be helpful to summarize the main policy events and institutional changes that have affected Spanish television.

The first policy event, the RTVE Statute, was generated in a period of compromises, impasse resolutions, and pacts among the major political parties in the late 1970s. The 1980 statute established norms to ensure a plurality of political influence over the national network, Radiotelevisión Española (RTVE); to order state guarantees that broadcasting be treated as an essential public service; to protect open and free expression; and to suggest that the autonomous regional communities of Spain might have new broadcast channels operating in their zones. Two institutional changes followed: the eventual democratization of RTVE (still, some argue, in transit) and the parallel decentralization of television, an aspect of the wider pattern of political reform associated with the reorganization of the centralist state.

Without approved legislation from the central state, the parliaments of the Basque Country and Catalonia approved their own television systems — the Basques in May 1982, the Catalans in May 1983. These actions constituted the most significant institutional change of broadcasting since the nationalization of radio during the Spanish civil war.[1] Together they were a direct assault on the national law that had regulated radiowave communication for more than seventy years, contravening a 1908 royal decree that gave the central state the right to control all technology using the electromagnetic spectrum. Nevertheless, and missing the mark by many months, the central government approved in December 1983 its own Third Channel Law to regulate the establishment of additional networks in the Autonomous Communities.

The Third Channel Law came into force in 1984, months after the Basques and Catalans had begun broadcasting (experiments started in December 1982 and August-September 1983, respectively). It was designed to decentralize the state broadcasting system and thus was a very important policy event for the transition to democracy. In principle, it was meant to cause controlled denationalization of television by creating channels that responded to the plurality of cultures, languages, and communities within the Spanish territory — a multinationalism suppressed since the end of the civil war. The law ordered, however, that decentralization be carried out in line with norms established in the constitution and the RTVE Statute, especially the sections of these that retained the state's control, and RTVE's dominance, over the airwaves. The two regional parliaments in Catalonia and the Basque Country, and later the Galician parliament as well, balked at this; they understood that their separate right to broadcast was not dependent on the state. They maintained that their own statutes of autonomy, in combination with relevant clauses in the 1978 constitution and the RTVE Statute, protect independent action in this area. For more than a decade now, the contradictory mandates within and between these legal documents have been deployed in battles over rights of access to regional airwaves.[2] On a smaller scale, a similar battle developed over local, village-level television, which passed from a situation characterized by what some Spanish writers affectionately call "alegal" broadcasts to one regulated by a posteriori legislation to normalize spectrum use and state regulation.[3]

By 1990, eleven autonomous broadcast organizations were approved, six of which had already begun broadcasting on a daily basis.[4] In 1989, the directors of these systems had agreed to merge into a national federation of autonomous broadcasters, known as FORTA (the Federation of Autonomous Radio and Television Organizations), creating a network of public broadcasters to rival RTVE. Participating in FORTA are regional corporations from the Basque Country, Catalonia, Andalusia, Galicia, Valencia, Madrid, and Murcia.

RTVE remained throughout the transition a commercial (albeit not-for-profit), state-controlled system with two television channels and two radio networks. For obvious reasons, when the state was the only television broadcaster, the private media promoters, regional authorities, advertisers, and advertising agencies saw RTVE's hold over the airwaves as a monopoly over audience attention—a monopoly, moreover, with both economic and political value. The regional autonomous systems broke this monopoly, and with FORTA competed within a short-lived duopoly of publicly owned, commercial, not-for-profit television networks. By the late 1980s, with three regional television networks and an expanded national network, the total investment in television advertising had been pushed upward of 1,000 percent over investment in 1975—and privately owned, commercial TV had not yet even started.

The most controversial policy battle during the transition concerned the development of a law of private television. Indeed, in many ways the legalization of commercial, for-profit TV became emblematic of the problems of political transition to democracy. Most commentators argue that privatization was held up for over a decade because the process became "politicized."[5] Though this is true in the general sense that official politics took over the process of privatization, apparently restricting decision making to the closed ranks of a political class, "politicization" is, as this book shows, a narrowly contentious way of understanding media reform in the transition.

The outcome, however, was the third major media policy event of the Spanish transition, a 1988 law and technical plan for private TV.

Law 10 1988, May 3, of Private Television furnished three licenses for the bidding of private corporations, a three-phase framework for the extension of universal territorial coverage, and restrictions on legal ownership to promote conglomeration and multiple partnerships rather than monopoly control. The technical plan (Royal Decree 1362 1988, November 11) created an independent public company, Retevisión, to manage the technical infrastructure, effectively delinking RTVE from the central source of its economic and political control over the airwaves. Today all broadcasters must pay an access fee to use the public infrastructure.[6]

By the end of 1989, three new private television channels had begun test broadcasts; regular transmissions began in 1990. By 1991, the market share of national audience attention broke down as follows: two TV channels of RTVE together registered 55.4 percent (down from nearly 90 percent in 1989), FORTA companies received 15.4 percent, two private broadcasters brought in 27.8 percent (Telecinco, 17.0 percent and Antena-3, 10.8 percent), and a third private company, a pay-TV outfit called Canal Plus, reported 1.0 percent (the market share of private channels has since increased). The remainder, 0.4 percent, was attributed to the municipal and local television systems (over one hundred such systems exist in Catalonia alone).[7] These figures show that the national system remains a prominent force, but they also demonstrate how the national state system alone no longer regulates the daily routine of nationwide audiences. Moreover, once they are broken down to reflect the region-by-region competition for audience attention, the fortunes of private, state, and regional systems can be shown to range widely (see chapter 14).

In a little more than fifteen years, Spanish television made the transition from absolute state control to a regulated, competitive system of national and regional networks of mixed private and public ownership. About 98.9 percent of Spanish households own a television. Before 1980, less than 1 percent of Spanish households had a VCR; today about half of them do, and a little over 10 percent per day watch a video. On average, people watch about three and a half hours of television each day, mostly in the afternoon and late evening hours.[8] Except for the occasional strip show or pornographic film, the programming of all channels is very similar to American broadcast television (not to mention the dominance of U.S. products as a percentage of all telefilms, series, and feature films broadcast). Though this book does not address program content, a matter of deserved attention, chapter 14 discusses some of the programming strategies of the different firms. The quality varies as much as in any broadcast system, and like most national media industries everywhere, the various Spanish TV channels repulse and attract on a pretty even score across their audiences.[9]

A few points should be added to this summary. First, revenues have been slacking off in the past few years. The initial euphoria of promoters, managers, and advertisers has begun to be tempered with doses of the economic reality of rising costs and downward adjustments for regular viewership; and the need for public subsidy for mass media increases at the same time that public budgets shrink. Second, the integration of Spain into the European Community (EC) played a significant role in shaping the legal framework for private TV and the technical plan. The most disruptive effect of EC membership, however, has been the monetary submission of the Spanish peseta to the deutsche mark, via the exchange rate mechanism, resulting in serious devaluations of the national currency (this issue as it relates to the media industry is taken up in the conclusion). Also related to EC membership were the major reform law of telecommunications (LOT) and the investments leading up to the 1992 exposition held in Seville and the Olympic Games held in Barcelona, which placed Spain and two important regions in the international limelight — recall the media baptism of Spanish democracy in the international TV coverage of the 1992 Olympics. And finally, new channels and new reforms continue to emerge: a second channel each in the Basque and Catalan systems; a third requested by RTVE; further privatization campaigns sponsored by the conservatives of the Partido Popular, who did not get anything from previous reforms (they were earlier called the Alianza Popular); satellite channels, with and without cable enterprises; and many grassroots adventures that include — besides local TV — closed circuit community video, urban radio pirates, and video and audio piracy.

At least three salient issues in the preceding summary call attention to the problems facing international media theory in the 1990s. These can be formulated in terms of privatization, globalization (or transnationalization), and regionalization (or decentralization). Although each of these issues can be identified and analyzed in other locations, the Spanish media experience is illuminating because of the clearly defined bonds and collisions among regional, national, and transnational media spaces. This chapter aims to clarify the problems faced by international media theory when it confronts this nexus of global to local media spaces.

Privatization and the Transnational Phenomenon

Michèle and Armand Mattelart argue that the "era of accusatory testimony against the imperialism of the transnationals has given way to an era of banalization of the transnational phenomenon, which tends to become further diluted under the appellation of 'globalization of the economy.' "[10] Change has occurred, they argue, at the point where the directors of national economies and defenders of national cultures can no longer afford to denounce transnational capital—the patron saint of international economic growth among industrialized countries in the postwar period. The key boundary points are protectionist barriers. Throughout Europe, for example, these barriers have been removed, leaving little of the grand agency once enjoyed by national state powers (most particularly during the interwar years).[11] As the Mattelarts put it, "the macrosubject is in sharp decline," but, they hasten to add, "this is not the case for all macrosubjects."[12]

Herbert I. Schiller, who along with Armand Mattelart is often credited for developing the cultural imperialism thesis, is succinct about which "macrosubject" is not in retreat: "Though no one has suggested that transnational corporations should run the world (not even their executives), no other candidate has stepped forward."[13] Schiller also observes a marked banalization of the transnational phenomenon among media scholars. He notes with dismay how the growing transnationalism of the "informational-cultural apparatus" is "treated by the currently dominant school of social analysis and cultural theory as hardly worth noticing."[14] At the political level, what gets noticed are the declining fortunes of nations, the fiscal crisis of states, and subsequently the crisis management of the nation-state, which now promotes—to escape crisis—alliances with the same external powers that not more than two decades ago were regularly accused of being cultural colonialists.

One explanation for the "banalization of the transnational phenomenon" among some Western intellectuals is that throughout Europe—where only a generation ago the most highly centralized and protectionist media in the world could be found—liberalization policies have opened the door to foreign investment, both private and public, in national television and telecommunications. There are, of course, regional projects promoted by the European Community (such as the directive *Television without Frontiers*) that have been established as defensive responses to regulate stable integration of European culture industries within the global economy, but such initiatives are far from being protectionist in the strict sense, and are viewed as barriers to trade only by U.S.-based megacorporations like Time Warner.[15]

In Europe, then, globalization of national media industries proceeds apace. It is in this context that many theorists of international communication have revised their accounts of national sovereignty and cultural imperialism in an adjustment to the reality of new transnational media spaces that surround them. The decline of state safeguards and the liberalization of national public media systems have understandably been the primary focus of these revisions.[16] As a consequence, the agitation against the breakup of the old cultural territory of the sovereign nation—a central, adversarial role played by cultural imperialism theorists in debates of the 1970s—is today not very fashionable. An irony of imperialism, informational or otherwise, is that in the dominant theory-producing countries of Europe and North America a general trend in published work downplays the role of national sovereignty and cultural imperialism, and somewhat complaisantly accepts transnational hegemony.[17]

This theoretical trend can also be appreciated in the context of dependency theory, the conceptual home of much of the writing on cultural and media imperialism. As Andre Gunder Frank, who advanced the theory of global dependency in the 1960s, argues, transnational determination of national outcomes is more formidable than ever; and political safeguards decline as a result. He notes that within the interdependent global economy today there is little freedom of action for governments, right or left, east or west, developed or not. After reviewing the economic policy choices in dozens of countries (some industrialized, some liberal-capitalist, some socialist, some authoritarian, some in Eastern Europe, others in Latin America, Africa, and Asia), Gunder Frank asks, "Why did and do *all* these governments follow essentially the *same* economic policies in the face of the same material economic circumstances?" He answers bluntly, "Because they *had to*. That is, they all *had* to do, not what 'the people' wanted, but what economic circumstances demanded." He adds that national social conditions and politics were not decisive of these circumstances. Rather, it "was and is first and foremost the *dependence within the world economy* that sets out the narrow margins of 'democratic' choice and policy."[18]

Gunder Frank presents a scenario of states powerless to determine their own destiny. It is a scenario in which, besides economic policy, national policies of communication are overdetermined by transnational economic circumstances. The transnational phenomenon is the focus, the hegemony of transnationalism the conclusion, and national politics the loser.

The Mattelarts note that one problem with models of dependency (and they imply world-systems models too) is that some theorists are prone to extend dependency so far as to instrumentalize the role of the nation-state within the international economy. What happens within national politics is explained away as a function of impersonal global systems.

Instead of this instrumentalism, the Mattelarts suggest that it is not politically practical to think that a plan to downsize the nation-state in the service of the international economy came off some corporate drawing board fully designed.[19] After all, they imply, don't global institutional preferences meet with some form of opposition, encouragement, or alteration? The Mattelarts argue that within each national political context a distinct "play of struggles and negotiations" significantly shapes the manner in which transnational phenomena get reproduced.[20] In other words, transnationalization cannot advance, or be contained, without political intervention at the local (national) level. Without denying the systemic extension of transnational power, the Mattelarts urge social and cultural theorists to indulge in reconceptualizing the nation-state in light of its "deterritorialization." The question this raises concerns what role there is for national politics and policy formulation in the era of transnationalization.

To advance this theoretical point, this book starts from the conviction that national politics still matter even if the national state is overshadowed by transnational phenomena.[21] This commitment trivializes neither transnational hegemony and global dependence nor the crisis of national states. Action counts, rather, and so too the interventions to organize cultural industries at local, regional, and national levels — the social dimensions of *infranational* processes.[22] The political history of broadcasting in Spain bears this out. In each of the episodes of television reform, new players and new styles of negotiation emerged that could not be foretold or easily explained by functionalist models, though dependent ties to the global political economy can be identified (for instance, by revealing class positions, and interests, favored by political action).

Part II of this book develops these political terms in an analysis of privatization of television in Spain. Leading this procedure is a premise that political actors only know what to think about causes and consequences of social transformation through ideology. Their preferences for democracy, and broadcast reform, furnish them with the frames (or what used to be called mediations) on the world that in turn define their courses of action — action that has social effects. In this sense, part II aims to identify primarily ideological determinations of material outcomes; that is, the politics of privatization.

At stake is the normative expectation that the central state will protect national culture against transnationalization, or, if you prefer, against cultural imperialism. Gunder Frank and others argue that the state can no longer be universally relied upon to serve as a deus ex machina; such an expectation stands up rather weakly to the whirlwind liberalizations of national markets during the past two decades.[23] How then do international scholars study the politics of media reform, given this deterritorialized national state?

Politics and social action have to be accounted for; decisions are made by different individuals and groups, intentions are not all allied, outcomes are unpredictable. The question, as always, is how and why individuals come together to act in unison, i.e., to act as a class. Whether a political alliance, an economic alliance, a religio-cultural alliance, or a nationalist alliance, the social interventions analyzed in this book are respected as human efforts to change or conserve existing institutions. At the same time, a healthy respect is accorded to the wider coordinating power of political economies that limit the purview of human action.

In chapters 4, 5, and 6, the analysis of TV reform shows how privatization was discursively legitimated but not instituted because the contending political ideologies that defined the transitional state had effectively stalled that outcome. These chapters examine the contested nature of policy discourses, and show how commercial TV was only "naturalized" once the language of market freedoms became the dominant idiom of the policy debate over media expression. The commercial press was especially active in eliding market ideology with democratic issues of expressive freedom, a point that cannot be emphasized enough.

The simplest lesson to be drawn from the episodes related in part II is that capital investors who want commercial media properties will use whatever means within their control to get their way. That's obvious enough. The harder lesson of part II is that such elite demands don't have to be privileged. The principles of democracy and free expression do not have to be abandoned to commercial media promoters.

Still, as these and the remaining chapters of part II show, noncommercial, democratic media systems were rarely considered by the major political parties in Spain. Specifically, ideas for alternatives remained poorly developed by the left opposition. In the absence of critical leftist media policies, there was a lack of constraint on commercial media. The failure of the left to legitimate an alternative cultural politics among decision makers came at a time when no natural link between commercial television and democracy existed. This crisis of commercial cultural hegemony, though short-lived, provided a range of possible outcomes, limited but not predetermined, that the left failed to confront. The reasons for this are addressed in more detail in chapter 1 and throughout part II; there is, however, little evidence to show that the left's failed cultural politics resulted from anything but its own bad analysis and strategy.

Major changes in the politics of privatization followed the Spanish Socialist Workers Party (PSOE) to power in 1982. At first, the PSOE resisted all reform of television (left and right) except for the RTVE Statute. Its eventual acceptance of private TV was anchored to its liberalization policy of the entire ensemble of telecommunication systems. The episodes related in chapters 7 through 11 show how the socialist party's reform reflected the growing importance it attached to informational-cultural industries as a key for solving the economic problems of the nation. The PSOE moved to enlarge electronics and informatics industries, privilege business usage of telecommunications, sell off parts of the public communication system, and manage the entry into Spain of global media interests. This policy helped make Spain one of the fastest-growing economies in the world in the 1980s, while opening the floodgates for foreign investment in its communication media.[24]

The socialist response to economic crisis appears to bear out Gunder Frank's assessment that government actions are overdetermined by global dependency. Thus, even as the analysis moves from structures to political action and back again, supranational formations are acknowledged as already and always putting cultural and political self-determination at risk.[25] Dependency of the Spanish economy results from a historical economic reliance on international markets at the expense of internal markets (see chapter 3). This link to the world system generated historically distinct cultural forms through the dictatorship, the early years of transition, and into the present; cultural forms that nonetheless have had progressive outcomes in one moment, reactionary effects in the next. The socialist management of privatization is analyzed as yet another ideological expression of this obdurate transnationalism, although one without socially progressive consequences.

My account of contemporary media politics in Spain reflects a small part of what Eric Hobsbawm ventures will become the conventional history of the late twentieth century, which he says "will inevitably have to be written as the history of a world which can no longer be contained within the limits of 'nations' and 'nation-states' as these used to be defined, either politically, or economically, or culturally, or even linguistically." Hobsbawm suggests that the world of the late twentieth century "will be largely supranational and infranational," but he cautions that "even infranationality, whether or not it dresses itself up in the costume of some mini-nationalism, will reflect the decline of the old nation-state as an operational entity." Thus an account of the local-global nexus begins with the withering historical force of state nationalisms; it begins, in Hobsbawm's words, with " 'nation-states' and 'nations' or ethnic/linguistic groups primarily retreating before, resisting, adapting to, being absorbed or dislocated by the new supranational restructuring of the globe."[26]

More decisive than national mass media in this context are the emergent forms of infranational and supranational cultural production and distribution.[27] The failure to account for the growing hegemony of this local-global nexus can be characterized as a kind of national masochism; resting all hope on the national state only improves the chances for further subjection of cultures residing within a national community.[28] Nonetheless, what this book aims to capture is how a particular "play of struggles and negotiations" within the national polity can make a difference for people. Even in the era of transnationals, hope rests on popular action and political participation. What this might mean in the end, as Armand Mattelart notes wryly, is that "every society gets the kind of modernity it deserves."[29]

Regionalization and the Local-Global Nexus

With the nation-state caught between supranational and infranational processes, specialists in international media theory and policy analysis have begun to rethink national cultural sovereignty. If the state no longer represents the key macrosubject, then theory has to account for a world in which interstate relations are an inadequate basis for understanding cultural sovereignty. Instead, research must focus on "the process of deterritorialization and reterritorialization, decomposition and recomposition of territories as meaningful units for collective identities."[30] This shift in thinking represents greater sensitivity to discrete differences among human collectivities; it welcomes a new ethic grounded in respect for alterity.[31] At the same time, however, much of this new thinking has neglected the transnational dimension, what Hobsbawm calls the "supranational restructuring of the globe."

In the absence of the cognitive maps of the global dimension, what counts is familiarity with what is near and particular to "us": the enhancement of life seems a local affair, its political economy distant and meaningless.[32] The classic agitation of the cultural imperialism thesis against transnationalism gets muted in this new thinking; denunciation of cultural imperialism seems to dishearten the joy that greets the abundant attention to the local, to the zones of cultural difference, to the folks who have hitherto been excluded from resources, participation, and expression within the national culture of the national community.[33]

The new thinking thus treats the imperial model as an anachronism. No longer is the emphasis on the global ubiquity of American cultural goods, the U.S.-hegemony in the world media market, the powerful U.S. government media apparatus (the world's largest), and all the other sources of an ideology rationalizing the spread of global capitalism. The revisionist thinking in international media studies opposes this sender-oriented world dominated by one international communicator, the United States.[34] As Annabelle Sreberny-Mohammadi puts it, the notion that there is "a hegemonic media pied piper leading the global media mice appears frozen in the realities of the 1970s, now a bygone era."[35]

Many compensations have been made for the shift to a receiver-oriented world without a central presence. Few have been simple, for while reception analysis appears concerned with popular rather than institutional preferences, more often than not research on media audiences maintains an institutional bias by inverting but not transcending the dominant sender model. For example, Ien Ang has shown how two receiver-oriented models—uses and gratifications and cultivation analysis—reproduce notions of passive media audiences through the construction of statistical typologies that serve the interests of media owners and paternalist policymakers.[36] People's agency is ironically figured out of such receiver-oriented equations.

These simple notions of receivers—along with other fictions in rational choice, functionalist, and utilitarian models—have been challenged along the way by various Marxist approaches in ideological criticism, especially by those inspired by Frankfurt school theorists and analyses of cultural subjection inspired by Althusser. These last have in turn been challenged for maintaining a view of receivers still constrained by top-down, institutional preferences.

Presently emerging as convention in the new thinking are poststructural approaches influenced by the work of Bakhtin, Bourdieu, and Foucault.[37] Human collectivities are identified not as senders or receivers but by positions they inhabit as acting subjects within a flexible though determinate range of social conditions. The old macrosubject, abstractly posited as the "United States," no longer constitutes a source of absolute, singular power. Instead, and besides the other a priori macrosubjects (the transnational corporation, the EC, Japan, national governments, white Europeans, and so on), there is a multiplicity of power relations *experienced* at the microlevel. "Counterpower" to cultural imperialism resides at the microlevel. That is, in *the local,* human collectivities resist becoming modern, misrecognize commands from the center, and escape the orientalist's imaginary. In these and many other ways, "the people" impose their own microregimes of truth—reactionary or progressive—on the international flow of media and cultural goods.[38]

By a curious twist of intellectual history, this revisionist emphasis on cultural experience rather than on global economic relations of capitalist expansion appears to have achieved what the original critique of cultural imperialism, first uttered over two decades ago, could not: namely, to break with the economistic tradition of the working-class movement and focus on the representational spaces where the struggle over hearts and minds takes place.[39] In principle, both approaches reject ethnocentric worldviews, both deplore the idea that elites in North Atlantic countries produce most of the knowledge about life on the planet, both seek to find ways to ensure balanced flows of expressions among the world's regions, and both want to end the stratification and segregation of cultures. The difference between revisionist reception studies and the cultural imperialism thesis resides in their orientations to political economy.

As the critique of cultural imperialism developed through the late 1960s and 1970s, it focused increasingly on institutional preferences and macroeconomic organization. This was due in no small degree to the rapid extension of new communication technologies, such as satellites, from the United States to Latin America, India, and other parts of the Third World; to the quadrupling of television households worldwide from 1961 to 1979 (reaching 453 million); and to the surge of investment from the United States, Japan, and Europe into the Third World that began in the 1960s.[40] With the onslaught of privatization campaigns that began in the 1950s in Britain, enveloping remaining public and state-regulated systems in Europe and North America in the 1970s and 1980s (Spain was a late target by comparison), the global merchants of communications had come home to take over the rest of the roost as well.

The theoretical response to these material fronts of imperialism was the stress on sender-oriented models. These models assumed correctly that technologically advanced, capital-rich states (headed by the United States) were causing global imbalances of informational-cultural exchange. Such imbalance, according to this model, privileges the ruling elites of these states and reproduces their worldwide hegemony. Around the world and in the core of these informational empires, the media industry was being removed from publicly accountable controls. In place of social controls, an ethos of accountability emerged that looked to the bottom line rather than public needs for guidance. It made sense that the messages, at least according to a sender-oriented model of cultural imperialism, could mean little else besides a sale of the goods, ideas, and sentiments in support of the established order.

The revisionist audience position shifted the burden onto the receiving end of cultural flows, perhaps, as Ang suggests, to counter with ethnographic evidence the disempowering effects of top-down models (either left or right).[41] Fred Fejes, in his 1981 review of the literature on media imperialism, put it this way:

> Little progress has been achieved in understanding specifically the cultural impact of transnational media on Third World societies. All too often the institutional aspects of transnational media receive the major attention while the cultural impact, which one assumes to occur, goes unaddressed in any detailed manner.[42]

In detailing the microprocesses of "the cultural impact," however, revisionist audience studies moved further away from the institutional aspects of media flows until, as Schlesinger observes, culture for the revisionists somehow managed to recede from the international political economy altogether.[43]

By delinking culture from the global political economy, the localist-experientialist thrust of the new thinking rhetorically "did in" and theoretically "outdid" the cultural imperialism critique. Rhetoric notwithstanding, its theoretical advance cannot be denied. The disaggregation of receiving publics into the actual human collectivities using media and communication *for themselves* is a welcome improvement, especially for understanding "counterpowers." However, as the new thinking advanced, what it left behind, as Schlesinger has suggested, is a sense of both the supranational restructuring of the globe and the stratifications inherent in the international political economy. As H. I. Schiller documents in his book *Culture Inc.*, the intellectual de-emphasis of political economy in cultural analysis and media policy has pleased to no end the ideological supporters of the transnational phenomenon.

This separation poses a great theoretical problem for international media theory. It distances the world of transnational cultural domination to a sideshow, a backdrop, a stage. It risks neglecting the staggering register of the global cultural institutions whose preferences for media use overdetermine, more than ever, those of nation and community—a list that includes AT&T, Time Warner, IBM, Young and Rubicam, Dun & Bradstreet, Capital Cities, GE, USIA, and others from within the United States; and Dentsu, WPP, Bertelsmann, Havas, Murdoch, Berlusconi, and others outside. This list is well known and much longer; it is a register of global informational-cultural businesses. The combined actions and influence of these companies and players highlight one central structural reality: the transnational media phenomenon has been produced by a remarkably unified class, one whose members' institutional preferences for capitalist expansion diverge only to the degree of state, military, and financial power supporting them.[44]

If the interstate bias of international media studies does not hold up to the changing operations of national states, then cultural sovereignty devolves from the state to infranational and supranational influences. If the focus is too narrowly pursued at the infranational (indeed at the local-experiential) level, a gaping hole in international media theory opens up. If, in contrast, theory holds stubbornly to a focus on the supranational scale, other gaps, much older and just as problematic, remain uncontested. What framework is there, then, for understanding the persistent conflicts over uses of communication technology at the interstate/international scale, or the conflicts among stratified and segregated cultural logics at the infranational scale (popular, traditional, modern, postmodern), or battles over the competing geostrategies of megacorporations?

This book does not pretend to provide a full answer. What part III acknowledges is that new modes of political expression have marked an emerging framework for international media theory with the language of the local (i.e., of locales, regions, small-nation nationalisms, and so on). In respect to this challenge, this book advances an analysis of regionalist television in democratic Spain. The theoretical issues that part III addresses generate from the nexus of local to global media spaces discussed here. This approach joins with the work of others who have recently sought a rapprochement between culture and political economy, between the near and the distant, and between local and global contexts — a rapprochement that has come to warrant a place on the agenda for international media studies in the 1990s.[45]

Within the landscape of electronic regions of Spain, part III examines the identity politics of the regional networks. Founded on a cultural politics of nationality, these networks instituted a new daily routine for the construction of a regionalist identity against the centralist culture of the nation-state. Such a routine established the boundaries of a distinct cultural space, where a national identity framed by a regionalized TV screen could invoke a nationalist practice opposed to the central presence of national state television. At the same time, however, this new regionalized "counterpower" furnished media marketers and advertisers with an effective demographic marker.

The analysis of part III is animated by the voices of those who fought over regional media spaces in Spain. Specifically, an experiential context is furnished by extensive interviews with policymakers who occupy positions representing center and region. The premise suggesting this procedure is that the geographical-historical tensions between centralism and regionalism are likely to be embodied by the statements of those tied to contrary territorial sentiments. In other words, the interviews make the abstractions of political theory and political economy concrete. Part III brings together the near and the distant and enlivens the conceptual issues it aims to advance in international media theory.

From the perspectives of cultural studies and what Cornel West calls a new cultural politics of difference, the battle to regionalize television within the territorial state of Spain represents a progressive, historically significant process. It might even be described as a casebook example drawn to support "the vocation" of cultural studies, which, as defined by Stuart Hall, seeks "to provide ways of thinking, strategies for survival, and resources to all those who are now—in economic, political, and cultural terms—*excluded from anything that could be called access to the national culture of the national community.*"[46] By establishing broadcast institutions to encourage identification with nationality, regionalism (or more precisely, small-nation nationalism) in Spain presents a radical challenge to the cultural hegemony of the nation-state, especially to the territorial ideology that omits ethnic or linguistic identification.[47]

Moreover, regional media politics in Spain challenge the interstate bias of much international media research. Regional and local firms are happily trespassing within the cultural borders of national broadcast systems. In terms of defining their publics, regional firms displace the national citizen of the modern nation-state. Their mode of address represents a realignment of audience identities with the felt nationalism of the local. Against the culture of the nation-state, which hails its public as citizens of a nationwide community, regional television calls on its public to act locally—to insist on the multicultural, multilinguistic, and multinational character of Spain.

However, as previously noted, mass mediated regionalism runs the risk of slipping from a politics of national identity to becoming another marketing appeal of consumer demographics—actually, part of a strategy known as localization (see chapter 14). Against the culture of the nation-state, regional broadcasters also hail their publics as global consumers, as shoppers in the EC, as participants in a transnational cultural exchange. For this reason, the shift to an infranational analysis is adequate as long as it is carried out in the context of a political economy of international media—that is, as long as the supranational does not recede from view. At the very least, this cautions international media theory against a romantic account of regionalist movements. Obviously, there is an inherent danger of "folklorizing" or "anthropologizing" regional television, or, worse, of seeing autonomous regional television in Spain as a treacly and quaint grassroots phenomenon. The movements of autonomy and decentralization of cultural power form part of the crisis of the nation-state; they are rooted in political nationalism and the conflict between regional authorities and the central government. Yet they are also affected by liberalized (deregulated) investment of transnational capital in Spain.[48] If we are going local, we must avoid being ingenuous.

There is no more prominent example of this dual character of regionalism than the programming choice for the opening night of the new Catalan channel, TV-3. In an effort to spread the language and culture of Catalonia to the widest possible audience, TV-3 broadcast the hit episode of *Dallas*, "Who Shot JR?" All the autonomous broadcasters have followed similar programming strategies, choosing to dub popular imported series into the local idiom rather than pursue a strategy based on pure autonomous production. Pure autonomy is shown in the end to be an impossibility.

At the infranational scale, regional and local movements for cultural autonomy have put great pressure on the centralized practices of the national state culture to recognize and respect cultural difference. Chapters 12 and 13 focus on the tensions between regionalism at the media periphery and media regionalization from the center. Chapter 12 identifies the early regionalization of the electronic space of Spain and the actions taken by the regional authorities to alter this. Chapter 13 examines the play of struggles and negotiated outcomes that were far from those preferred by the central authorities, and also reveals the contradictory links of the regional broadcasters to a system of commercial expansion that inherently drives them across the borders of their politically defined regions. The play of trespass and containment that this gives rise to is analyzed in the national context where state and private TV are dominant.

At the opposite extreme, transnational forces bulk large, pressuring both national state and regional authorities into a secondary role in the international economy. Part III closes with an analysis of the political economy of Spanish television at both the infranational and supranational scales. In the distant region of political economy analyzed in chapter 14, global media space merges with the politics of nationality. It is a territory of cultural sovereignty that lies beyond the reach of existing safeguards.

The conclusion brings the story to 1993. The privatization process made feasible the dominance of commercial TV by global media giants, Berlusconi, Murdoch, Kirch, and Radiotelevision Luxembourg. Foreign ownership now surpasses levels allowed by law. Also very present are banks, which hold almost a quarter of the commercial TV business. This is a difficult situation for communications freedom. Financial dependence led to three major devaluations of the national currency in 1992–93. Without any restrictions on transnational capital flows since 1992, Spain has been at the mercy of stronger currencies; its shrinking reserves and growing foreign liabilities severely hamper new participation by national communications firms. As a result, everyone is trying to go global, seeking assets in markets with stronger currencies or selling their assets in Spain to get ahold of stronger currencies. The losers are local, the winners have deep pockets.

Part I

Political Transitions, Media Transitions

The transition is an imaginary line, like the equator ... postmodernity. An imaginary line that obliges us to bear all of history on our backs, to help find the before and after of the facts, until it is finally packaged, and falsified. ... For a boxed-in culture, the dictatorship of imaginary lines is logical, as is the repugnance toward the idea of history as a totality without end. A day is an imaginary line. An hour. A minute.

Manuel Vázquez Montalbán,
Crónica sentimental de la transición (231–32)

Scholars of recent Spanish history tend to agree on at least two of the key conditions that greeted the transitions of media and politics in democratic Spain. The first we can call, after Poulantzas, the crisis of the dictatorship. The second is the reemergence in 1976 of strong regionalist projects of the so-called historic nationalities of Spain: the Basques, Catalans, and Galicians. In addition, no account of the social conditions in transitional Spain would be complete without identifying the place of Spain in the international economy.

The crisis of the dictatorship began long before the death of General Franco with the expansion of an educated middle class during the "boom" years of the 1960s. Already in the late fifties, an oppositional culture was forming through alliances of students and working-class resistance, which, from a parallel zone of influence, were aided with persistent, if somewhat blinkered and opportunistic, international pressure.[1] This crisis lasted beyond the dictator's death in 1975 and shaped the early years of the political transition of the Spanish state.

Democratic media for the new Spain was defined against Francoism and against the state. This negative definition—i.e., what democratic media was *not*—was part of a more general movement of civil society. In other words, the organizations of civil society in democratic Spain defined themselves against the institutions of dictatorship; they were not going to have any of the characteristics of the past. As models and alternatives for a new media were developed in this battle between past and present, it became clear that television's relation to the state was seen as the main object for reform. This situation, as chapter 1 argues, anticipated later problems of legitimacy for state-related media within democratic Spain. In particular, it limited the symbolic value of the public service model.

Regionalism has been a significant historical force within the territorial state of Spain since the end of the nineteenth century. Democratic Spain inherited an old problematic that will continue to define political and social processes for some time. Chapter 2 presents the geography of the regionalist movement and the historical tensions between centralism and regionalism that are manifest in Spanish media and society.

Technological dependence is another inherited feature of the environment in which the young democracy found itself after Franco's death. Direct and indirect ties between the electronics sector and the mass media require some basic understanding before judgments about policy choices can be made. Likewise, the advertising sector in Spain is highly internationalized, dominated by British and American multinational agencies. These aspects of dependency in Spanish communications will resurface in later chapters in more concrete historical situations; chapter 3 has been written as a brief introduction to economic dependence, and it maintains a narrative style not much burdened by numbers or economic jargon.

1
The Death of the Dictator and the Twilight of National Mass Media

In 1975, a joke on the American television comedy program *Saturday Night Live* reminded viewers that the former dictator of Spain, Francisco Franco, was "still dead." The macabre joke referred to Franco's extended agony before dying. For months, the world had watched as the eighty-three-year-old dictator was returned repeatedly from near death, surviving dangerous surgical operations and living beyond medical expectations with the help of machines.

When he finally passed away on November 20, 1975, the public seemed uncertain, as if reassurances that he would stay dead were needed. *Saturday Night Live*'s joke expressed both an emotional release and an underlying anxiety that is complex in meaning although very familiar to Spaniards, for Franco left the world having done everything in his power to ensure continuity of his regime in Spain. "All is tied up and well tied down," he said, in reference to the key social institutions prior to his death.[1] Even the manner of his suffering death seemed emblematic of a legacy well planned to survive into the future. Accounts depict his body suspended among rows of life-support machines in a net of wires and tubes, with the mantle of the Virgin of Pilar draped over him as he clutched furtively the embalmed arm of Saint Teresa. His corpse nested like a symbol of his dictatorship: "a modern industrial ... consumer society haunted by the relics of a Catholic, traditional state."[2] This specter of *franquismo* seemed to obsess Spanish culture and society as the transition to democracy stumbled into 1976.

The king, Juan Carlos I of Borbón, who was appointed by Franco in 1969 to assume the supreme leadership of Spain, emerged at the forefront of political reform, a surprise to both continuist and reformist forces. Juan Carlos, thirty-seven years old at his coronation, had to make dramatic changes in the political culture of Spain or risk losing the legitimacy of his monarchy in the eyes of Western leaders and in the court of "liberal opinion" in Spain.[3] There was high expectation and pressure among European leaders that the king should dismantle the authoritarian institutions. The king's first pronouncements made it clear that his hold on the throne, and its "dubious origins," depended on his determination to create "a constitutional, democratic, and parliamentary monarchy."[4]

When Juan Carlos became head of state in 1975 he indicated a preference for reformist initiatives, which he saw as the only viable route to maintain the monarchy. Yet his ability to achieve this in the first government was severely hampered by the dominance of Francoists in the Cortes (the Spanish parliament), the National Council of the Movement, and the Council of the Realm. The Francoists (in popular parlance known as *el bunker*) were well entrenched in the Cortes. The National Council of the Movement was a leftover of the National Movement party, which brought together fascists, monarchists, Catholics, and military into a political coalition of nationalist forces under the leadership of Franco during and after the Spanish civil war.[5] The National Council was "by 1970 the ideological watch-dog of the regime, guarding the Principles of the Movement as the communion of all Spaniards who shared the ideals of the Crusade, that is, the negation of liberalism and all its implications."[6] The Council of the Realm was another of the medieval revivals established by Franco. It was set up as an advisory group empowered to name political appointments, among which was the president of the government (prime minister). Only after the failure of the first government did the Council of the Realm provide the name (among a list of three) of a moderate Francoist, whom the king then appointed as the new president in July 1976.

The appointment of Adolfo Suárez, a young former minister of the Movement, civil governor, and (coincidentally) former director of Televisión Española (TVE), appeared at first as another incarnation of Franco's spirit. This image of Suárez came from his association with Francoists loyal to a former prime minister, Admiral Luis Carrero Blanco. Many believed that Carrero Blanco was destined to become the first president under the monarchy until the Basque separatist group, ETA, assassinated him in 1973.[7] When Suárez was appointed it was clear that Franco's death alone had offered no guarantee of a safe passage to a period beyond Francoism; reformists were making little impact, and the left opposition was still illegal. Finally, as the new year of 1977 approached, the Suárez government charted a fresh direction toward a post-Francoist order, ironically with the Francoist constitution as a guide. The political reforms of the first Suárez government were both surprising and extraordinary. Suárez turned out to be extremely skillful at bridging the gap between the past regime and the transitional government. Carr and Fusi give a partial list of his accomplishments:

July 1976: Amnesty was granted that freed four hundred political prisoners.

September 1976: Catalonia was allowed to celebrate its national day.

November 1976: Creation of a bicameral system based on universal suffrage; approved in referendum in December.

January 1977: The Basque flag was legalized.

February 1977: A new Law of Political Association legalized political parties.

March 1977: A new amnesty was granted, and the Francoist syndicates disappeared after new legislation reestablished the free trade unions.

April 1977: The government dismantled the Movement and legalized the Communist party.

June 1977: The first elections in over forty years, from which the party Suárez headed, the Union of the Democratic Center (UCD), emerged as the dominant political force in the nation.[8]

When the democratization process opened up in the summer of 1977, broadcast policy reform moved to the center of the political project of the new Spain. The importance of broadcast media, especially television, as a keystone of institutional reform is best explained by the role played by radio and television under the Franco dictatorship.

In the year of Franco's death, Radiotelevisión Española (RTVE), the broadcast corporation owned by the state, had two national television networks, a centralized national network radio, and a network of locally and regionally oriented radio stations. The television network, Televisión Española (TVE), had two channels, and no competitors. It was highly centralized and tightly controlled by the dictatorship, more so than any other medium. According to Spanish media scholar Enrique Bustamante, TVE had become, since the 1960s, the regime's "principal instrument of ideological domination."[9] Typically, TVE's management came from the ranks of political appointees associated with the National Council of the Movement. Because of the Movement's influence, RTVE was known popularly by the epithet used for Francoists, *el bunker*—a stronghold of Francoism.

The status of RTVE as "the bunker" was unique, however, in one very significant way: it was the most visible and popularly known daily evidence that things remained unchanged. Of course, television and radio were not the only or the most important institutions held by el bunker. Francoists continued to block educational reform, control key government offices, and resist strategic political reform through control of military powers, the militarized police force, secret police, and paramilitary civil guards. In fact, a biographical sketch of the government elected in 1977 showed that two-thirds of the members of the majority party (the UCD) were linked to the National Movement.[10] Soldiers patrolling the streets and fascist youth congregating in preppy gangs in upscale neighborhoods of large cities were common sights, but, more prominent than soldiers, police, or fascist gangs, the most public of all Francoist institutions was television. Francoism defied the search for civil society in many spheres; indeed, elimination of this central presence — the institutions and culture of the dictatorship — became the very definition of civil society projected onto a democratic Spain. But it was the intractable evidence of Francoist TV that absorbed the attention of reformers. The transformation of RTVE became a living metaphor for the transformation of Spanish society.

In this context, the symbolic politics of attacking the state control of media were quite serviceable to opposition forces. Such attacks led to intense debates over the proper course for broadcast reform and transformed the Cortes into a showcase of transition drama. Yet despite the position of TV reform as the most prominent cultural expression of democratic change, consensus and legislation for new policy were actually minimal during the first decade of the transition to democracy. Until 1983 most changes in broadcast law favored the central government's control over television.[11] The lack of achievements in broadcast reform during this period is overshadowed, and perhaps explained, by political and economic crises that accompanied the transition.

After the political transition to democracy began in earnest, political forces coalesced into significant parties, while antisystemic movements emerged and new coalitions of reactionary conservatism formed. This new mix of political classes came together in the midst of a "historical accident" when the "onset of and adjustment to the economic crisis happened to coincide in Spain with the critical transition from dictatorship to democracy."[12] Primarily because of the global recession, outdated economic development models, and the oil shock of 1973–74, Spain suffered a dramatic reduction in economic growth throughout the 1970s and early 1980s. The annual average growth rate of gross domestic product (GDP) dropped from the 7 percent of the boom years (1961–74) to only 2.3 percent in the first three years of the transition. Inflation jumped over 10 percent between the same two periods. By 1977, inflation had reached a high of 26.4 percent, while growth stagnated. Under this "stagflationary" strain, unemployment began to rise sharply, and by the early 1980s rose to the highest level in Europe, over 20 percent. By that time the rate at which the GDP was expanding had diminished to almost nothing (with the low of 0.3 percent in 1981).[13]

The effects of political and economic crises on the agenda for broadcast reform are hard to disentangle. On the one hand, political forces who backed broad economic liberalizations, including the privatization of television, faced a conservative national elite of investors, manufacturers, and employers. Franco had ensured Spanish capitalists a level of protection for their goods and markets; therefore, calls for liberalization and for increased investment with unknown prospects seemed to them to put many fortunes in jeopardy. On the other hand, the remaining vestiges of the dictatorship, including protectionism, were seen as unnecessary by many of the reformist parties and younger entrepreneurs. This led to a political stalemate in the midst of the stagflationary period. Spanish capitalism—or what can be termed properly as the national economy—was caught between an ineffective political class that had just recently begun to redefine itself and a conservative capitalist class that balked at institutional change.

The old alliance of state and business elites faced an emerging group of younger reformers who were willing to make decisions, forge strategic coalitions, and create a new hegemony. This threw many of the continuist options posed by the Francoists into a legitimation crisis, which was further challenged by the radical left opposition. At first, the left pushed for a complete dismantlement of the old regime and the establishment of a democratic break with the past in a manner that was known then as "democracy without adjectives." What emerged instead from this impasse was a balance of compromise and sacrifice, mostly at the expense of the people hardest hit by the economic crisis, i.e., the working class and rural populations. With Eurocommunism and social democratic platforms defining official politics of the major leftist parties in Spain, most of the radical proposals for a transitional state were muted. Strategies of the left turned to evolutionary, rather than revolutionary, political practice.

The most prominent political strategy emerging from this evolutionary type of politics was characterized by the leader of the Spanish Communist Party (PCE) as the *ruptura pactada,* or negotiated break with the Francoist past.[14] The *ruptura pactada* suggested a solution to the political impasse that followed Franco's death. The left opposition offered to ease social tensions by negotiating for "democracy without adjectives" (a notable contradiction) rather than demand radical reform or revolution. In this sense, the opposition set aside revolutionary goals in order to establish democratic political institutions across the board. In exchange they would help to ease economic strains on Spanish capitalism.[15] To put it somewhat differently, it was a time of pacts and deals.

The most important social pact of the period was signed in October 1977 in the Moncloa Palace, the official residence of the president. With the Moncloa Pacts, as this set of agreements became known, the left agreed to wage ceilings, credit restrictions, and a conservative fiscal policy. In exchange the government was supposed to reform, among other things, regional policy, the structure of the general economy, and the police forces, as well as loosen restrictions against public protest, legalize contraceptives, and decriminalize adultery.[16] This "contrived unanimity," as Hooper calls it, sought to ensure political peace and protection for the UCD's legislative package until a new constitution could be written, approved, and enacted.[17]

To many activists, workers, and members of the popular opposition, however, the Moncloa Pacts were evidence that the left leadership had betrayed democracy and progressive principles. Moreover, in signing the deal the leftist reformers recalled the style of ex-Francoist reformers who sought to "bestow" democracy from above.

Though the RTVE Statute was developed as a result of the Moncloa Pacts, as chapter 4 explains, it did not emerge from its paper existence until 1980 under the second UCD government. In fact, no reform for television came out of the first UCD government. Meanwhile, anti-RTVE sentiments continued to rise in the press and among opposition parties and intellectuals. At issue was the nature of democratic mass media and their relation to the state and civil society. In general, liberal democracy—the social and political order sought by the majority of opposition and reformist forces—provided only two models for national mass media: public service broadcasting, and the commercial model. In order to understand the orientation of Spanish policymakers and intellectuals to public service and commercial broadcasting, a clarification of the principles and archetypal practice associated with the two models is worthwhile.

Basically, public service broadcasting aims to provide universal access to radio-television signals across the territorial state, regardless of community status but within a framework of a liberal enlightenment project. Such a project promises the proper mix of entertainment, information, and education to each individual citizen of the national state in order to enhance the individual's contribution to the national community — be that in voting intelligently, in purchasing goods in national marketplaces, or in cultivating appreciation for the best of the national culture on offer. The archetypal public service system is the British Broadcasting Corporation (BBC). Much of the rhetoric associated with public service therefore derives from the British experience; this is especially true regarding the Victorian tone of social reform and ideas concerning the "betterment of the masses." The rhetoric is also applied to most paternalist frameworks of cultural policy that are fitted to Matthew Arnold's precept that the proper culture is what enlightened publics understand as the best that has been thought and written.[18]

The other major model of broadcasting in liberal democratic societies is one based on commercial organization, its fundamental goal being profit making. The commercial broadcaster is in the business of attracting public attention, through programming and advertising, for commodities produced by national industries. Most TV economics texts put it this way: commercial TV produces audiences, not programs. Because the television service is competitive, for audiences and for contracts with national advertisers, it is encouraged to be innovative and growth-oriented. That is, to compete successfully it must find new ways to attract larger audiences and reduce technical costs at the same time; to grow it must maximize particular high-status audiences (i.e., those with money to spend). As Bernard Miege points out, this keeps commercial media in a permanent crisis of creativity.[19] To survive in this crisis system, however, formulas that have proven attractive to audiences in the past come to dominate programming strategies — repetition is the ironic result of commercial competition.[20]

In addition, universal service across a territorial state cannot be guaranteed by this model until concentrations of populations reach a certain density. The threshold is usually defined and graded according to the potential sales of commodities, i.e., according to the buying power of the population. This results in uneven quantity and quality of broadcasting services across a given territory. The United States furnishes the archetype of a commercial broadcasting model: the concentration of broadcast service is patterned on population density and graded on a numerical scale of markets. If it were not for the establishment of cable communications, some communities in the United States would still be without service under the commercial model (although many communities are simply priced away from the cable or satellite connections anyway).

In principle, programming for a commercial system is aimed at giving whatever the local community deems is sufficient and acceptable, regardless of its intent to inform, educate, or entertain. This local service principle notwithstanding, there is no national programming philosophy attached to the commercial model. Taking the U.S. case as an example, however, the state and businesses can be shown to work closely to ensure a market-oriented philosophy throughout the national system.[21] The national community is, in turn, envisaged as an agglomeration of localized markets for goods. A public thus conceived is not primarily of national citizens but rather is a mosaic of consumers.

A final point about these models. The national community of citizens is the sovereign in a public service regime, subordinating the individual to the culture of the national community. In the commercial model, the individual consumer is the sovereign, subordinating corporate and government institutions to the individual voter-shopper. Where the people pay a tax or fee for their citizens' media in a public service model, the commercial system offers programming in exchange for the viewer attention to the business message.[22] These institutional and philosophical differences will resurface in the policy debates explained in later chapters. The key element is that both public and commercial systems claim to serve people, not politics.

Spanish intellectuals who supported each of these models argued, on a pretty even score, that the other model fails to serve the true principles of liberal democracy. Both camps argued together that a state-controlled system is in essence not democratic. In practice, both models have problems, and most media scholars tend to agree on this point—the one is elitist and paternalistic, the other tied in the extreme to economic imperatives. Nevertheless, both models offered to Spaniards already well established systems of national media that are *in principle* beholden to people—no matter how fuzzy or utopian the notions of citizens and consumers—and not controlled directly and soley by the state.

Other experiences also determined how these two models were received in Spain. Although the principles of public service television were well known in Spain, a public service ethos was never consolidated in Spanish television. Televisión Española had been organized on a principle of absolute state service, and its function was to impart the state's informational propaganda and an identity for the national community modeled on the National Movement's self-image. The only thing it shared with the public service model was the goal to provide universal public access to its signals.

Under Franco, TVE was a state-controlled universal service with mixed state and commercial funding. In contrast to other mixed models, such as those of France and Italy, TVE made absolutely no pretext of furnishing a balance of information or opinion; it simply spoke for the state power that was unified in the singular figure of Franco. Except for a pseudopluralism restricted to the "families" of the National Movement,

TVE was Franco's vision and voice. Contrary to both commercial and public service models, TVE held a monopoly with advertisers as the only television outlet for commercial messages in Spain.

Given the lack of both public service experience and the closed market for advertising, it is not surprising that in the rhetoric of reformers (policymakers, journalists, and intellectuals), public controls suffered from a legitimation problem.[23] As a result, the policymakers eventually "bowed to a neoliberal ideology which ... accused the public service of being a burden on the taxpayer compared to the 'free' service provided by private television."[24] The commercial model was in part legitimated by this intellectual context, and eventually came to dominate debate and policy (see chapter 6). In contrast, public TV retained a checkered reputation because of an unexamined notion that it necessarily has to be tied to state controls.[25]

In the end, the media reform initiatives were almost entirely authored by the younger, middle-class reformers—aided by the free traders in the transnational sectors of advertising, communications technology, and finance—whose voices sounded most clearly on the pages of newspapers like *El País* and other commercial media. Indeed, the private, commercial press was an instrumental force in setting the agenda for broadcast reform, as part II of this book shows. After its establishment in 1976, the newspaper *El País* became the standard bearer of the image and project of a liberal democratic media. Along with other privately owned dailies (most notably *La Vanguardia* and *Diario 16*), *El País* began a two-pronged attack on the state television, going after TVE's mismanagement by the state, while offering an alternative in the image of a "nonpartisan," democratic, commercial press.

Despite the evidence that similar press wars in Italy, Britain, and France helped commercial media promoters gain a foothold in private TV, it was not widely understood in Spain what motivations lay behind the press's rhetorical strategy to link democracy to a private, commercial model. What was clear was the symbolic value of dismantling RTVE. Without question, RTVE represented the specter of *franquismo*; both its organization and orientation were entrenched in *el bunker*. RTVE was indeed tied up and well tied down.

2
The Regional Question

A key element of the transition to democracy in Spain can be understood by analyzing the genesis and structure of the political economy of regionalization. Regionalism emerged as a direct response to the spatial hierarchy, the regionalization, created by centralism in Spain. This regionalized hierarchy privileged the center politically and constrained the regions economically — especially the more dynamic capitalist regions of Spain, Catalonia, and the Basque Country. The tension between centralism and regionalism was decisive in shaping the organization, and orientation, of Spanish radio and television throughout the twentieth century. This chapter digresses from the question of media regionalization to furnish a general perspective on the political and economic regionalization of Spain. Though the geography of television is described in chapter 12, the basic issues related here will help clarify the workings of regional politics, regional nationalisms, and, perhaps most important, the highly stratified structure of the interregional economy.

In 1978, the Spanish people approved in referendum a new constitution that contains the basis for the dismantling of the centralized state apparatus and the reorganization of the Spanish state into a democratic parliamentary monarchy. A "State of the Autonomies," as it was called, replaced the centralized structure of the state. The process that codified this new State of the Autonomies required that provincial leaders join together and write a statute that justified and defined the autonomy of their regional bloc of provinces as a distinct cultural, political, or economic community within the Spanish territory. They were then required to submit the statute to referenda to legitimate it with a show of popular support. Eventually, this process led to the parceling of the fifty provinces of Spain into seventeen regional autonomous communities (see maps 1 and 2, and table 1).

The State of the Autonomies materialized slowly after the 1978 constitution, however. The devolution process stumbled over two obstacles, both structural and intractable: the uneven historical development of political regionalism and the inconstant geography of Spanish capitalism. Decentralization of political authority would have to overcome the spatial hierarchy of the Spanish regions—some were rich, some poor; some had a history of self-governance, some did not. The genesis of this politico-economic regionalization is related historically to the rise of centralism in the modern Spanish state.

National centralism in modern Spain crystallized under the constitutional monarchy of the early nineteenth century, which divided the territory into fifty provinces and eight thousand municipalities. These divisions destroyed the historic provinces and territorial boundaries that emerged during the Reconquest (711–1492). Throughout the nineteenth century, for the most part, administration and control of the provinces and local institutions rested in the hands of agents of the throne.

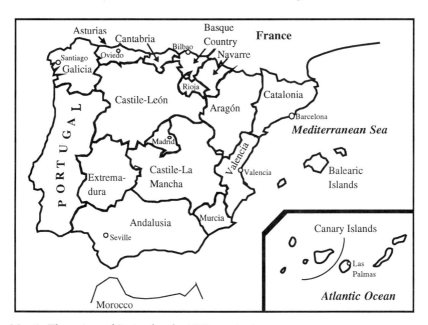

Map 1. The regions of Spain after the 1978 constitution.

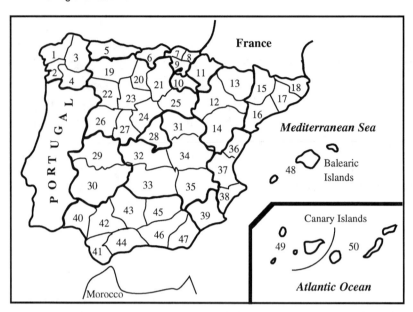

Map 2. The Autonomous Communities and provinces of Spain.

Galicia	Aragón	26. Salamanca	Murcia
1. La Coruña	12. Zaragoza	27. Avila	39. Murcia
2. Pontevedra	13. Huesca	**Madrid**	**Andalusia**
3. Lugo	14. Teruel	28. Madrid	40. Huelva
4. Orense	**Catalonia**	**Extremadura**	41. Cádiz
Asturias	15. Lérida	29. Caceres	42. Seville
5. Asturias	16. Tarragona	30. Badajoz	43. Córdoba
Cantabria	17. Barcelona	**Castile-La Mancha**	44. Málaga
6. Cantabria	18. Gerona	31. Guadalajara	45. Jaén
Basque Country	**Castile-León**	32. Toledo	46. Granada
7. Vizcaya	19. León	33. Ciudad Real	47. Almería
8. Guipuzcoa	20. Palencia	34. Cuenca	**Balearic Islands**
9. Alava	21. Burgos	35. Albacete	48. Baleares (Menorca,
La Rioja	22. Zamora	**Valencia**	Mallorca, Ibiza)
10. La Rioja	23. Valladolid	36. Castellón	**Canary Islands**
Navarre	24. Segovia	37. Valencia	49. Tenerife
11. Navarre	25. Soria	38. Alicante	50. Las Palmas

Appointed by the central government, these agents exercised the will of the central power through their assigned positions as civil governors and mayors.[1]

Although the Basque nationalist movement drew on existing cultural and social resources to legitimate itself, generally speaking most traditions of modern Basque nationalism are early-twentieth-century inventions. The "apostle" of Basque nationalism was the philologist Sabino de Arana

Type of region	Type of autonomy	Name of region	Population in thousands (1990)	Gross domestic product, in billions of pesetas (1990)	Unemployment rate (1991)
Charter regions	Greater, fast-track, and tax autonomy	Basque Country	521	799	10.6
		Navarre	2129	2982	18.5
Regions established by article 151 of 1978 constitution	Greater and fast-track autonomy	Andalusia	6920	6142	25.8
		Canary Islands	1485	1752	24.5
		Catalonia	6008	8620	12.2
		Valencia	3787	4380	15.7
		Galicia	2804	2526	12.2
Regions established by article 143 of 1978 constitution	Limited and slow-track autonomy	Aragón	1213	1570	9.9
		Asturias	1126	1236	15.9
		Balearic Islands	682	1041	9.9
		Cantabria	527	610	16.0
		Castile-León	2626	2776	14.9
		Castile-La Mancha	1714	1696	13.0
		Extremadura	1128	862	23.8
		Madrid	4878	7307	12.2
		Murcia	1027	1180	18.1
		La Rioja	261	333	9.6

Table 1. The regions of Spain. Data from OECD, *Economic Surveys, Spain*, 1993.

Goiri (1865–1903), a Castilian-speaking Basque who sought to create a proper national language for the Basques through such efforts as codifying correct spelling, fabricating Basque names for Spanish ones, and cleansing the existing Basque language of traces of what he thought were Hispanicisms.[2]

In addition to reviving and codifying the language, Sabino de Arana was the first to associate territory with Basqueness (he also designed the Basque flag). It is significant that Arana invented the word to describe the land where Basques lived, Euskadi. Prior to that, there was no name attached to an ethnic "homeland" as such. Rather, the region was called Euskal Herria, the place of Basque speakers. Euskal Herria described something akin to a "language land" as opposed to "homeland." Until Arana's intervention, then, language, more than place, anchored ethnicity. Nevertheless, the foundation of cultural tradition in the Basque Country, Euskadi, rests most firmly in ancient linguistic history, although this seems equally difficult to trace because of the primarily oral diffusion of the numerous dialects of Basque.[3]

Historical accounts of the nationality are often filled, not surprisingly, with myths and legends of ethnic tradition, and are occasionally suffused with scientific racism, as supports for an ethnically distinct homeland.[4] Sabino de Arana inspired the rise of nationalist separatism and racialist determinations of Basque nationality. Disgusted by "Spanish" immigrants to Euskadi, he inveighed against miscegenation and sought the establishment of a pastoral, Catholic society in which only authentic Basques would live in a separate, preindustrial regime.[5] He was imprisoned by the central authorities twice for his propaganda of radical independence from the Spanish state. The second incarceration was for a telegram he sent to U.S. president Theodore Roosevelt congratulating him for the "liberation of Cuba from Spanish rule."[6] In 1910, seven years after Sabino de Arana's death, his followers founded the conservative Basque Nationalist Party (PNV), today the dominant political party in the region.[7]

In contrast, Catalan cultural nationalism was able to draw on an earlier renaissance of its literary and intellectual past. Almost forgotten between 1750 and 1830, the cultural traditions of Catalan "land, race, and tongue" were revived in the midnineteenth century in the works of Carles Aribau and Rubio i Ors, and with the inauguration of the *Joc Florals,* a national poetry competition, in 1859.[8] But, as Vilar argues, "recovery of the language ... followed rather than preceded political enthusiasm for independence. This means that the true issue does not lie with these 'differentiating factors' (geography, ethnics, language, law, psychology, history) but with other reasons which had inspired a given region at a given time to bring these factors forward once again."[9]

Between 1870 and 1914, nationalism throughout Europe became increasingly political, while the appeal of the nation-state spread with the hegemony of industrial capitalism.[10] The regions of Spain had been linked administratively to the state since the sixteenth century, to form one of the first modern nation-states in the world (absolutist, to be sure).[11] In general, however, the centralized state system that developed in the nineteenth century worked against the consolidation of commercial and industrial capitalism in Spain. Political centralism thus crippled attempts to form a national market of a kind that served as the basis for the industrial revolution in Northern Europe during the nineteenth century.[12] The capitalist mode of production in Spain developed unevenly as a result, and a pattern of regional economic differentiation was established that eventually assumed political form.

Barcelona (Catalonia) and Bilbao (in the Basque province of Vizcaya), though once the periphery of Spanish society both politically and administratively, were the first sites of capitalist development in Spain, followed by Madrid.[13] The south of Spain was dominated by large landholding oligarchies that resisted industrialization, and this resistance extended north with the support of the central state against the hegemony of an emergent northern bourgeoisie. Peripheral to this was the small farm economy of Galicia. This split diminished the structural interdependence between agriculture and industry, keeping the most dynamic sectors of a burgeoning Spanish capitalism — located in the Basque Country and Catalonia — from making the Spanish national economy one of the "first comers" of the industrial revolution.[14] Under these conditions cultural nationalism in the Basque Country and Catalonia became politicized.

This emergent regionalism took political form during the First Republic (1872–74), when attempts were made to establish a federal system attentive to regionalist sentiments, only to be crushed by reaction of the oligarchy. The regionalist movements in Spain received growing support from the urban middle classes, which were most developed in Catalonia. Industrialists in both regions, and banking interests in the Basque Country (30 percent of all Spanish financial investment by 1908 was Basque), became increasingly intolerant of their marginal political role and subordination to the centralist oligarchy.

This undercurrent of nationalism, what Tamames and Clegg call "subjacent federalism," emerged again at the end of the nineteenth century to unite these forces into a movement for independence.[15] For the regional bourgeoisie, the imperial Spanish state was characterized by two intolerable qualities: the excesses of *caciquismo* (the abusive exercise of power by local authorities) and a disgusting global impotence, which was seen as leading to the loss of Spain's last possessions in Latin America (Cuba and Puerto Rico) and in the Far East (Philippines) in 1898.[16]

In 1914, with regional reform under the constitutional monarchy of King Alfonso XIII, a limited autonomy over cultural affairs, education, public works, and local government was devolved to the reunited Catalan provinces on an experimental basis. With the industrial revolution complete after World War I, basic industries came to be concentrated in the Basque Country and assembly industries in Catalonia. Limited autonomy was about to be applied to the Basque and Galician regions, but in 1923 the military dictatorship of General Miguel Primo de Rivera reasserted centralist control over Spain with the blessing of the monarchy. Under the dictatorship of Primo de Rivera, all actions that might tend to question national unity were outlawed—regionalism was treated as treasonous.[17]

Regionalists eventually united with other democratic parties in a broad movement to overthrow the dictatorship. Primo de Rivera was forced to resign in January 1930 after the military, financial, and industrial powers withdrew their support from the regime. The following year the constitutional monarchy of Alfonso XIII collapsed and the Second Republic (1931–39) was born.[18]

The Republican constitution of 1931 reopened the way for the regional communities to establish their political autonomy. The Catalans obtained autonomy in 1932, the Basques negotiated their own regional autonomy in 1936, and the Galicians eventually approved a statute of autonomy by plebiscite. The fascist uprising and the civil war (1936–39), however, blocked any attempts to further the political devolution process.[19] Franco's victory reestablished a centralized, authoritarian regime and erased the political gains of the autonomous regional movement.

As the Axis powers captured territory across Europe, Francoism focused on two fronts: the restless diplomatic pursuit of a campaign against the Soviet Union, and the establishment of the dictatorship's national economic reforms, which appeared modeled on the German directed economy. After the Allied forces landed in North Africa, Franco was forced to yield to their diplomatic pressures, although he still campaigned for a Western alliance against the USSR despite the lukewarm reception for his anticommunism. With concessions to the Allied powers, Franco was able to acquire some material imports that saved Spain's manufacturing industries. The economy had nonetheless been devastated by the civil war: Spain was isolated, roads and rail were destroyed, hunger and deprivation prevailed. The nationalist propaganda failed to fill stomachs, and Spain became further isolated from the international community.

Franco refused international demands to democratize Spain, leading the United Nations to denounce the regime and France to close its border with Spain briefly. Many commentators foresaw in this period after World War II a quick end for the Franco regime, but, as Vilar argues, the "formation of a world-wide anti-communist bloc" saved Francoism from extinction. The cold war allowed Franco, a surviving fascist, "to parade himself as a 'forerunner'" of anticommunism. Because of this, Franco "acted towards the USA … as a creditor rather than a debtor."[20] Franco's negotiations with the United States concluded in 1953, and a bilateral aid agreement was signed. The United States gained use of Spanish territory for military base operations; in exchange, Spain received investments "to strengthen the bases of the programme of military cooperation."[21]

With Spain's piecemeal integration into the international economy in the late 1950s, the government began to implement a policy of regional development. This policy, the Stabilization Plan of 1959, was based on a growth-pole/growth-center model. The growth-pole model relies on forced relocation of industry to counter the "inherent" backwardness of underdeveloped regions.[22] This plan, along with the First Development Plan of 1962–63, established special pricing structures and subsidies to encourage transfers of surplus produced in the south to industrial growth poles throughout Spain. This process eventually led Spain on a path of rapid growth and increased industrial productivity in the 1960s, bringing it inside of what Arrighi calls the "perimeter of the core" of capitalist economies.[23]

Despite these successes, the rigid structure of regional inequality persisted; moreover, it was extended by growth-pole industrialization. Capital and labor became more concentrated in already-developed zones around Bilbao, Barcelona, and Madrid. Vast areas of rural Spain were abandoned as laborers moved to these industrial centers, while economic development in Andalusia, Extremadura, and Galicia remained at a standstill.[24] In the course of the 1960s, as Spain's gross national product grew, the gap between regional economies widened, "making regional underdevelopment a price of national development."[25]

Although this inconstant geography of Spanish capitalism has been inherited by the present generation, important changes altered the regional economic map during the 1970s. The global economic bust of 1973–74 gave rise to a shift in sectorial dynamics of regional growth. For example, though the strength of the Basque economy once rested on industrial sectors very prominent during the "economic miracle" of the 1960s, these same sectors were hit hardest by the oil shocks of the 1970s (e.g., steel and shipbuilding). As a result, the northern Basque provinces, especially

in the zone of Bilbao, fell back in their overall contribution to the national economy, while local per capita income and employment sunk,
and general social well-being declined.

Indeed, most of the older industrial zones lost their preeminence in
the economic hierarchy of Spain during this crisis. The entire northern
coast—known as the cornice of the Cantabrian Sea—has been in steady
decline since the 1970s.[26] Other regions have experienced notable favorable changes as a result of organizational and technical innovation; for
example, the Ebro River Valley, Catalonia, and the Mediterranean regions
south of Catalonia have all had rising fortunes.[27]

Historically Spain has been plagued by immense demographic movement from the central regions outward (and toward Madrid) and by
urban expansion in industrial areas. This trend accelerated in the 1970s
and early 1980s. In addition, unemployment figures surged, though with
crucial regional differences. In Andalusia the average unemployment rate
in 1987 was around 30 percent, while in Madrid the average was about
17 percent. The total average for Spain rose from 16 percent to 22 percent through the 1980s, giving the country the highest unemployment
rate in all of Europe during the decade.[28]

According to Julio Alcaide Inchausti, Spain can be divided into four
distinct economic regions: one on the rise, another in crisis, one that can
be called "the abandoned Spain," and finally "the Spain that survives."[29]
Except for a few cases, the political regionalization of Spain (i.e., provinces and Autonomous Communities) cannot be matched identically with
these economic regions. The borders of economic regions are much more
flexible, overlapping the fortunes and failures of distinct political regions
(see map 3). As a result, some regions share the indisputable core of
Spanish capitalism, crossing the axes of the Ebro River Valley and the
Mediterranean coast. Others lie in zones of extreme decline, stretching
west from Bilbao into the north of Galicia. Some correspond to neglect,
depopulation, abandonment—a large inland territory that circles the
region of Madrid. The survivors are those regions that tend to comprise
provinces that have historically remained less rooted in Spanish capitalism. They are generally more traditional societies: small peasant farming
or tenant farming in semifeudal, agricultural economies.

In 1978, when the constitution issued a new map for Spain's fledg-
ling democracy, two hundred years of political and economic geography
could not be ignored. Nor could two decades of state-managed, export-
oriented, and financially dependent industrialization, for these years had
sharpened the distinctions created by earlier disparities.[30] With reason,
then, the Spanish constitution called for "the establishment of a just

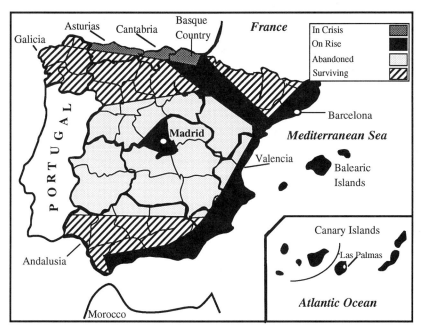

Map 3. The four economic regions of Spain, 1973-85. See Julio Alcaide Inchausti, "Las cuatro Españas económicas y la solidaridad regional."

and adequate economic balance between the different areas of the Spanish territory" (article 138, I).

Yet a two-tiered process of slow and fast decentralization created new social cleavages in the political workings of the nation. Regional authorities saw the Basques and Catalans as being privileged, and began to worry that they themselves would be left missing the train to full and rapid autonomy. Through this "demonstration effect," the onlooking regional elites and voters feared their relegation to the status of second-class citizens within the State of the Autonomies.[31] Devolution was thus stuck in the dilemma about how to redistribute political authority to the equal satisfaction of the historic nationalities and the rest of Spain without at the same time exacerbating "the problem of inter-regional economic inequality."[32]

Nonetheless, opinion polls showed preferences for centralism were declining rapidly throughout Spain during a three-year period that followed the 1979 statutes of autonomy in the Basque and Catalan regions—the first such statutes in Spain. A general agreement seemed to be developing that the "decolonization" of the Spanish regions should respond first and most forcefully to the historic rights, privileges, and experience at self-government possessed by the Basque and Catalan regions. The rest of the regions, as Shabad observes, were content to receive a "profound degree of administrative decentralization."[33] Successive surveys throughout the 1980s and early 1990s registered continuous decline in the preference for centralism.

After a 1982 electoral victory, the Spanish Socialist Workers Party (PSOE) presided over most regional and local administrations with the significant exceptions of the Basque and Catalan governments. This allowed the PSOE to stall the process of devolution to the remaining regions seeking equal status with the Basque Country and Catalonia. Gradually, nationalist sentiment among the regional leadership of the PSOE grew despite the central leadership's resistance to devolution. As an Andalusian official in the PSOE put it, "Autonomy, at least for Andalusia, can be used as a means to get out of a situation of economic dependency and underdevelopment; it is a means, moreover, with which to fight inter-regional inequality. That is the principal merit that autonomy has for Andalusia."[34] Though the PSOE eventually acquiesced to normalize the State of the Autonomies, it did not solve the regional development problem.

In sum, the political and economic regions of Spain are not just stratified but are interwoven into a structured hierarchy that has been generated over two hundred years of inconstant development. As part III of this book explains, these spatial inequalities have had (and will continue to have) a profound impact on the Spanish television industry.

3
Transnational Phenomena in Spanish Media

This brief chapter has one simple goal: to describe the ties of Spanish media to the wider international economy. Two areas need to be introduced: technological dependence and multinational advertising. Spain does not control its own technological destiny, and most of the large advertising agencies are in the hands of the British and American firms. The period examined here precedes the multiplication of TV channels, though later chapters will have occasion to explain the importance of these two points of structural dependence as commercial media promoters and regional authorities push for new channels.

The well-known litany about our contemporary political economy is worth repeating: after World War II, possession of half of the world's resources was effectively under the control of the United States, the U.S. military had ensured American hegemony beyond both Pacific and Atlantic Oceans, the value of national currencies was anchored to the U.S. dollar, and technical and organizational bases of U.S. corporate capital emerged from the war intact and undamaged while much of the global competition lay dormant or annihilated.

As World War II marked the apogee of the American Century, the 1950s kicked off what *Fortune* magazine called "the electronics era."[1] Fundamental for the technical and organizational expansion of U.S. interests were information and communication technology. Long the basis for efficient control and management over distances, innovations in communications technology were significantly speeded up after the war, on the heels of increased military demand and new developments in mass market products of electronics hardware. Among the last stands the very prominent TV system of transmission, distribution, and reception.[2]

Spain finished its industrial revolution in the early part of this century in the absence of any significant institutional interest in technology. By the 1920s Spain was heavily dependent on foreign expertise in communications technology, transport, and capital goods. Obviously, given the tumultuous history of the subsequent years, Spanish businesses and government could not develop an independent sector in this area. Telecommunications, in fact, developed neither as a national commercial enterprise (as in the United States) nor as a national government enterprise (as with European ministries of posts, telephones, and telegraphs). In Spain, the multinational firm International Telephone and Telegraph (ITT) held control over telecommunication diffusion through its absolute ownership of the national telephone company; with its manufacturer, Standard Electrica, S.A., it established a monopoly over the production and distribution of hardware as well. Though this direct foreign control of national communications was common in (U.S.-dominated) Latin America, the only other European country that accepted complete dependence of this sort was Romania.[3]

This loss of control to a foreign firm came when the Primo de Rivera dictatorship stopped a nationalization project that was in process in 1924. Also during the dictatorship, in 1926, the penetration of multinational advertising firms began in Spain with the arrival of J. Walter Thompson. This was followed by two French agencies, Havas and Publicitas, just prior to the founding of the Second Republic in 1931. There were efforts to reverse this situation under the Second Republic, when a project to limit ITT's control was proposed. The intervention of the United States was this time decisive in forcing the Republic's abandonment of the reform project.[4]

Under the Franco dictatorship, a law was passed in 1946 to nationalize the control of the telephone company. The government gained a position as a principal shareholder and manager, but did not retain majority of the controlling interests. Franco created a separate network infrastructure for radio and television, tying broadcasting more firmly than the telecommunications system to the politics of the national state. This did not change until 1988, when the socialists finally loosened a bit of the state's grip on the television infrastructure and brought it under the umbrella of a comprehensive telecommunications policy (see chapter 11). Advertising remained much as it was in the 1920s, i.e., without significant Spanish agencies. This would not change until the boom years of the 1960s.

After World War II, the United States invested nine billion dollars through the Marshall Plan to bolster production and financial markets in Britain, France, Belgium, the Netherlands, Italy, West Germany, and Greece. One of its aims was to ensure European demand and payment for U.S. exports; another aim, of course, was to lure these countries away from communist and socialist politics, which had become attractive and viable options under postwar conditions.[5] There was no Marshall Plan for fascist Spain, perhaps because there was no need to invest in making Franco an anticommunist. Nonetheless, the internal market suffered from too little foreign assistance at a time when the rest of Europe was being rebuilt. Indeed, the amounts of U.S. aid that Spain managed to receive in the 1940s and 1950s were not even enough to be regarded as significant of foreign penetration by leftist commentators.[6]

Though the economy was starved for new injections of capital, food rationing ended in 1952. Franco signed the Concordat with the Vatican and the military base agreement with the U.S. government in 1953. Two years later, Spain was admitted to the United Nations. The dependence on imported technology became more central for Spain after 1950, and was further institutionalized by the U.S. base agreement and by three national development plans in 1959, 1962, and 1972.

By 1957, a slightly recharged capitalist economy had outgrown the policies in existence, and new political and economic forces emerged from the shell of autarky. Labor and student conflicts became more frequent; the children of the growing middle and working classes were becoming increasingly discontent with the regime. The crisis forced Franco to form his sixth government, which included technocrats from the Opus Dei.[7] This marked an important shift in policy, as the new government set out to introduce an economic plan to create the conditions for industrial growth, namely, "a market economy in Spain ... and the integration of that market in the capitalist economy of the West."[8]

With the market liberalizations of the 1960s, an attempt was made to diminish the control of ITT over the telecommunications sector, as the national telephone company (Telefónica) established partnerships with Swedish, Italian, and American firms.[9] Though Spain's modernization can be understood as "dependent, uneven, and distorted," as Casanova reports, Spain came to be regarded as "a highly diversified, internationally competitive economy."[10] What most characterized this period was the state-managed internationalization of the Spanish economy.

One of the key cultural aspects of the internationalization period was the reform created by the new administration to liberalize communications law. As minister of Information and Tourism between 1962 and

1969, Manuel Fraga Iribarne introduced legislation that made more flex-ible censorship rules affecting the press, book trade, and theater. These reforms did not apply to television, however; in fact, Fraga's law codi-fied censorship of TV where once only loose administrative sanctions could be found. Fraga brought TVE under more direct control of the Ministry of Information. TVE was seen as an important tool for the dis-semination of the regime's ideology, having reached about 65 percent of the national territory at the time; with only 1 percent of the population owning TV sets, communal viewing received official patronage. None-theless, television was the one instrument of information control that the dictatorship could not afford to abandon to the pseudocultural plu-ralism that Fraga sought to project as Spain's international image. While Fraga promoted Spanish culture with the slogan "Spain is different," the regime continued to propagate its own image of the "one great and unified" nation.[11]

As a point of contrast, this period in the mid to late 1960s witnessed the rise of "new Spanish cinema," an increase of Marxist publications in Spanish bookstores, new leftist publishing houses, and other symbols of reform—though by no means should we exaggerate their impact. Television did not experience this sense of "opening up," but rising view-ership combined with the social routine of communal viewing to make television "exceptionally important" in the 1960s.[12] By the end of the sixties, the number of TV receivers equaled about 16 percent of the population (163 sets per 1,000 inhabitants). Despite these relatively low figures, social gatherings for television viewing were quickly becoming a new cultural resource for Spaniards. Some moralists even considered TV to have achieved cultural status as "the Spanish vice."[13] Whatever the case, there is anecdotal evidence that when people gathered to watch TV, for example in the Tele Clubs fostered by the Ministry of Informa-tion, their meetings became "vehicles for a nascent political opposition" rather than places where "passive viewers absorbed the propaganda of the regime."[14]

As the cultural uses of television expanded, economic international-ization of Spain's professional electronics market deepened. In 1975, Spain's dependency on foreign technology in the sector of electronics components reached an estimated 93 percent. At the same time, Spain was investing less capital on research and development as a percentage of its wealth than any other European country. Further, Spain was notably weak in contracting license agreements and even weaker in assimilating the technology it was licensed to use.[15] The share of the gross domestic product attributed to the communications sector grew from 1.4 percent to nearly 2 percent between 1975 and 1985.[16]

By 1986, besides ITT—which controlled Standard Eléctrica, S.A., the Compañía Internacional de Telecomunicación y Electrónica, S.A. (CITESA), and Marconi Española, S.A.—other important foreign telecommunications and informatics hardware companies operating in Spain were AT&T (United States), Corning Glass (United States), Bull (France), Fujistu (Japan), IBM (United States), Digital (United States), Siemens (Germany), NIXDORF (Germany), Olivetti (Italy), Hewlett Packard (United States), Philips (Holland), L. M. Ericsson (Sweden), and Telettra International (Italy). Of the consumer electronics corporations, the list was topped by Philips (Holland), Grundig (Germany), Thomson (France), Sanyo (Japan), AEG-Telefunken (Germany), Sharp (Japan), Matsushita Electric Industrial (Japan), and Sony (Japan).[17]

Like most aspects of the internationalization of the Spanish economy, the most significant multiplication of firms came after the 1959 Stabilization Plan, designed in part by Opus Dei technocrats.[18] This was the case for advertising as well. Advertising took off as the consumer society expanded in Spain during the 1960s, but the sector was already dominated by transnational firms. In 1978, between twenty-five and thirty-one of the leading fifty advertising companies could be linked to foreign owners. Four of the top five firms were J. Walter Thompson (United States), McCann-Erickson (United States), Davis Benton Bowles (United States), and a Belgian firm, Univas.[19] J. Walter Thompson and McCann-Erickson as well as five other multinational firms were wholly owned by their "mother" firms, indicating a distinct preference for foreign direct investment in this sector.[20]

By all accounts, the TV advertising market in Spain had experienced regular annual growth throughout the 1960s.[21] However, the monopolistic relation between the state-controlled Televisión Española (TVE) and the advertising market provoked much ire among private commercial media promoters. Obviously for these businesses, state-controlled TV offered only limited growth potential. While TVE expanded its advertising throughout the decade following Franco's death, perceived caps on this growth pushed advertisers into other media. Marketing strategies receiving the most dramatic investment since 1970 were in fact direct mail advertising, mail order, and other forms of commercial communication.[22]

Nonetheless, record investment in TV advertising in Spain buttressed the power of this sector, while the Spanish state provided the weakest record of any European country to safeguard against commercialism on television. By 1977, 94.1 percent of TVE's financing came from advertising, with only the foreign-controlled broadcasters in Luxembourg and Malta recording higher levels of dependence. Comparative figures for 1979 provide a telling contrast: France, 35.4 percent; Finland, 24.3

percent, including private TV; Greece, 29.2 percent; Ireland, 48.9 percent; Holland, 25 percent; Portugal, 38 percent; Sweden, 0 percent; Switzerland, 26.8 percent; and Britain, 55.2 percent, including commercial TV.[23] TVE actually boosted advertising income by 1,200 percent between 1975 and 1985.[24]

The challenge of foreign domination to national sovereignty in the electronics and advertising sectors cannot be turned back easily, if at all. Unlike the United States, OECD countries of Europe, and Japan, Spain's internal market has provided a much smaller contribution to its growth than has its participation in external markets. As Manuel Castells et al. note, Spain's economic well-being is "fundamentally" dependent on its participation in the international economy, the most important sectors being cars, electronics, oil, chemicals, finance, and tourism.[25] Though the Spanish economy is inextricably bound to the ups and downs of foreign markets, the government has not (and probably cannot) do anything about it.

As a rule, nations cannot easily compete for parts of global economies that are monopolized by global businesses. Such monopolies internalize many functions and remove them from impersonal, competitive, and unstable market conditions that would otherwise furnish opportunities for new participants. Among the areas most highly guarded by foreign firms is control over technological processes. As noted, Spain has little productive capacity of its own in this area, and the only hope for expansion has come from multinational transfers. By the late 1980s, however, there was no evidence that any of the large firms were going to share their knowledge. Most of the arrangements made between these firms and the Spanish government were limited.

The only thing the Spanish state could do under these circumstances was to regulate capital flows and negotiate some control over technical processes. For instance, flows of capital in the electronics sector could be regulated, at one time, because the majority of billings would go through the national telephone company of Spain, Telefónica. The management of this company was controlled by the state, although the company itself was controlled by ITT. As Fregoso has demonstrated, as a regulator of foreign purchases, Telefónica also served as the national bridgehead for penetration of communication transnationals in Spain.[26] When new and privileged participants entered the national market, such as the regional governments, purchases could bypass this regulatory filter. After the liberalization policies in the 1980s, new contracts with foreign firms were approved that did not include Telefónica. As a result, capital now flows through the electronics sector more freely.

Even when Telefónica controls the technology process, as in the guarantees it received from AT&T when it negotiated to build a microchip factory with the American firm, there are no real means to ensure technology transfer. As Castells et al. asked, "Is AT&T really willing to transfer, *for the first time in its history,* its technology for high-density circuit design just so it can come to Spain?"[27] This question applies to all transnational firms in Spain (the only currently viable source for new technology and know-how) and reflects a crucial weakness of a sector dependent on international markets. It highlights the problem that Spain might forever remain a production and assembly plant for foreign companies, limiting its capacity for innovation and competition.

The enormous power held by transnational electronics firms, and the transnationalized telecommunications providers, gives this branch of the communications sector great influence among Spanish business and political elites. During the transition period this influence was decisive in the formulation of Spain's telecommunication policy.[28] That policy, known as the Ley de Ordenación de Telecomunicaciones (LOT), was a key element of the socialist party's liberalization plan to end most of the quasi-protectionist aspects in the Spanish electronics and communications market. LOT paved the way for a new technical plan for private TV and changed the relation of RTVE to both national and regional scales of broadcasting.

This instance alone warrants a better understanding of the transnational presence in Spanish telecommunication and electronics. Other examples also illustrate the power of this sector. As chapter 13 shows, from the point of view of the regional authorities LOT represented the government's attempt to take back the regional airwaves from the Autonomous Communities of Spain. In addition, as chapter 10 explains, the campaign to promote LOT and the broader plans of reindustrialization (i.e., liberalization) employed a rhetorical strategy that relied on the specter of Francoism to scare businesses and voters into supporting the socialist reforms. Rejecting the failures and fears of the past, the socialists instead offered the pillar of technological modernization to bolster confidence among national business leaders and voters. The PSOE's campaign surrounding the union of Spain with the North Atlantic Treaty Organization, which was subject to a popular vote, and the European Community relied on this rhetoric of modernization. As they took Spain further into the international political economy, the socialists guaranteed that Spain would never again be haunted by the specter of *franquismo.* In exchange they asked Spaniards to accept the military union, the European market, and foreign investment.

Part II

The Politics of Privatization

Broadcasting systems of the world conceal layer upon layer of suppressed conflict; many of the unresolved neuroses from which nations suffer can be found reflected in the ways they choose to organize radio and television.
Anthony Smith, The Shadow in the Cave (3)

Bertolt Brecht once conjectured that from the perspective of a tennis ball in play the laws of physics must not make any sense—objective conditions are experienced as chaos. From the point of view of official politics of the Spanish transition, very little of what was happening must have made sense. With proverbial hindsight an analysis should produce a clear image of the objective forces that set political decisions and actions in motion during the transition. For this reason, writing about the past, and about political situations in which historical actors found themselves, is always a test of the clarity of analytical perspective, a challenge to make sense of the laws of motion obtaining at the time.

Yet one of the deceits of hindsight is to correct the subjective position of political action, to tidy up the details of missed chances, false starts, and aborted projects. Pushed to neglect the chaos experienced at the moment of decision making and action taking, analysis might miss the very rhythms of play and negotiation that characterize policy formulation.

To account for this inherent unruliness of the politics of broadcast reform, the investigation can proceed in two directions: it can remove away layers of suppressed conflicts that get nested around the broadcast system (as noted by Smith in the epigraph to this part of the book), or it can follow, in a more linear fashion, the layering process itself. Both ways seek to make sense of the past while respecting the point of view of the historical agents.

Part II of this book opts largely for the second procedure. It unfolds as a presentation of the layering of political conflict that led to TV reform in the new Spain. Part II aims to maintain an important balance between explaining what the polity experienced and understanding what its decisions and actions meant in the long run. As one state functionary told me, the best analysis of Spanish broadcast policy in this period is one that furnishes "a clear idea of the chaos." This suggests that in the midst of the transition, while everyone knew there was a crisis of state and society, no one knew exactly what would come of it. Likewise, the possibilities for broadcast reform appeared at first to range widely.

4
It's Private: Policymaking for Television in Spain, 1977–82

With only a relative majority through two elections, the Union of the Democratic Center (UCD) presided over the Spanish government until 1982, when this party finally disintegrated. Throughout its tenure it was forced to manage the state through the negotiated break with the past. Basically, the *ruptura pactada* defined the government's actions on three levels: the government had to minimize its own internal battles to keep a very loosely formed alliance of liberals, Christian Democrats, and Social Democrats from collapsing; it had to regulate the schedule of reforms in such a way to avoid aggravating the remaining Francoist institutions, especially the military, which advocated continuity; and it had to negotiate consensus on these reforms with the left opposition, primarily with the Spanish Socialist Workers Party (PSOE) but also with the still-influential Spanish Communist Party (PCE).

In general, the first transition government of the UCD attempted to develop a "high policy" of democratization, that is, a democracy bestowed from above. In the area of cultural policy, the transition to democracy also followed a set of procedures that could be contained and planned from above. In this the government worked from the basis of the Moncloa Pacts of October 1977, the comprehensive and conciliatory agreements over future legislative plans signed by major party heads. As Hooper puts it, the pacts created a "widespread feeling that the politicians, having taken the electors' votes, were now deciding what was good for them."[1] The *ruptura pactada* represented a tacit confinement of social policy to parliamentary negotiation, and the narrowing channels to political power came at a time when the political process might have been opened to greater popular participation.

All attempts to resolve a particular impasse were restricted to this high politics of negotiation. This is especially clear in the framing of the Spanish constitution. The constitution was drafted within a year of the elections and ratified by a public referendum in December 1978. Gunther's study of the constituent process demonstrates how the *ruptura pactada* shaped the thought and behavior of policymakers. In his "Constitutional Change in Contemporary Spain," Gunther shows how the conflict resolution at the center of the constituent process required the active participation of most of the major political parties. Examining the relative weight of private, backroom deals versus up-front parliamentary negotiation, Gunther found that private meetings were favored. Such negotiations led to predebate consensus and successful resolution of opposing positions. The main public opposition to the constitution came from the Basque Nationalist Party (PNV), who refused to vote on the draft on the basis that the Basque natural right to nationhood was denied.

If we could read these inclusions, exclusions, and resistances as so many tea leaves in the cup of democracy, we might have predicted the outcome of TV reform as well. Ideally, the range of choices was open. In practice, the *ruptura pactada* encouraged the reduction of outcomes of television policy to three: (1) maintain the status quo; (2) radically transform RTVE; or (3) legalize private television. At least in appearances, the first was unacceptable to a transition government, especially given the latter's eponymous mandate. The second appealed to the opposition—at least rhetorically—but not the ruling party, which benefited from the inordinate amount of control over TVE conferred to it by existing law. And the third held no legitimacy, as yet, with the majority of either continuist or reformist factions in the government. When private TV became a real option, it had the impact of a first shot fired in battle—it split ranks and destroyed the basis of political negotiation.

Franco had been dead a little over five years in the spring of 1981 when a faction within a new UCD cabinet, recently formed by President Leopoldo Calvo Stelo, announced plans to present a bill that would legalize private TV in Spain. This factional action exacerbated tensions within the UCD, primarily between Social Democrats on one side and Christian Democrats and Francoists "of liberal spirit" on the other. (Ironically, the split in the UCD was generated by a fight over a new divorce law staunchly opposed by the Christian Democrats. The fight over TV somehow seemed a fitting corollary to these divorce proceedings.) The private TV bill served as a catalyst to undo the alliance that had kept this coalition party in power since 1977. The external appearance of a steady alliance of reformers was a key element of the party's legitimacy.

At the same time, the ruling party's ability to manage all reforms of transitional politics with consensus was a crucial external factor. Political negotiation was, after all, the sine qua non of the pacted transition to democracy, and any breach of this implied social contract promised to make the UCD vulnerable, to both internal stresses and external pressures.

Eventually the act of proposing a private TV bill helped fragment the ruling coalition party, causing new political alignments. From these realignments emerged a moderate socialist party claiming a new, and more centrist, majority, cast with some of the defecting Social Democrats of the UCD and characterized by a new anti-Marxism (around this time González presented the PSOE with his ultimatum: "Marx or me"). The right coalesced with the defections of the Christian Democrats to Alianza Popular. In the end, the crisis that precipitated the fall of the UCD proved to be a major influence on the politics behind the first (and failed) legislation of private TV. As a consequence of this episode of the political transition, private TV became a legitimate feature on the agenda for a democratic society.

Before Private TV: The UCD Tries a Little Media Reform

Ineptitude and conflict defined UCD media reforms. Between 1977 and 1981, the ruling party seemed to pursue reform halfheartedly, largely in response to external pressure or to minimize damage done to its image. One commentator noted that the policy events sponsored by the UCD served only to confirm that "the government was not disposed to give up a single bit of its rigid political control over the territory of television."[2]

The two most significant reform laws were aimed at liberalizing radio licensing and at making the state-controlled system, RTVE, more democratic. The first promoted a boom in independent radio stations. The second was a bust.

About the same time as the Moncloa Pacts, a law for radio was passed by the UCD government and put into force.[3] This reform lifted the Francoist ban on radio news reports and initiated the so-called boom in radio broadcasting of the 1970s.[4] The boom continued as AM radio spectrum allocation was reorganized and rationalized in 1978, followed by FM spectrum reallocations in 1979.[5] In less than a year, the number of FM stations doubled. Radio reform was not altogether unexpected, nor was it perceived to threaten the government. A number of popular private radio stations had existed prior to the new law with the blessing of the Franco regime (the most important was SER, or La Sociedad Española de Radiodifusión).[6] Far from being a rational part of a coherent media policy, these early reforms of radio under the UCD were actually more of a public relations campaign. According to Moragas, the Suárez administration needed a quick policy event that would portray the UCD as a maker of democratic reforms and a true believer in freedom of expression. The radio law expedited a quick make-over for the transition government at a time when inaction would have aggravated reformist forces.[7]

In contrast, the government appeared to have neglected TV reform altogether, until scandal forced it to act. Against the wishes of the ruling party, the workers' assembly of RTVE set up a committee in 1977 to investigate the internal mismanagement of the state broadcast industry. Although no detailed history of the Anticorruption Committee exists, a series of newsletters produced by the committee revealed private business deals, fraud, censorship, strange procurement procedures, and general disaster.[8] "There are those who earn, literally, twice as much as the king," one magazine reported, summarizing the reports about RTVE.[9] Despite the Anticorruption Committee's investigation, as well as others (one of which described RTVE as a company "on its deathbed"), no action to reform the state system was taken.[10] At least, no action had been publicized. In actuality, the government was working on two fronts but had kept this information from going public.

First was the legal reform of RTVE. Behind the scenes, on the heels of the Moncloa Pacts, the UCD had drafted a reform statute for RTVE. The Estatuto de Radiotelevisión Española (RTVE Statute) was not well known during the investigation of the Anticorruption Committee. Indeed, it was not yet an element in the press accounts of the state system. As happened frequently in the early moments of the transition, the public did not discover what was going on until the government deemed fit. Eventually, scandal, government leaks, and an independent press encouraged disclosure and government action. Years later, it was discovered that in 1977 and 1978 the UCD and the opposition had been haggling over the wording of the final text of the statute, which the UCD cabinet finally approved in December 1978—but to no avail, for the parliament dissolved for the general elections of 1979, preempting debate of the statute.

Meanwhile, Suárez had ordered his own audit of RTVE in 1978 (though this too was only revealed years later). The Ministry of Finance, headed by the Social Democrat Francisco Fernández Ordóñez, had been charged with the duty to get to the bottom of the financial black hole that RTVE had become. The subsidy for RTVE was growing, but the money remained unaccounted for. Graft and other personal excesses combined with disastrous bookkeeping and a general free-for-all production system that evidenced "a degree of inefficiency and dishonesty that at times beggars belief," as one chronicler stated.[11] Once again, the government tried to conceal its investigation — to publicize this account would have clearly announced the UCD's inefficiency and sloth.

Nevertheless, in January 1980 *El País,* one of the most widely read daily newspapers in Spain, got hold of the auditor's report and published a half-dozen articles that told of the official audit from the Ministry of Finance as well as the findings of all prior investigations.[12] The scandal of RTVE became too hard to manage and now even harder to keep out of the press. *El País* made public what the government and the workers' assembly already knew: management made no calculations for income and outgoings; production costs ran on a confusing system of bonuses for regular hour employment, where extra payments were rigged with "production assistants presenting programs, reporters who direct, directors who present, commissionaires who film, and even radio announcers who'll do their job in front of the cameras"; so-called *depósitos personales* (personal stashes) were created by individuals who accumulated clothing, valuable objects, and even the master duplicates of programs as if these were personal property. The audit told of extreme cases of hoarding in which people flatly refused to return programs to RTVE, thus perhaps causing the absence of archive material available for broadcast.[13]

The burden on the UCD government to reform RTVE weighed heavier with each publicized bungle. The press learned well a lesson about its influence through this episode, and would come to repeat the tactic in the future. The government also learned a lesson, namely, that the appearance of inaction only increased pressure from the press and opposition. Shortly after *El País* exposed the state broadcast company to public scrutiny, the government finally enacted the RTVE Statute. Only then, in January 1980, was it reported that the law had been approved thirteen months earlier and drafted as far back as 1977.[14]

The RTVE Statute, as designated in Law 4, January 10, 1980, recognized the necessity to formalize the organization of radio and TV within a set of clear and precise norms. The first and most important of these was the definition of radio and television as "essential public services, the responsibility for which falls to the state." The statute proposed creating an administrative council that was publicly accountable, subject to commercial law in its external relations, and elected by a two-thirds majority of the parliament. The ruling party held the right to appoint the director general, who for a five-year period was allowed to attend council meetings as a nonvoting member. The council was directed to guarantee objectivity (i.e., nonpartisan information), review finances, and enforce the statute.

In calling for the RTVE administration to be nominated by a majority of parliament, the larger parties, UCD and PSOE, did not really give up control to other political forces, though the principle of the statute's article 7 was that RTVE should reflect the mosaic of political parties in parliament. This advantageous position of the larger parties is produced and maintained by existing electoral law, which is modeled on the D'Hondt system of proportionate representation. Article 1 of the statute reinforced state control over spectrum management, although in principle it also urged the polity to define TV and radio as it would any basic necessity; that is, as an essential feature of the spiritual health and cultural well-being of all Spanish citizens. The statute also codified the process whereby regional authorities could build and operate a third channel under state control (article 2).

Although the statute was generally viewed as a sign that the state-run media were effectively being democratized, implementation of the law was conspicuously slow.[15] The Spanish Communist Party and the Catalan minority in the parliament argued that the statute actually caused a setback for disenfranchised and minority groups. They pointed out that centralized control over the national development of new channels explicitly excluded the smaller, less powerful, and more popular broadcasters from cultural policy and from the social means of cultural and political expression.[16] This point of contention would return to spark the events that led to the development of local and regional adventures in broadcasting (see chapter 12).

Further tensions developed in absence of real efforts in RTVE to allocate broadcast time to major social and political groups and to respect the right to reply and correct errors, both of which were guaranteed by the statute. This problem amplified the protests of those groups that were excluded, especially the smaller and extraparliamentary parties. One party leader in particular, Manuel Fraga of Alianza Popular, would have his revenge based on the government's neglect in enforcing this aspect of the statute (see chapter 10).

The press pushed on with its war against state broadcasting, playing up the rhetoric that expressive freedom and democracy would arrive only with commercial media, and encouraging the belief that a social transition in principle called for private TV. With the reports of scandal and sclerotic media policy, it was easy to believe that nothing was going to change. Yet the press's delight in the prospect of private TV compromised its objectivity, for in fact nowhere on the agenda of official government negotiations had private TV appeared.[17] The discourse of TV reform was still incoherent, or inchoate at best. In general, policy discourse was phrased in terms of public expenditure, or how to resolve the embarrassing situation of the national company, or how to correct the bad management of the UCD.

An alternative to the status quo had to be found, but why private TV? The obvious answer is that it was a project of the commercial press and the object of capital investment. Yet the government still had not accepted commercial TV. What was behind this resistance, and why did a faction within the UCD finally choose to propose private TV? The answer can be found in the crisis of the ruling party that followed the elections of 1979 and the breakdown of consensus politics within the government.

5
Unlikely Hegemony, Unfinished Party — UCD in Crisis

By 1980 Adolfo Suárez could no longer control the deterioration of the UCD alliance. He stepped down as president of Spain on January 29, 1981, under conditions that were not clear at the time.[1] The great personal strain associated with the disintegration of the UCD coalition was one likely reason for his resignation. Under Suárez, the party had won two general elections, and, although the historical role he played is often exaggerated, Suárez had achieved some rather astounding reforms.

Adolfo Suárez was virtually alone in getting real consensus for reform among continuists and reformists, using the Francoist constitution and legal apparatus to gain support for open elections.[2] In many ways, "Suarism" and the *ruptura pactada* were synonymous; a crisis of Suarism meant a crisis of consensus, the end of the negotiated break. But the balance of powers would always be precarious under a *ruptura pactada*. The social and political transition to democracy exploded the last vestiges of the hegemony of Francoism with an impact to overwhelm any single leader, no matter how charismatic. The fragmented pieces of the UCD re-formed into factional disputes between Social and Christian Democrats. The anger keeping these factions at odds precipitated a UCD party congress that would turn into a hunt for a scapegoat; Suárez expected to be the hunted. On the eve of the UCD congress, he resigned.

The social hegemony of the state was in question — the center was still undefined. Indeed, in its political form the UCD mirrored this uncertain center. Maravall had called the UCD an "unfinished party." Huneeus described the UCD as a "consociational party," one that was built around a politics of accommodation among bourgeois elites.[3] The accommodations were always perched to go awry: the UCD was neither Social Democrat nor Christian Democrat, liberal nor traditionalist, and the fourteen miniparties and groupuscules that formed the coalition held out more promises of confusion and conflict than consensus and reform. It was also true, as Antonio Bar Cendon notes, that the party system was still in formation in Spain until at least 1982. Until then, it was a highly volatile polity—polarized, fragmented, and characterized by very little popular participation in actual party politics.[4] The socialist Maravall disagrees, and argues instead that there was great stability within the party system, except for one notable failure: the UCD.[5]

In the streets, meanwhile, was a palpable sense that the transition to democracy would either end with state repression or open up to a cultural horizon shaped by revolutions of sexuality, performance, words, and images. Among the more memorable if incidental popular protests were anti-NATO demonstrations, including a festive though long march from Madrid to the U.S. air base in the nearby city of Torrejón; the rallies and reform to legalize abortion (women who chose abortion still faced a sentence of six to twelve months in prison); the marches against church and state led by gay, lesbian, and prostitute activists seeking reform of the penal code governing sexuality; the movement to end public subsidy of the Catholic church and get it out of education; the major prison riots demanding better conditions; widespread protests against the street and jail tactics of police, including many documented cases of torture; the radical reforms to democratize the military; and the movement and marches for freedom of expression, especially after the military trial of the theater group Els Joglars in 1978 (unchanged military laws—enforced despite the constitutional guarantee of free expression—entitled the military to prosecute, jail, and censor artists, journalists, and conscientious objectors).

Anyone who lived in Spain under the UCD government witnessed, or participated in, countless similar episodes of revolt, resistance, and movement. It was precisely this external pressure on the government that ensured democratization, however, even if such pressure polarized parliamentary and extraparliamentary political practice.

Behind the political and social transitions lay a deteriorated economy, strained further by popular demands for equitable development and social integration. A prolonged drought brought great losses in the agricultural sector, and productivity stalled while inflation soared. Spain continued to record the highest unemployment levels in Europe. A militant working class flexed its muscle, as laborers in the post-Franco era struck together for 150 million working hours in 1976, an unbelievable surge from 14.5 million hours in 1975. Strike hours continued to defy the state and commerce, even though they decreased to 110 million hours in 1977 and 68 million hours in 1978.[6]

An equally powerful test came from the regionalist movements in the Basque Country and Catalonia. These movements of self-government combined with economic power and parliamentary strength to challenge the ability of the UCD to maintain steady state relations. The 1978 constitution stipulated that Spain was a "State of the Autonomies." In such a state, the regions and provinces could achieve a certain amount of political and economic independence from the central powers in Madrid. This reorganization of the Spanish state created another source of tremendous strain, as massive investments were needed to cover the overhead costs of creating regional administrations. In addition, fiscal assurances of healthy autonomous governments had to be created under economic conditions that had fractured the Spanish territory into very unequal and stratified parts (see chapter 2).

The UCD leadership was notoriously reticent about devolution of powers to the regions—if not for fiscal reasons alone, then also because the coalition was dominated by members opposed to the nationalist movements. For their part, the political leaders in the Basque and Catalan regions became increasingly angered by the slow devolution process.

Under pressure from the Basques and Catalans to implement the reforms guaranteed by constitutional mandate, Suárez broke ranks and promised to advance the process of devolution. This helped Suárez gain support from the regions for the UCD coalition prior to the elections of 1979, but it also increased the tensions within the party and aggravated differences within the government over the schedule of decentralization.[7] Decentralization was a risky balancing act. If the process of devolution was not carried out, the ruling party would appear to be stalling the transition to democracy. Suárez needed the cooperation of the Basque Nationalist Party and the Catalan elites. If the ruling party agreed to the statutes of autonomy, there was the chance that the new regional governments (to be voted into existence) would exclude the UCD; the risk for the center lay in the unknown strength of separatist forces. It seemed imperative that Suárez court the more moderate nationalists, though in doing so he was also courting disaster. The fact was that nobody knew the extent of regionalist sentiment among the voters before the 1979 elections. Fear that the center would fall was commonly expressed in words like Balkanization, the possible disintegration of the Spanish state.

Already after the elections of 1977, UCD's hold on the fragile transition government was very tenuous, given the aggressive nature of the opposing forces that had to coexist within it.[8] Following the 1979 general elections, which Suárez called after the ratification of the constitution, the political environment became even less stable. The UCD had held its ground, but its support was concentrated in the conservative and less-developed regions of Castile, León, Galicia, Extremadura, and the Canary Islands. As for the opposition, a striking rise in the nationalist vote in the Basque and Catalan regions deprived the PSOE of any gains. Voting blocs were changing, electoral loyalties could not be predicted by polls, and abstentions were on the rise.[9] Nationalist parties had grown in size and influence in the Basque and Catalan regions. In the municipal elections of April 1979 (the first in forty-six years), the UCD was beaten miserably by the nationalists and by the left. As Carr and Fusi stated, the "UCD would control the central administration without any power base in the provinces."[10]

Suarism was in crisis. The government Suárez formed at the close of 1979 said as much: the transition and consensus were ending. He appointed his cronies and close associates to high government posts. He effectively canceled the negotiated reforms of education and divorce. He pursued regressive labor laws and new free market rhetoric. From the left's point of view, Suárez seemed to move in a decidedly rightward direction. In contrast, his negotiations for statutes of autonomy for the Basques and Catalans appeared, from the Francoists' point of view, a betrayal of Spain. Suárez became remote, confiding only in his closest associates; he even refused to appear on television. The heads of the various parties and groups in the UCD, the so-called barons, were becoming increasingly dissatisfied with his behavior. Shaken even more were the lives of everyday folks, threatened by an upsurge of violence. The number of women raped had risen alarmingly. In 1979 and 1980, the number of deaths attributed to terrorism totaled 131 and 124 respectively, compared to 88 in 1978, 29 in 1977, and 20 in 1976.[11] By the spring of 1980, the problems within the UCD leadership led to what the press called the "revolt of the barons." The factional powers of the UCD challenged the monocolor government of Suárez, and the opposition moved in with a vote of censure.

Suárez won, however briefly, a small reprieve. He recovered consensus within his party by reconciling with the barons, while he acted to regain political support by offering further deals to the regional authorities, especially to moderates in Catalonia. Carr and Fusi argue that Suárez made these decisions rather than risk new elections, or form new alliances with the left or right.[12] In the summer of 1980, he formed his fifth and final government. He brought the barons back in and gained the public support of the Catalans. His new government, pushed by Andalusian regionalists, worked to bring Andalusia onto the fast track to autonomy. Eventually, the government accelerated all the negotiations over the statutes of autonomy for the remaining provinces of Spain. The quid pro quo for a generous policy toward the nationalists was moderation and cooperation with the central administration. This was clearly the moment of the transition, when democracy in Spain had finally become "indissolubly linked to the autonomy of the regions."[13]

There were those who saw the nation-state as under threat of extinction, and their anxieties were privileged and well publicized by right-wing newspapers like *Ya, ABC,* and the explicitly pro-coup newspaper *El Alcázar* (which was also regularly distributed to the military garrisons). In 1979, for example, General Jaime Milans del Bosch, military commander of the motorized division at Valencia, summarized the transition for the newspaper *ABC* as follows: "Objectively speaking, the balance of the transition period appears negative: terrorism, the collapse of law and order, inflation, the economic crisis, unemployment, pornography, and, above all, the crisis of authority."[14] It would be a mistake to underestimate the presence of "unreformable" military powers and other nostalgic followers of the old regime. Amid the popular protests and party politics, they were *the* central presence against which civil society had come to be defined in Spain. Eulogies and demonstrations honoring Franco were still regular occurrences during this period. These Francoist meetings, together with publicized threats of military uprisings—mostly veiled, like those of Milans del Bosch—often precipitated fascist youth gangsterism, thuggery, political assassinations, and rumblings inside the armed forces.

A key element of the transition had been the military's acquiescence to democracy; after all, its own self-image was to be "the defenders of the will of the citizens."[15] This respect for the new order was focused on the king, the supreme commander in chief, who frequently called on the troops to remind them that their first duty was to democratic society. This balance of forces led some historians of the period to underplay the threats of those like Milans del Bosch.[16] To others it was clear that "ultra-right elements in the armed forces might take it upon themselves to cut the Gordian knot" in which Spain had become entangled—the knots of devolution to the regions, the end of the one great and good Spanish nation, anarchy and the crisis of authority.[17] Stories of secret plans of a military coup were common currency among rumormongers, and such a threat was very palpable in these days of crisis.

The military intervened less than a month after Suárez resigned, on the day when the parliament was scheduled to vote on the appointment of his successor, Leopoldo Calvo Sotelo (this was a second round, after a split vote two days earlier failed to elect Calvo Sotelo). Protagonists of the transition converged on the morning of February 23, 1981. The entire government—centrist, socialist, communist, nationalist, and (the one) fascist—was present when a group of soldiers from a unit of the Guardia Civil burst into the congressional chamber firing machine guns. Led by Colonel Antonio Tejero Molina, three hundred troops had been rousted out of their barracks with orders to proceed to the parliament and save the government from an attack by Basque terrorists. When they arrived, brandishing pistols and firing machine guns, they found no terrorists—only a terrified congress. The minister of defense, who was sitting next to Suárez, was pushed back in his seat as he tried to order them to stop. Suárez stood in response and was threatened, as were all, with a round of fire; orders to sit were shouted and scared everyone to the floor. (Legend has Santiago Carrillo, the communist leader, resisting this posture until forced at gunpoint to the floor.) Tejero announced that the parliament was dissolved for good and that the proper military authorities would soon take control.

For eighteen hours, the country was traumatized with the prospect of the return to the past. Rumors floated that political leaders in the regions were fleeing the country. Other tales in the street spoke of armed peasants in the south of Spain and heroic leftist militants rushing to their party offices to retrieve and hide documents, archives, books. Friends called friends to ensure their safety, offer a drink or a hand to hold; others celebrated.[18] Horror stories circulated fastest—leftist journalists, among others on a prepared list of victims, would be captured and killed in the Bernabeu football stadium, in mimicry of Chilean and Argentinian coups.

The national police were mobilized to protect citizens against insurgent military factions. This created a confusing image: police tanks aimed their guns at the occupied building, and civil guards aimed theirs oppositely. News circulated that Valencia was captured by insurgent troops. Yet no one was very sure if the coup covered the territory or if the only uprising was in Madrid, where one could see the parliament under siege, or see and hear that the RTVE offices had been captured. The national radio played military marches, while TVE presented blinkered news reports about events, with newsreaders, eyes shifting in fright, saying all is well. Later TVE showed an old Bob Hope movie in which he played a buffoon-pirate.

After midnight, and after many helpless hours, Spaniards watched as the king of Spain appeared on TVE. No one knew for sure until then that he refused to join the coup or that he had not been killed; it had been a very long while before he appeared. It was not clear that TVE had been recaptured by troops loyal to the government, and the king was the first to report that there was going to be no uprising and no end to democracy. He calmed fears and, as if speaking directly to them, commanded the insurgents to withdraw. Later it was revealed that the king had rallied all but two divisions to the defense of Spanish democracy. The next day international news reported how the U.S. government refused explicitly to aid the democratic government of Spain, declaring the situation an internal affair; France could only offer an airplane to retrieve the king from harm's way. Liberal democracy failed to practice its internationalist rhetoric. That night, many believers in democracy became monarchists, if only for a brief time.

Tranquillity had barely settled in when, one month later, a draft of the first bill to legalize private TV in Spain was announced among the leadership of the UCD. The events of the preceding months—the crisis of Suarism, the return of the barons, the accelerated devolution process, and the attempted coup d'état—had polarized the ruling party. The new president, Leopoldo Calvo Sotelo, could not manage to bring it together again. The Christian Democrats fought the Social Democrats, and the Social Democrats cozied up to the socialists. The RTVE Statute notwithstanding, the UCD had failed to consolidate its control over television. Reform battles within the ruling party centered on divorce, which the Christian Democrats opposed. When the draft of the private TV bill was presented to the UCD cabinet, the internal dispute it created revolved almost entirely around political process; content did not seem to be an issue. Members who saw the bill for the first time primarily fumed about their associates: "They hadn't consulted anyone!"[19]

The discussion of a private TV bill in March 1981 must have seemed rather mindless to onlookers given the turbulent days that the country had just suffered, but the right-wing members of the UCD executive who prepared the bill turned out to be quite mindful that private TV was going to be their last chance to win a national forum. The next elections promised little for this party, and the right-wing conservative factions in government had some way to go before they could consolidate a democratic, non-Francoist image. Meanwhile, the socialist opposition and the nationalist parties were well positioned to absorb the political center that the UCD failed to manufacture. The PSOE had only to appear more democratic when it came to the private TV bill, and for that reason, perhaps, opposition to private TV came to rely on the symbolism of consensual process represented by the negotiated break—a process that the proposal from the UCD executive threatened to violate. Over the next year, the spectacle of democracy, staged as official politics, would come to divert attention from the search for an intelligent, viable alternative to both state-controlled TV and private TV.

6
Political Failure, Broken Rules, and the Symbolic Advance of Private TV

Following the example of the Italian Christian Democrats who proposed private TV as the alternative in Italy in the mid-1970s, a faction within the UCD used the bill as a preemptive tactic to gain control over future channels. The tactic, as Costa argues, was meant to subvert reform of the public service system in order to undermine the opposition.[1] The Spanish Socialist Workers Party (PSOE) had gained in the polls with every failure of the UCD, and the internal crisis of the ruling party helped even more to further the socialist alternative. The PSOE was placed to make considerable gains in the next election, then scheduled for 1983, and most commentators assumed that it would win.

The socialists could then augment their control of RTVE either by enforcing the 1980 statute as the opposition, or by operating exclusive control of RTVE as the ruling party. When the Italian conservatives faced demands for reform of television, they too were suffering a crisis of their hegemony and rushed to legalize a privately controlled TV.[2] It might seem simple mimicry, but the politicization of TV by a faction within the UCD was generated by a crisis of legitimacy of the Christian Democrats and other former Francoists "of liberal spirit."[3] They had lost their claims for hegemony within the government and saw television as the next best forum for manufacturing consensus. Whether they would be able to control television was still a question, though *El País* soon reported that the UCD held strong connections to private interests willing to invest in a commercial TV enterprise.[4]

In the spring of 1981, word began to circulate that the UCD was bringing the bill to the parliament. *El País,* a perennial promoter of private TV, reported months later about the outrage that surged among the ranks of the PSOE, which rushed to champion opposition to private TV. A spokesperson for the PSOE predicted that presentation of the bill would provoke a "juridical conflict of grand proportions" and said it represented further evidence of the inability of the UCD to lead Spain into a democratic future.[5]

Basically, the public had no way to know what private TV was about. The communists explained: "Private TV does not mean more freedom of expression because only the few with the means at their disposal to start up a broadcast station would have this freedom."[6] The press chimed in: the UCD needed a medium sympathetic to it for the next election campaign, so it would create one. To add to the confusion, *El País* also alleged that the leadership of UCD and PSOE had made a secret pact to postpone TV privatization until after the elections scheduled for 1983.[7] And the PSOE lectured: "In countries with long-standing democratic traditions, studies suggest that the technical application of new TV channels can lead to foreign influence on national sovereignty."[8] Private TV was about economic stratification, serving the rich. Private TV was about political control and propaganda, serving the political classes. Private TV would mean a loss of national sovereignty, a Trojan horse deploying external influence. In all these accounts private TV seemed more trouble than it was worth.

Some measure of its worth had in fact already been established. After all, an additional channel was long thought to be a way to overcome the dominance of the "bunker" RTVE. The idea of public service television had been discredited with great force by the publicity surrounding the scandals in the state-controlled broadcasting company. As noted in chapter 1, the tainted RTVE was the only real experience that Spaniards had of a public service regime. It seemed simple: the value of a new channel was measured against its appeal as not-state-TV. The option of the political classes' controlling TV was out, having been cast in a negative light. The problem for the UCD was that this shadow spilled over onto their proposal for private TV. One force remained to turn a positive spin on the prospect of a commercial television system—namely, the press.

The press war against RTVE had not subsided. On the contrary, the rhetorical sorties that had served the private press well—linking private TV to innovation and expressive freedom and state TV to corruption and unfreedom—increased, the damage becoming even more severe after the February 1981 coup attempt. During the coup, the RTVE studios were occupied and controlled by insurgent troops. Old Bob Hope movies showed on TVE and military music played on the national radio. In a fortuitous turn of events, the commercial radio remained untouched by the renegade troops, who did not seem to have done their homework on the changing media environment in Spain.

Commercial radio vigorously sought to keep the population informed about troop movements around the country, while a popular sports-caster gave blow-by-blow coverage of the takeover from outside the parliament building. Even the captive members of parliament listened to these reports on their transistor radios. Until the soldiers confiscated the little receivers, the members could compare the radio version of the coup's progress to their captors' version. The commercial radio announced how Valencia had fallen under a state of emergency, declared by none other than Milans del Bosch, and how a tank division was seen rolling toward Madrid; but other garrisons seemed quiet, unwilling to join the rebels. The commercial radio reported how many of the young soldiers inside the congress defected in the middle of the night once they realized their folly. For the government and for the people of Spain, there was perhaps no better demonstration of the dangers of total state control over the electronic media. Nor would there be a more memorable event that revealed the democratic potential of new, independent audiovisual channels. (The fact that the work of individual journalists and technicians of TVE played a key role against the coup that day is still often forgotten.)[9]

The press got a further boost from the increasingly inept government, as old political antagonisms reemerged in July 1981. Pío Cabanillas, general director of social communication under the presidency, solicited a legal study from the Council of State to determine whether the UCD could push the bill through parliament by means of a simple decree, also called an ordinary law.[10] Cabanillas had been one of the founding members of the UCD, a key "liberalizer" who served under Franco as minister of information. His attempt to find legal support for a decree enraged the Social Democrats, and the feud became headline material for some months.

The dispute centered on the fact that a decree or ordinary law does not require two-thirds of the parliamentary vote for passage, as does an organic law. The tacit accord of the *ruptura pactada* would be violated if passage of the bill were pursued in this manner, especially when consensus about the bill had not been negotiated among the major parties prior to its introduction. Consensus politics had already been lost within the UCD, and it was obvious that consensus would be impossible to achieve in an open parliamentary debate.

Within the UCD, opposition to the bill was led by Francisco Fernández Ordóñez, then minister of justice and leading member of the Social Democrats. Fernández Ordóñez will be remembered as the finance minister during the state's investigation into corruption of RTVE. As minister of justice he was the primary force behind the highly divisive divorce law. A Harvard-educated economist and former tax inspector and president of the National Institute of Industry under Franco, Fernández Ordóñez had been a key player in the UCD coalition. By bringing his strong liberal convictions to the coalition, he conferred the democratic legitimacy that Suárez alone could not provide. Under Calvo Sotelo's direction, the rightward tendencies of the party were well on their way to antagonizing the Social Democrats, especially Fernández Ordóñez. Tensions increased as dozens of UCD members joined with the Social Democrats and the opposition to pass the divorce law.

In July 1981, the same month that the divorce law went into effect, Fernández Ordóñez joined with the PSOE and PCE in opposing the ordinary law for private TV. This combined opposition further stalled the development of a private TV law, but it also paradoxically made feasible the continuance of government control over television.[11]

This was a key moment in the symbolic advance of private TV. The political maneuver to create a law by decree altered the course, and discourse, of TV reform within the polity. The mode of transitional politics that had served to promulgate some semblance of stability through consensus among political forces — namely, the *ruptura pactada* — had been jettisoned with the proposal of a law by decree. The UCD had broken the rules of the game. In doing so, it had redirected the attention of the opposition from the question of private TV as a suitable, desirable alternative in itself to the issue of the legislative process per se. Decisive too was the timing of this attempt to finagle a decree law, for it happened in the midst of the government crisis, splitting like a wedge the irreconcilable divisions left by the divorce legislation.

Only a small minority of the parliament spoke out against the actual premise of the bill, though all were furious at the impropriety of the proposal of a decree law. The PSOE, for example, accepted the idea of private TV as an alternative on the condition that certain restrictions be placed on advertising. The socialists offered no reason for supporting private TV, nor did they give any indication what the nature of the restrictions on advertising would be. This weak response exposed for the first time their lack of a developed platform on cultural policy. Only the PCE opposed the idea on the reasonable grounds that economically privileged groups would be the sole beneficiaries of private channels, citing a similarly hasty and ill-conceived legislation in Italy that had created the conditions for the commercial television oligopolies of Berlusconi, Mondadori, and Rusconi.[12]

Throughout the summer, the fight over the decree law reached a high level of political debate, intensified with the usual accusations and finger-pointing. An important change took place in the government at the end of August, when news leaked that President Calvo Sotelo had received an official letter of resignation from Fernández Ordóñez.[13] As Fernández Ordóñez formed new parties and moved closer to the PSOE, the instability of the government worsened. The public now focused more than ever on the internal problems of the UCD.

In the midst of this public spectacle, Pío Cabanillas was appointed minister of justice to replace Fernández Ordóñez. Cabanillas's successor in the office of the presidency, Matías Rodríguez Inciarte, immediately issued a statement saying that the bill for private TV would be tabled and studied more closely. But with the opposition now absent within the UCD, the government reintroduced the bill in less than a month. Years later Fernández Ordóñez told a reporter at *Tiempo* magazine that "to have approved that piece of junk would have caused a political earthquake." It seemed he could not tolerate the unilateral action of the UCD leadership, the use of the ordinary law, or the rightward turn of the party—all of which the private TV bill came to embody for him. In the same interview, he said, "I opposed the bill because it was an aberration of juridical process to legalize private TV by decree, and I asked that it be negotiated with the PSOE."[14]

In September 1981, the UCD let it be known that the Council of State had approved the process of a law by decree. Furthermore, the UCD said, the Council had issued provisions for licensing private television channels and allocating frequencies.[15] At this time, the UCD appeared to have legal consent to push its previous bill through parliament. Indeed, private TV might have been legalized were it not for one of those historic ironies that give these plots their interesting twists and diversions. A certain lawsuit had been filed with the constitutional tribunal a month earlier by a private TV promoter seeking the right to start a commercial channel. The court's decision promised to determine once and for all the legal process for creating a private TV law. The UCD government was made to wait again, this time because of actions taken by like-minded interests.[16]

In early August 1981, Antena-3, a commercial radio company, filed a suit against RTVE. Antena-3 was part of a conglomerate that owned, at the time of its lawsuit, the two largest publishing houses in Spain and a private news agency. Having been denied a broadcast license two years earlier, Antena-3 charged RTVE with operating in violation of article 20 of the Spanish constitution. Article 20 guarantees freedom of expression, which Antena-3 claimed was restricted by the lack of competition within a television market controlled exclusively by TVE. It argued that the constitution mandated the multiplication of TV channels, with private TV among them, as a guarantee of free expression. If the constitutional tribunal found that article 20 stipulated as much, then the government would be forced by law to issue new broadcast licenses.

The press, government, and TV promoters awaited the decision of the tribunal through the autumn of 1981 and into the next year. In the meantime, Calvo Sotelo reiterated that his goal was to legislate some form of private TV regardless of the high court's decision. Again, such apparent belligerency in the face of the democratic process worsened the split inside the UCD.

Finally, the tribunal issued its judgment at the end of March 1982. The news was leaked by Europa Press, the news agency of Antena-3, three days before the official notice. The leak said that the tribunal ruled in favor of Antena-3 and that the law is explicit in its mandate for private TV. This notice raised expectations of the TV promoters only fleetingly, however, for when the official version of the tribunal's decision was released it contradicted the Europa Press story and dashed hopes for a fast-track decree of private TV.

"It isn't a juridical-constitutional exigency," said the tribunal about private TV, stipulating further that private TV is not "necessarily a derivation from article 20." The creation of private TV is "rather a political decision that can be adopted within the framework of the constitution *by means of an organic law.*"[17] This decision took the UCD and promoters of private TV by surprise and sent them steaming back to the drawing board. They had expected that a year at most would be all they would have to wait for new commercial licenses for broadcast television.[18] "We are where we were a year ago," said the technical secretary in Cabanillas's ministry of justice. "The debate is still open."[19] Robles Piquer, Calvo Sotelo's appointee as director general of RTVE, noted indignantly that "the constitutional tribunal has forced the government to submit to an organic law and parliamentary consensus."[20] Antena-3 published a book a few months later with a title that translates to "The reasons for private TV."[21]

The opposition was satisfied that the issue had been returned to the negotiation table. One exuberant communist administrator on the RTVE council exclaimed that the will of the legislature had been vindicated in the high court's decision, "making private TV impossible."[22] Only the RTVE Statute remained as the guiding principle of television reform.

Immediately after these revelations, the UCD government promised that no new proposals for private TV would be forthcoming. In less than a week's time, however, the UCD reneged and said it was ready to present two new bills to the parliament. Rodríguez Inciarte, general director of social communication under the presidency, announced on April 7 that one of the bills proposed a law by decree and would cover concession of broadcast licenses (it was purely technical), and the other would be developed as an organic law to address issues of freedom of expression.[23] Suspicion arose, for obvious reasons, that the "new" laws had been drafted prior to the tribunal's decision.[24] Although this might have appeared to some observers as foresight on the part of the UCD executive, the proposition that licenses could be handed out for private TV without parliamentary debate showed contempt for the tribunal and the democratic process.

Nonetheless, the announcement of a private TV law raised expectations in the press and among the private TV promoters. These reached a peak on April 11, when copies of the proposed bills appeared in the pages of *La Vanguardia,* the Spanish newspaper with the greatest circulation at the time and whose publisher formed part of the Antena-3 conglomerate. Once the proposed bills were published, it was clear that the UCD was adamant about private TV, pleasing commercial promoters, who celebrated with abundant coverage of the event.

The development of the government's new logic behind the legislation represents the second key moment of the symbolic advance of private TV. Once the first advance of private TV was achieved after the decree maneuver (that is, making the issue one of process rather than content), the UCD was able to keep private TV on the legislative agenda. Now the UCD readily agreed that article 20 was not the principle to follow, for, with respect to the constitution, article 20 called for political negotiation and consensus in matters of freedom of expression. So the UCD shifted the support of its claims for private TV to article 38, which, in contrast, required government intervention to support freedom of commercial enterprise. Private TV was now about business freedom and the freedom to do business.

The new logic worked as follows. Article 38 explicitly "recognizes free enterprise within the framework of a free market economy" and further stipulates that "the public powers guarantee and protect its existence . . . and if necessary, its planning." Hence, a separate organic law could be reserved for social and political questions such as fair access, expressive freedoms, censorship, right of reply, and the like. But where the technical and economic questions of free enterprise were concerned (as if absent social and political content), an ordinary law could be expeditiously deployed—in fact, the UCD argued, it was necessary. The UCD had in effect offered to guarantee, protect, and plan commercial TV with the backing of a constitutional mandate.

Adapting the language of article 38 to their cause also provided a powerful new element to the rhetoric of the private TV promoters who had hitherto pegged their arguments to notions of free expression. From this moment on, the discourse of private TV no longer relied exclusively on the cultural politics embedded in calls for a transition to democratic freedoms — though this rhetoric endured. Instead, the political and business classes who wanted commercial TV made the more narrow argument that legalizing private commercial TV fell under the juridical-constitutional exigency to liberalize the economy. For them, the transit from dictatorship to civil society devolved from the previous negative definition (not-Francoism) to a positive definition that made the commercial marketplace the end point of democracy.

But it was too late for the UCD. The two TV bills it proposed were never debated and, as it turned out, would be among the last efforts of a moribund UCD to make any laws. Its alliance had weakened to the extent that it could no longer withstand the attacks of the socialist opposition — an opposition that had become more powerful and popular in the same measure that the UCD had declined. Yet the crisis had produced a lively new discourse to back the efforts of private TV promoters. At this stage, it might be said that the concepts of free enterprise, private TV, and democratic communication had become interchangeable. As these episodes demonstrate, the origins of this elision can be traced to that same slippery foundation that gave Spain the UCD.

It's Still Private: The Rise of the Spanish Socialist Workers Party

The Spanish Socialist Workers Party (PSOE) gained much ground after the elections of 1979. In its twenty-eighth congress, held in May 1979, the leader of the PSOE, Felipe González, engineered a radical reformulation of the party's orientation. This change started when the party voted to reassert its Marxist-democratic identity against the protest of González, who resigned as a result. In the aftermath of this ploy, he was begged to rejoin the party and was reelected as secretary, forming an executive leadership that included none of the critical Marxists. He then turned the leadership full face toward a center-left orientation that the left-wing Social Democrats of the UCD found appealing. González began to speak of a "new majority" and portrayed the young technocrats of the PSOE as the only "realistic" alternative for a democratic Spain.

One key area in which the socialists were gaining a base of support, and where the UCD was ineffective, was among the national business elites. In its program of economic recovery, the PSOE argued that Spanish capitalism needed to be developed, with the strategic assistance of the state, into a full-fledged member of the international economy. This required a concerted effort to dismantle the remaining relics of protectionism and invite increased international investment, while providing the necessary subsidy to potential growth sectors within the national economy. What the PSOE offered was a type of assisted (state) capitalism combined with a free market reduction of trade barriers. This attempt to find an "appropriate strategy for integration" into the international market was proffered as the least harmful option for traditional national businesses.[25]

The UCD, in contrast, was dominated by free market ideologues who had found uneven support from national industries. Calvo Sotelo had followed Suárez's last initiative in urging the party to accept free market principles, reduce state expenditures, offer incentive to the private sector, and keep wages artificially low. Yet most attempts by the UCD to make modest liberalizations in the economy (private TV among them) were resisted by national business leaders. The conventional wisdom appeared to be with the PSOE, whose revised form of assisted capitalism seemed a safer route to recovery.[26]

Assisted capitalism—an inheritance from the Franco era—offered reassurance to these financially conservative interests. The very powerful Spanish Confederation of Business Organizations (CEOE), for example, insisted that the tradition of assisted capitalism should be continued but under conditions that provided a greater degree of social control.[27] In other words, the state should manage the economy in concert with the CEOE, a clear call for a corporatist framework to guide national economic policy, and also an implicit rejection of UCD free-market demagoguery. The tension between proponents of assisted capitalism and the advocates of competitive capitalism tended to color many of the schisms among members of the UCD.

By withholding state support to the ailing economy, the UCD projected an image of incompetence that alienated the leaders of the Liberal and Social Democratic wings of the UCD coalition. This schism would eventually convince the "left" within these parties to join the socialists in the 1982 elections. This new PSOE—the new majority—promised to implement a more "realistic" policy of assisted capitalism, one that would combine notions of competitive and assisted capitalism as a way to bring national investors into the process of privatization.[28]

The character of these platforms came down to a kind of free enterprise with a safety net, precisely the mandate of article 38. By the time the last UCD-sponsored bills for private TV appeared, however, the ruling party had forsaken whatever confidence among business leaders it might have had. The authors of the two bills, whom Moragas identified as notable advocates of a free-market ideology of competitive capitalism, did not understand how little support or trust there was for their management.[29]

With reason the confidence level among the PSOE leadership rose as the reputation of the UCD sank. "Don't forget," said the spokesman for cultural affairs for the PSOE, "those laws approved by simple decree can also be revoked by simple decree."[30] Thus spoke a future government. Needless to say, when the proposed bills were presented to the parliament at the end of April 1982, they fell into obscurity without debate. Still, in the following months expectations for broadcast reform rose to such a pitch that over seventy groups claimed to be ready to begin commercial television broadcasts within the year.[31] The symbolic advance of private TV had been complete.

Out of the clamor arose the first applicants for private TV licenses. These initial applicants included *La Vanguardia,* who joined Antena-3 and Radio 80 to form the promotion company TEVISA; La Sociedad Española de Radiodifusión (SER, the private radio company) with Tele 80; the newspaper *ABC* with Izaro Films in a venture called Canal 7; a promotion company called Radio-TV 16 (later Tele 16), of the group owning the magazine *Cambio 16* and newspaper *Diario 16*; Grupo Zeta; and Teleunión.[32]

All the excitement subsided as soon as the parliament dissolved in an open crisis and early general elections were scheduled for October. To no one's surprise, the PSOE won an absolute majority of seats in the government, Felipe González became president of Spain, and the agenda of TV reform was redrawn.

That private TV would be placed permanently on the political agenda because of a failed attempt to put it there is one of the most fitting ironies of the transition in Spain. Though obviously hard to unravel, political conflicts entangled with all the little internecine battles set the agenda of broadcast reform during the years of UCD rule. Broadcast policy was contingent on the *ruptura pactada,* the political game rules of the transition to democracy. In contrast, the political economy of private TV — i.e., the long-term economic, social, and political character of TV reform — proved to be less of an influential problematic to the policymakers. Their focus was the project of winning and maintaining consensus for the proper management of the political transition.

The UCD was incapable of holding together a very fragile set of institutional arrangements, especially where it sought to appease the old guard while compromising with the new. The reforms the UCD pursued in concert with the democratic reformers, especially devolution to the State of the Autonomies, aggravated the ultraright and the military. At the same time, its belligerency in the face of the organic legal process and its contempt for the constitution alienated the liberal and Social Democratic wings of the UCD coalition. As the crisis of the UCD became more acute, the PSOE gained momentum for an electoral victory by adhering to a politics of negotiation, by developing a program of economic recovery acceptable to dominant business interests, and by achieving a consensus among a "new majority" of center-left Social Democrats. In the process, the PSOE accepted a situation that legitimated as the dominant discourse of broadcast reform the language eliding private TV with free enterprise and democracy.

7
The PSOE: New Rhetoric, New Pressures, and New Strategies for Media Reform

At first, the new government established after the October 1982 elections greeted the issue of television reform with silence. For obvious reasons, media policy was a far less pressing concern than the transference of power to the socialists, their creation of a cabinet of ministers, and the shuffle of appointments at the subministerial level. In response to the silence, however, another lawsuit was filed with the constitutional tribunal, which reached a decision in December 1982 that reiterated its previous verdict in March of that year.

The PSOE did not begin to articulate a position on private TV until the first weeks of 1983. At that time a bill for an organic law of private TV was defeated by the socialist majority. The bill was a product of the rightist party Alianza Popular (AP), now the largest opposition party. With the defeat of the AP bill, the PSOE indicated that it had no intention of furthering the process of TV privatization. The defeat also demonstrated the extent to which the socialists held absolute control over the issue of broadcast reform. Unlike its predecessors, the PSOE represented the absolute majority of the parliament — it did not need to make pacts or deals or coalitions.

This new configuration of political power changed the course of media policymaking, for now the ruling party alone could make or break legislation of new TV channels. If the socialists chose to make private TV a reality, the only remaining official and organized opposition to private TV was the Spanish Communist Party (PCE). The PCE showed miserably in the elections, dropping from 11 percent to 4 percent of the national vote and losing three-quarters of its deputies from the former government. The UCD dropped to 7 percent of the vote, marking its virtual disappearance with the elimination of 156 of its previous 168 deputies. The PSOE had a substantial mandate with 202 deputies and 46 percent of the vote, followed by Alianza Popular, with its 25 percent of the vote and 106 deputies.

Predictions, Promises, and Surprises

Just past midnight on February 11, 1983, Felipe González made what is perhaps his first public statement as president on the issue of private TV in Spain. The following is an excerpt from that interview, which took place on the privately controlled radio chain SER.

> GONZÁLEZ: If you are referring to private television, let's deal with that. First of all, private television is important only to a few people. It may be important for those who are interested in it, yes, but it's not important to many citizens. What most people want is good public television — most people want good television, public or private: they don't get into distinguishing between whether it's public or private. This battle is colored by ideological twists, at other times with certain vested interests ...
> I look around and find that France has public television, I see that Belgium has public television, and that West Germany has public television, Switzerland has public television, and Sweden and Norway, and on and on and on ... governments of the left, of the right, progressives, conservatives, all maintain their public television. Why do they maintain it? I say that there are two other models: a model that is English, or the British model, and another that is Italian. Both are equally respectable.
> What I cannot accept, and I believe nobody would commit this grave error, is that if there is no private television there is no freedom of expression or that, as is sometimes said, "liberties are restricted." In Spain, we have been enjoying liberties since five, six, seven years ago. In France, a few more years. In Belgium, a few more years. And nobody ever thought of saying, "Look, no freedom exists here because we don't have private television."
> Therefore, the problem has to be stated in its proper terms. There may be problems of defense and of sovereignty, in the sense that we want to avoid cultural dependence or cultural colonialism. It seems that in the future it will be practically inevitable that we receive satellite television programs that have nothing to do, I don't say with public or private television in Spain, but that have nothing to do with Spain. A citizen will press a button, tune to Channel Nine, and unavoidably there will come out via satellite whatever the Soviets or the Americans want to

give us; they'll be the ones who have those satellites with those communications to try to, shall we say, continue in their policy that divides the world up in zones of influence.

SER: In conclusion, what will happen between now and 1986?

GONZÁLEZ: With private television? Probably there won't be any. I say probably. Probably there won't be any.[1]

The rhetoric of this statement foreshadows many of the decisions that the socialists would make over the next three years. The reference to the will and desires of the people is used here and in future statements as the supreme justification for socialist media policy. In principle the discourse of orthodox political democracy is laudable, and it clearly marks out a transitory path beyond authoritarian politics. In practice, the rhetoric was unmatched by acts to open up the process of media reform to public debate and participation.

The reference to the external experience of the older democracies of Europe would also play an ongoing role as a standard against which to measure Spanish development. Within the polity but more prominently within press accounts of media policy, this rhetoric gained its power from another kind of political orthodoxy, which might be called the politics of imitation. What Spain's democratic neighbors were doing would come to be an important guide for socialist policy and for a press determined to promote private TV.

This attachment to orthodox political democracy and to a politics of imitation stands curiously against the statement about cultural defense and political sovereignty. Soviet imperialism notwithstanding, González portrays Spain as subordinate to the imperious world power of satellite technology. It's inevitable, he says, that Spain will get new channels, but these are channels Spain does not need. This rhetoric actually matches more closely the Spanish government's real weakness in safeguarding cultural borders. It presumes the end of protectionism.

The interview with the SER radio chain is on the whole a curious mixture of predictions: no government action to make private TV, but such inaction is what the people want; no government power to stop new channels, but such passivity is what external powers demand. The only obstacle to private TV in this scenario is the Spanish people. If the people change their minds, then it follows that Spain will get its private TV. The transnational framework is assumed.

If rhetoric were reality, then González would have controlled the media environment in the way he rather obliquely described. However, some premises were already clearly established, while others were changing as he spoke. Established was the alternative of private TV, which enjoyed a privileged position on the political agenda and in press headlines, despite González's claim to the contrary. The legal foundations for private TV had been normalized under the previous government and were now harder to remove from the legislative memory. External to official politics were other pressures on the new government that pulled it along a path of unexpected media reform, changing the rules once again.

The most decisive of these new pressures came in two stages from the Basque and Catalan regions of northern Spain. First, regional laws creating the legal entities of Basque Radio and Television (EITB) in May 1982, and the Catalan Corporation of Radio and Television (CCRTV) in May 1983, marked the beginning of the denationalization of the state-controlled airwaves.[2] With this action, the Basque and Catalan governments put into practice a legal right afforded them by the 1978 constitution, by the 1980 RTVE Statute, and by their own statutes of autonomy enacted under the UCD government. The second and most consequential political step was the beginning of experimental broadcasts by Euskal Telebista (ETB, or Basque Television) of the EITB system on January 1, 1983, followed by TV-3 of the Catalan CCRTV system in August 1983.

These actions had tremendous objective force on media policy in Spain; they are perhaps the most decisive element, apart from Franco's death, in the history of broadcasting in democratic Spain. Most significantly, they constituted the first major institutional change of broadcasting since the Spanish civil war, when all broadcast media were nationalized. The first regional television broadcasts in 1983 were also a direct assault on the national legal framework that had controlled broadcasting for more than seventy years (see chapter 12), an attack particularly on the stipulations—reiterated, moreover, in the 1980 RTVE Statute—that gave the central state exclusive control over radiowave communication. The broadcasts therefore took place in the absence of a law allowing the building of transmitters or the use of the airwaves by anyone but RTVE.

Presented with a de facto change in the national media system, the government of Felipe González was forced to legalize a posteriori these two broadcast networks. On December 26, 1983, Law 46 was enacted, which regulated the licensing of a new, third channel to each of the autonomous regional governments. The Third Channel Law maintained centralized state control over the technical infrastructure for use in the Autonomous Communities according to the terms of the RTVE Statute and the respective statutes of autonomy (articles 1 and 2).

The contradictory nature of the Third Channel Law has been problematic from the beginning. How else could it be, given that it enforces centralized state control over the means of communication while condoning the principle of decentralized control over regional culture. The Basque system, for example, tested controversy from the start as the regional government claimed the legal right to build and control a separate technical infrastructure. Obviously, EITB reached this interpretation of the law in opposition to the central government's interpretation of the very same legal norms.

At the heart of the debate are three key documents: the statutes of autonomy, the constitution, and the RTVE Statute. Together these documents support the establishment of autonomous broadcast networks. The RTVE Statute both asserts the control of the RTVE network over all new technical expansions and encourages the development of regional channels, but the Basque government insisted that the constitution and its statute of autonomy gave preference to decentralized control. As a result, the Basques argued that in fact they created a fourth channel, reserving the right to start another channel under the provisions of the Third Channel Law. Aside from the legal dispute, the material outcome was the construction of a new technical infrastructure that literally ran parallel to the RTVE system of transmitters and relays.[3]

This and other controversies surrounding the Third Channel Law are taken up in more detail in chapters 12 and 13, but two changes in policymaking especially important to the present story followed these events. The first figures as part of the longer and more durable changes in the political economy of nation-states. In particular, it concerns the decline of centralism in the Spanish national state. The actions of the Basque and Catalan governments confronted the political authority of the central powers of the state, which was forced to act positively on the legal norms embodied in the constitution, the RTVE Statute, and the statutes of autonomy. These legal norms called for major changes related to the devolution of state power to the regional authorities. Thus, as a real and legal force of devolution, broadcasting in the autonomous regions helped set in motion key practical aspects of the transition to democracy. (One must remember that this degree of influence results from the special power held by the regionalist movements in the Basque Country and Catalonia. The codification of autonomous status among the regions was central to the democratic process in Spain, but the political and economic status of these specific regions was, for historic reasons, much weightier.)[4]

The second change in policymaking was more practical and immediate. The efforts of the Basque and Catalan governments rearranged drastically the agenda of the González administration. The obvious result of the forced change in attitude was rapid reconsideration of the technical problems of frequency allocation and transmitter distribution; discussion of subsequent legal issues related to licensing; and concern with the over-arching question of the political economy of new competition for advertising and audiences.

With enactment of the Third Channel Law, a new policy direction was charted and pursued at breakneck speed. About the same time that the Third Channel Law was formulated, news floated that Felipe González had raised the issue of private TV for debate among the socialist party leadership—some ten months after his SER interview.[5] This reversal of position came on the heels of González's reappraisal of poll data showing that a majority of the Spanish people favored more TV channels—a shift justified by the orthodoxy of political democracy, as previously suggested. Regardless of how attuned to the people González claimed to be, however, he chose private TV over other possible alternatives.

The story surrounding PSOE policymaking concerns the narrowing of potential outcomes of such a framework since the Third Channel Law in 1983. The UCD administration encouraged a limited range of variation of broadcast reform, but the potential outcomes of reform, though restricted, were still open. After all, there was no actual implementation of a private TV law, and the left opposition, which had stood in the main against private TV, was now in power. Witness González's predictions. Moreover, the UCD proved to be a very unstable coalition, and was thereby forced into a higher degree of collaboration with the left opposition. The UCD governed in a period of TV reform defined by the negotiated break. Those years of decision making were characterized by political pluralism, however chaotic the result.

Under the socialists, class alliances shifted, and the nature of broadcast reform shifted with them. The result was diminishing outcomes of broadcast policy reforms. Collaboration among key social actors continued, but with reduced participation of political parties in the opposition.

New Game Rules

The socialists managed a system known in the field of political science as liberal corporatism. The PSOE sought out limited socioeconomic agreements among itself, the socialist-affiliated labor union, and the CEOE, the largest association of business leaders (see chapter 6). The social and economic accord that this group fashioned in 1985 actually included no other major participants; notably absent was the communist labor union, Comisiones Obreras, which comprised the larger blue-collar labor membership.[6] Jessop has argued that social democracy pursues a liberal corporatist strategy precisely because it can secure the support of the largest dominated class.[7] The Unión General de Trabajadores (UGT), the union affiliated with the socialist party, furnished the government with this base of support and helped facilitate the management of the state by agreeing to wage levels, labor market restrictions, and so on. The UGT represented about 29 percent of wage earners in all sectors of the Spanish economy in 1984, and held majority representation of employees in the following sectors: energy (35 percent), retail (44.2 percent), transportation and communication (29.8 percent), and business services, i.e., finance and insurance (27.4 percent).[8]

Working on the principle of induced class collaboration, the socialist government was not obliged to tap into the full range of political and social forces that had defined the previous period of transition. The mandated pluralism of the negotiated break was over, and the political system that replaced it was liberal corporatism.

The decision-making system, or game rules, for the legalization of private TV did not promise to vary much from the paradigm of liberal corporatism. Indeed, if it weren't for the unnegotiated eruption of regional TV, broadcast policy would have been formed entirely by the template of induced class collaboration. Above all, the push for autonomous regional broadcasting proved that extraofficial political pressures could provoke, and actually expedite, reform.

As the story unfolds, a new set of political and corporate alliances emerges to help the PSOE extend its administrative control and consolidate its hegemony. The most striking moment comes when the socialist government is able to leverage itself into a second term using the mere promise of private TV. The symbolic capital of this political power was invested in the PSOE only when it limited the field of TV promoters to a few highly capitalized multimedia companies. Along with its establishment of liberal trade policy and the soft purge of opponents of foreign investment from its ranks, the PSOE was able to use the private TV promise to help bring about the opportunity of reelection. This was a state that came to promise to subsidize the modernization of the national communication infrastructure and to deliver a relatively docile union of laborers in the bargain. Spanish socialism ensured that all would be tied up and well tied down as Spain joined the economic community of European nations, the North Atlantic Treaty Organization, and the market for private TV.

8
For the Few: The Socialist Revival of Expectation for Private TV

The year 1984 was characterized by great expectations for private TV. In the press, the polity, and among businesses eager to advertise their wares, every mention of new commercial television channels generated hopeful signs that new opportunities for investment were around the corner. Also, in 1984 the PSOE clarified its position on television policy, reversing unabashedly its opposition to private TV.

Boosterism for private media competition often received support from highly publicized visits of international luminaries, including Walter Cronkite, who declared in sage tones that "without competition a government can suppress the news."[1] Roy Gibson, former director general of the European Space Agency, forecast that "if the Spanish government doesn't accept two or three private channels, there will be an invasion of pirate transmissions that no one will be able to stop."[2] Ominous references to the year of Big Brother aside (i.e., the state as prison guard of knowledge and expression), these expert opinions supported the reduction of power of the national state and an increase in the flow of international media contents. Echoes of González's statement regarding the inevitable invasion of Spain can be heard here.

The Spanish press enjoyed the rhetoric of this free flow doctrine inasmuch as it manifested the press's own desire to overturn the existing media order. The rhetoric of free flow fit well with the rejection of Francoist institutions that had traditionally relied on protectionist strategies. The appeal of antistate, procompetition declarations was directly linked to the disgust with totalitarian autarky that many associated with the political and economic stagnation of Spain.[3]

Internationalization was also apparent in this press penchant for finding, and often concocting, evidence that liberal democracies around the world were opting for media systems independent of the state. The effect was to portray the socialist government as an isolated stalwart among its peers. The strategy of the press was to exploit González's own appeal to imitate Spain's neighbors, but in a reversal that promoted private ownership, not public TV.

El País, for instance, thought it newsworthy to announce that socialists in Portugal and France had licensed independent television channels.[4] The newspaper reported that in Portugal a private license was issued to the Catholic church in early 1984 to appease the Vatican for the Portuguese abortion law. This account slyly portrayed TV as a protean medium of exchange between state and church, when in fact private TV was not officially sanctioned by law in Portugal for another five years. *El País* also reported—more accurately—that Canal Plus, a commercial pay TV, would soon begin broadcasting in France. *Diario 16*, another Spanish daily newspaper, told an outlandish story that Norway had issued over 430 private broadcast licenses in 1984.[5] Norway did not actually obtain a private TV concession until 1992, although satellite and cable operations had been active since the late 1980s. The press thus played an ironic role of misinforming the public about the downfall of state controls of the media in liberal democracies throughout Europe. Spain, RTVE, and the socialists were made to appear falsely as the last holdouts against the onrush of free expression sponsored by commercial media interests.

Raising further ire about government inaction were the TVE scandals of 1984. Each incident received widespread coverage in the press, which as always compared a corrupt and badly managed state TV to an ideal commercial media, typically depicted as self-regulating and innovating because of free competition. The most curious scandal concerned a very expensive telecast of a 3-D movie on TVE-1. As it turned out, the programmers had been duped into buying a film that was not of the standard they had thought, the technicians did not know how such a system worked in the first place, and TVE did not actually own the appropriate equipment anyway. Worse yet, the farce spread to the public, who had spent an estimated one hundred thousand dollars on special glasses for 3-D viewing, now worthless because of the bungling TVE.[6]

El País chronicled continuing episodes of mismanagement at this time. One of the worst revelations was that TVE had been buying telefilms from French public television through the distributor MGM-UA, which charged an extra 10 to 15 percent commission on top of the program price. The administration of TVE looked rather foolish after reports publicized that it was the only company in Europe paying this extra cost.[7]

The press war continued to ridicule in this manner the government, RTVE, and the notion of state-controlled television. The socialists countered these attacks with promises that television reform would be addressed within a more comprehensive reform legislation. On March 29, 1984, *El País* disclosed that the Ministry of Transport, Tourism, and Communication was in the process of finishing a bill that proposed to integrate telecommunications technologies, including the infrastructure for new TV channels. The draft of the bill was called the Ley de Ordenación de las Comunicaciónes, or LOC, and this was the first major reform bill that treated postal services, telegraphy, telephony, and television in one package. On the surface, LOC appeared to be a radical departure from previously fragmented attempts to reform communications in democratic Spain.

A week after this signal announcement, Felipe González confessed at a meeting of the Association of European Journalists a new belief that a "majority of the Spanish people could favor private TV." He told this group that feelings among the people were so strong that he "would like to take their preoccupation to the party so it will modify its position."[8] In these declarations, González referred to the impotency of the UCD government, which had failed to reform communications. In contrast he emphasized his own strength as a leader who would make democratic change a reality. The spectacle of machismo aside, the news of González's reversal of platform on private TV made front-page headlines.

For the press, expectation of private TV carried tremendous weight of newsworthiness. So much weight, in fact, that this issue shared headlines with an article concerning Spain's position within the North Atlantic Treaty Organization and with the announcement that Spain was going to begin diplomatic relations with Israel.[9] The value that news about the media possesses is in the main arbitrarily assigned. That is, information about the informational-cultural industries has no inherent worth; such news achieves its value largely as a function of the self-promotion of the media and of communication specialists. In other words, it's big news for those who stand (or fail) to gain some enhancement of investment, career, or standard of living because of it. In this case, however, the advance of new media channels was tied to democracy in clearly defined terms: it signified the enhancement of social well-being in the post-Franco era. Its newsworthiness might therefore be seen as value derived from a combination of economic self-interest and a journalistic ethos that advocated democratic reforms. This is only one possible explanation of the press obsession with media reform, but what cannot be disputed is the press support for private ownership.

The day after González had made public his change of position, it was rumored in the press that LOC already contained provisions for the legalization of one new channel to be licensed to private owners.[10] This made González appear disingenuous, especially as the reports said that technical and political information related to private TV was actually being gathered in conjunction with LOC. The contradictory information about LOC would later prove to be a product of a dispute between the president's office and the minister of Transport, Tourism, and Communication.

The radical turnabout of government policy in March and April 1984 was greeted with great skepticism from the opposition. Alianza Popular, the largest party in the opposition, said that the PSOE briefing was a ruse and that the socialists were not really committed to doing anything about private TV until after the elections of 1986. Cynicism reigned among many commentators who could not believe that such an about-face was anything but the result of a backroom deal struck between the PSOE and investors. The PCE attacked the character of the PSOE platform altogether, pointing out that this was one more broken campaign promise. (Throughout this period, the communists refused to support any legislation, including the Third Channel Law, that did not seek directly to reform and democratize RTVE.) The socialist turnabout had to be particularly painful for the activists of the PCE who helped put the PSOE in power in 1982 with the so-called *voto útil*, or practical vote, for the left. The sense of betrayal was palpable for the communists, who held fast to the position that "TV is too important to put in the hands of government, but also too important to be put in the hands of big private interests."[11]

Debates, suspicions, and accusations continued during this period, but the topic of private TV had not yet reached the parliamentary floor for consideration. At the end of April, González asserted his new thinking with ever-greater complacency and announced 1985 as the year that Spain would have private TV.[12] In a veiled reference to global media power, González added that "if the government doesn't do it [create private channels], then the techno-electronic revolution will."[13]

Finally in May the parliament reconvened, and the heated discussions were moved from the press and extraofficial debates to the floor of the Cortes (parliament). On May 2, 1984, González reiterated his intention to authorize private TV. He justified this official declaration with the latest round of public-opinion polls, which showed a majority of Spaniards favorable to private TV.[14] The parliamentary debates that ensued degenerated into finger-pointing battles between Alianza Popular and the PSOE. Each group accused the other of corrupt backroom deals and of hiding the names of investors and private media interests that had a stake in the respective proposals for private TV.[15] During this session a vote on another private TV bill sponsored by Alianza Popular was overruled by the socialist majority.[16]

As the PSOE apparently sought to slow the process of TV reform, the summer months of 1984 brought new pressure on the ruling party. Again, it was the regional Autonomous Communities that broke the regulatory tempo. Laws were passed to establish radio-television companies in the communities of Galicia (June 11), Madrid (June 30), and Valencia (July 4)—the latter two under PSOE regional governments. Even though the legal and technical framework of the Third Channel Law supported these ventures, the events increased the momentum of publicized demands for new media channels. Moreover, the regional authorities offered fresh political legitimacy to claims for reform of broadcast policy. The push of the regional television projects highlighted the slow pace of the democratization of RTVE and the rising expectation for new channels independent of the central state. It was clear that government reform of television was being pulled along by external events.

The official media politics of the PSOE finally crystallized at the party's thirtieth congress, held December 13–16, 1984. Prior to the congress, the PSOE made definitive its intentions to halt the legalization of any new channels until its studies were complete. This was an attempt to demonstrate control over recent legal and institutional changes; the government was determined to portray itself as a thorough and professional manager. The PSOE therefore announced plans in mid-July to send a multiparty exploratory group to Britain to study the public service model employed there. Members of the investigating team told reporters that future visits to Japan, the United States, and Italy were also planned. The leadership of the party said that it was prepared to explore all potential options given the limitations of spectrum, national expertise, and technology.[17] Still, the PSOE made no secret of its preference for the British model.[18]

By the time of the party congress, the membership was informed about potential legislation to establish private channels. In the official committee report of the party congress, *The Overcoming of Inequalities,* the promise of new communications channels was clearly made, although without clarifying who would own these channels. This was the first official manifestation of the PSOE's acceptance of private TV. According to Bustamante and Villafañe, after this proposal was publicized there was "a dizzying rise of expectation among various pressure groups" (politicians, press, and private TV promoters are cited as protagonists). Notably absent from the celebration were "the citizens"; Bustamante and Villafañe argued that the Spanish people would have no taste at all for private TV if these same pressure groups had not fed them daily promotions for it.[19]

The role public opinion played in the socialists' reversal is therefore problematic, and next to impossible to document. To follow Bustamante and Villafañe, the main influences that shaped the agenda of public opinion were the press and the political theater where debates about private TV had been staged. Private TV was not an option among the public until promoted as such. Also obvious was the fact that public debates over the future of TV — discussions that should have included citizen groups and other institutions of civil society — were never held. The determination of the future of TV was designated to elite groups, the most public of which was the press. The press is not the public, however, and the socialist claims that the public supported private TV were never proved. People did express interest in a plurality of TV channels, but the terms on the relevant public-opinion questionnaires varied among options as diverse and abstract as regional TV, another state channel, private TV, and more media in general.[20]

Viewed from within the political process, there was a lack of democratic participation in the determination of TV reform. Seen as a process of legitimation of the socialist party among the ruling elites of Spain, the acceptance and promotion of private TV was a political necessity. This appeal to political necessity characterized the so-called realism of the Spanish socialists. The thrust of this realism was to depoliticize media policy through a reduction of participation to private press, the party of opposition, and commercial promoters. Absent were those participants of civil society whose organizations, groups, and friends had a stake in broadening the democratic role of the media. There was no professional association of journalists to speak of, nor was there an association of TV viewers.

9

Social Democracy, Modernization, and Corporatism in Action

The events of 1984, notably the crystallization of the PSOE policy and the schedule for reform of the communications system, made 1985 the potential inaugural year for private TV in Spain. All pieces appeared to be in place for a radical restructuring of the media — yet the process of policymaking continued at a slow pace. Apart from the business of creating a cohesive and widely entrenched political class within the transitional state, the PSOE gave itself the task of integrating the communications infrastructure in the Ley de Ordenación de las Comunicaciones (LOC). These two problems combined to challenge the socialist claims of the previous months. Felipe González's confidence about his ability to establish a new media policy where his predecessors had failed now waned tremendously, and in February 1985 he confessed with typical hyperbole that "not even God knows how to create private TV."[1]

Complicating communications reform were larger political and economic processes that came to affect directly the prospects for private TV. Among these was the integration of Spain into the European Economic Community (or the European Community, EC — now the European Union). Spain was soon to sign the treaty of adherence, and the prospect of Europeanization of the Spanish territory shifted much of the debate over communications to questions of international standards, open trade, new investment, and modernization. The reform of television, telecommunications, and related industries moved away from themes of a social nature to the technical issues relevant to the integration of the Spanish economy into the European system. Conflicts inevitably arose around the impact on Spanish industry of EC integration and modernization.

The electronics manufacturing industry of Spain was highly dependent on foreign technology, and, as chapter 3 pointed out, the sector as a whole was already dominated by transnational companies. In 1985, for example, three-quarters of color television manufacturing in Spain was controlled by foreign companies; chief among them were Philips (25 percent), Grundig (18 percent), Thomson (10 percent), Sanyo (10 percent), and Telefunken (8 percent).[2] The interlocking partnerships of these oligopolistic firms showed that Philips owned a part of the Spanish firm Radiola and a major portion of Grundig (which owned 6 percent of Philips), and also collaborated with Matsushita (another Japanese transnational corporation). Matsushita was a partner with Bosch (FEMSA in Spain) in a venture called MB Video. Bosch, together with Siemens (the German electronics giant), owned Blaupunkt, the radio manufacturer. Matsushita also owned 51 percent of JVC, which was a partner with Thomson and Thorn-EMI in a venture called J2T in Spain.[3] The list goes on, but the point should be clear: in 1985, only about 10 percent of the national consumer electronics market was held by the Spanish electronics sector. This very small sector had been traditionally protected by a mélange of twenty-four separate taxes and a system of export rebates and compensatory import duties.[4] With Spanish integration into the EC, this system of taxes, rebates, and duties was to be replaced with a single value added tax. This planned liberalization of long-standing regulation of capital flows prompted the Spanish association of employers in the electronics sector, ANIEL, to foretell the death of the Spanish electronics industry during negotiations with the EC.[5]

In the face of such dour predictions, the government began a publicity campaign aimed at assuring the public and political forces that liberalizations associated with EC integration would be good for the country. Although Spanish businesses were weak in the electronics sector, the socialists insisted that certain planned enterprises would give new life to the ailing economy. The symbolic politics of modernization helped this delicate balancing act. The socialists had to convince people that growth and employment (understood popularly as good for society) would be the final outcomes of liberalization of trade, which everyone knew was bound to damage sectors of the national economy (obviously seen as bad for society). Among the future enterprises to serve as salves in the socialist scenario were telecommunication and information technologies, and new television channels. González wanted to sell the Spanish public on the idea that when he got a good private TV law passed, he would be able to reenergize the national electronics sector.[6]

The legitimacy of this plan was questioned by the actual political economy of the Spanish electronics and information technology sector. After all, new investment would be directed at a sector already dominated by transnational capital, suggesting in fact that capital flows would really be directed outward rather than into the national economy. Yet the widespread belief that new national markets would rise in the ashes of old with the introduction of new products held sway in socialist rhetoric. Private TV, among other wonders of the information age, was going to provide one of those new products.[7]

Concurrent with this shift in government rhetoric was an upsurge of all sorts of meetings, interviews, colloquiums, and roundtable discussions between private TV promoters and political parties. Intense public relations efforts surrounded these get-togethers as press announcements and reportage were orchestrated by two daily newspapers: *La Vanguardia*, which had joined the private radio company Antena-3 to form the TV promoter TEVISA, and *Diario 16*, whose parent (Grupo 16) created Tele 16 to promote private TV. These two companies publicized the discussions of early February 1985 without bothering to disguise their collusion—both newspapers published the same report by the same author.[8] Such an alliance demonstrated with force how the press was working in concert to promote private TV.

The pooling of the press reports and the increase in the number of meetings between the government and commercial television promoters forced the socialists to make public their intentions. Evidence arose out of the discussions that the PSOE was committed to a private TV system based on the principle of universal territorial service. Universal service is a benchmark of public service television, designed to provide equitable distribution of broadcast signals regardless of a community's socioeconomic characteristics. Parallel to the specific focus of such a media policy was a general mandate in the constitution to ensure "the establishment of a just and adequate economic balance between the different areas of the Spanish territory" (article 138, I). In addition, the Industrial Reconversion Program of 1981 started a system of "incentives for new investment in regions" aimed at counterbalancing existing interregional inequalities.[9] Universal service offered a socially fair framework for TV reform and met the criteria of the constitution and the reindustrialization directive.

Clearly, the socialists had affirmed their commitment to the spirit of the British model once again. But the platform of universal service not only mitigated against one of the known tendencies of commercial television systems (exemplified by the big-city-first development of television in the United States), it was also explicitly justified as protection against the kind of commercial TV service that had developed in Italy.

Words such as debacle, anarchy, and chaos were most often used in the Spanish media and professional literature to describe the Italian boom in commercial television. In 1974 the constitutional court of Italy ruled that the state held a level of control over broadcasting that was unconstitutional. Many local private TV stations had started broadcasting by the time that the Italian government passed the 1975 reform act that partially legalized local independent TV. This was considered a time of true independence of television in Italy. By 1976 another law was enacted that gave precise provisions regulating private TV, and an extraordinary surge in local commercial television followed. Little by little, many of the small TV businesses began to fail, outmaneuvered and outspent by larger investors. As the smaller companies were swallowed up by the bigger ones, broadcasts with a national audience became a necessity for the continued growth of the expanding firms. However, simultaneous broadcasts across the national territory were not legally sanctioned by the Italian TV law, a restriction meant to protect the state networks of Radiotelevisione Italiana. As the story goes, the commercial television owners (Silvio Berlusconi becoming ever more prominent among them) were undaunted by this rule and staggered the schedule of the local broadcasts in such a way that multiple stations showed the same program but with a slight delay between stations. For all intents and purposes, the large companies achieved regional network linkups of virtually simultaneous programming without, they claimed, breaking the letter of the law. Apocrypha notwithstanding, it became feasible to sell to advertisers national and regional audiences tied to regular program schedules, and competition with the national state system began in earnest.

Thus from the grass roots an unwieldy commercialism grew into large networks to rival Radiotelevisione Italiana. In 1980, Silvio Berlusconi brought together regional networks Canale 5 in the north and Rete 10 in the south to form a national network, called Canale 5. In 1982, Berlusconi took over Italia 1 from a rival entrepreneur, Rusconi. In 1984, Berlusconi added the Retequattro network of the Mondadori group. Berlusconi's company, Fininvest, thus became a commercial television monopoly—for which no regulation existed until 1990. His story is that of a veritable robber baron of the information age. In an interview with the Spanish newspaper *ABC* in 1984, Berlusconi reminisced about the advertising war that erupted between his media empire and Radiotelevisione Italiana:

BERLUSCONI: The rise of advertising is the result of the war with the state television, which offered reduced prices. Our reaction was immediate: on the Canale 5 network we gave away one spot with each one we contracted; on the Italia 1 network, for every spot contracted, we gave away two.

ABC: Who won the war?

BERLUSCONI: We did.[10]

From the Spanish government's point of view, this technical, commercial, and legal fiasco had to be avoided. Even Bettino Craxi, the socialist prime minister of Italy, warned the Spanish government against the mistakes of Italian private TV.[11] In principle, the platform of universal service promised to check uncontrolled commercialism of private TV and the establishment of spatial hierarchies of communication. Francisco Virseda, director general of social communication under the presidency, confirmed that the government wanted to avoid this spatial hierarchization by prohibiting localized media operations.[12] (It was thought that the most likely concentration of investment would have centered around Madrid, Barcelona, Valencia, the Balearic Islands, Bilbao, and Seville.) If the government were going to legalize private TV, it would do so with strong state safeguards against the tendency of uneven development. The principle of universal service offered a modernization plan tempered by social democracy's geographical morality.

The Spanish government, however, also applied this principle to grassroots media (the proverbial baby thrown out with the bathwater). In 1985, the prospect of a noncommercial system of local stations still existed, and indeed would grow more prominent in the coming years. In Catalonia alone there were seventy low-power, noncommercial television broadcasters. Some were run by municipalities, some were the project of local TV repairers or electricians (the so-called *chispas*, or sparks), and some were generated by village-level social clubs.[13] When asked about the government's position on local TV, Virseda repeated that the government was going to take a strong stand against the municipal systems, as it would in principle with local private TV. Indeed, many of the village-level stations were closed by police during this period on the grounds of piracy — although no legal framework existed that would define them as pirates. In all, there was little sympathy for the grassroots TV experiments. This undifferentiated opposition to local TV reflected, again, worries that a situation similar to that of Italy would arise; namely, that private investors would use the grass roots to enter the market against the will of the state. One of the unfortunate blindspots of the Spanish government was not to have incorporated the element of popular participation into the national policy framework at this time.[14]

The new direction for television charted by the policy of universal service encountered technical problems with the infrastructure. The only system with national territorial coverage was RTVE, which reported reaching 98 percent of the population on TVE-1 and 85 percent on TVE-2.[15] Investigations into alternative distribution technologies such as satellite discouraged the government at the time. As Barrasa noted in 1985, "Today the participation of the aerospace sector of Spanish industry in a first satellite could conservatively be put at 25 percent, while the participation of Spanish industry in a terrestrial network rises to 70 percent."[16] Technology transfer accompanied by foreign investment and expertise was an option discussed by the socialists, yet informed speculation still stood in opposition to increased dependency through such transfers.[17]

Private TV promoters did not like the remaining option, links to the RTVE network, which for them equaled dependency on the state. With the real-life experience of TV-3 in Catalonia showing technical costs much higher than expected, many investors found themselves between, as it were, the rock of big price tags and the hard place of the investment imperatives. Describing the demonstration effect of the operation of TV-3, the trade journal *Anuncios* said, "The five thousand million pesetas [about thirty-one million dollars at the time] necessary to transmit only a few hours a day ... has made more than one promoter come down from the clouds."[18] Despite the available evidence that technical independence on anything but a limited urban scale would be very pricey, none of the private TV promoters was adventurous enough to negotiate seriously for a national linkup through RTVE.[19] Subsequently, the promoters sought out another option, and partnership, with the national telephone company of Spain, Telefónica.

About one-third of Telefónica was owned by the state at this time, and the state was still licensed to control the company by law and by means of a government delegate appointed to manage the company.[20] As chapter 3 explained, Telefónica was effectively controlled by the American multinational corporation ITT, with large subsidiary interests held by Ericsson, Telettra, and American Cable.[21] When the socialists took over, they began a privatization campaign that resulted in a first-time sale of 13 percent of the company stock on European exchanges.[22] Also, in 1985 Telefónica negotiated to become the Europartner of AT&T in a microchip factory and experimental cable ventures. Telefónica operations were completely internationalized, formed by partnerships with those companies previously mentioned as well as with Philips, Fujitsu, Digital Equipment, Corning Glass, MBB (Germany), and Hormann (Germany).[23]

This portfolio was attractive to private TV investors, and private TV was attractive to Telefónica, which tried at one point to start a cable TV service.[24] Telefónica and RTVE controlled the two largest telecommunications networks in Spain (smaller networks, such as those of the Ministry of Defense and of the Ministry of Post and Telegraph, also existed), with the primary difference between the two being Telefónica's relative independence from the Spanish state. Even the Basques and Catalans had recourse to use the phone company links a few times just to avoid confrontations with RTVE.

The phone company soon prepared a study to "analyze two possible technical solutions ... that respond to the new demands ... of television" in Spain.[25] One was an expanded microwave network, the second was a multiplication of ground receivers for satellite reception. The satellite reception facilities were owned by Telefónica, which was authorized by the state as the Spanish representative to the consortia Intelsat, Eutelsat, and Inmarsat. Private TV investors were to pay for any upgrade (by today's standards, remarkably low estimates from 56 million to 116 million dollars) and then a yearly fee for access (25 million to 34 million dollars).

These costs would be largely shouldered by the best-financed private investors, but shared in part by the state because of its partnership in any proposed modernization. The government followed the Telefónica report with a suggestion that the RTVE communications infrastructure be united with that of the phone company, and that a public firm, insulated from state control, be formed to manage the system.[26] This integration of networks was rumored to be recognized in LOC. Other, less serious suggestions from smaller companies included requests for links to RTVE in exchange for a "symbolic" tariff (i.e., nothing). Regardless of the option offered at this time, any upgrade to accommodate private TV was "equivalent to paying for a good part of the benefits of private groups with public money."[27] For the moment at least, no viable technical plan appealed to the promoters, or to the state, although the scale of investment for a national network was now better understood.

Meanwhile, RTVE management had undertaken measures of internal reform that reflected its own expectations of a new competitor. In 1984, the PSOE gave RTVE orders to become self-financing, which meant that the state television, TVE, would have to rely completely on advertising revenues. As noted in chapter 3, TVE was already the most highly commercialized national television in Europe, but never in the history of Spanish television had evidence existed showing how a purely commercial finance structure might work.[28] By March 1985, the director general of RTVE, José María Calviño, tried to take advantage of this lack of experience among investors. He professed to have knowledge that there was only enough advertising for one TV company, that the market was saturated, and that growth had stagnated.[29] No one but the most gullible believed these claims.

Democratic reform and streamlining for efficiency in RTVE went hand in hand with another management campaign that encouraged early retirement — a move that can be seen as a generational cleansing of the old guard. The director general of RTVE held out the promise of working for quality public television to young professionals in order to discourage their acceptance of potential offers from new private competitors.[30] An administrative report circulated that foretold of further personnel reductions: the Plan Integral de Mecanización e Informatización suggested that such reductions would necessarily follow from the installation of computers to help regulate both technical and managerial functions.

All of these events — the socialists' call for universal service and their rejection of small, local TV enterprises; the evidence of high start-up costs; and the retooling of RTVE — presented a daunting situation to many private TV promoters. Yet the most significant act occurred when the government laid the issue of national territorial coverage on the negotiation table: with it, they had drawn the trump. Not a single promoter could alone come forward with a feasible project, and only the more stable partnerships that had formed in the early 1980s survived the most recent events. The marketing journal *Mercado* reported in May 1985 that the costs of national coverage were now known to be so prohibitively high that most of the major players would fall far short of the needed capital. The same report disclosed that the government was working closely with a reduced number of the existing multimedia partnerships, and it was suggested that LOC was actually being framed by these backroom negotiations.[31]

In 1985, evidence of one such web of negotiations between the government and a private media promoter emerged in a case involving Promotores de Informaciones S.A., or PRISA. Then, as now, PRISA owned *El País*, the Spanish daily newspaper whose readership had grown in the preceding years to surpass all other national dailies (an expansion of circulation that curiously coincided with the increase of electoral support for the PSOE). PRISA also owned Radio El País, a commercial radio operated by a subsidiary called PRESA. (The radio company has since disappeared, having apparently served its purpose as a speculative venture aimed at gaining a foothold in other, more lucrative radio businesses.) Jesús de Polanco, the head of PRISA, had close ties to the PSOE, and the degree of his influence became apparent as news surfaced about a government-sanctioned expansion of PRISA's media holdings. The intrigue included Bettino Craxi's visit to Spain in 1985, when the press disclosed that he suggested to the socialist government that it make a binding pact with Polanco. Although Craxi warned against the problems of privatization, especially the chaos in the airwaves that might result in a situation similar to that of Italy, the rumor of his support for a single corporate client circulated easily. After all, the socialist Craxi had given Berlusconi the protection he needed to build his monopoly outside of the law in Italy. The rumor linking the Spanish socialists to PRISA soon appeared to bear some truth.[32]

Between January and June 1985, PRISA increased its holdings from 25 percent to over 50 percent of the largest private radio network in Spain, La Sociedad Española de Radiodifusión (SER). By July of the following year PRISA controlled 71 percent of the SER network. Notably, the government controlled a 25 percent share of SER through the course of these buyouts. Key to understanding the SER buyout is that although the government lost control of the majority of SER properties, it maintained the legal power to authorize all sales and purchases of SER stocks (under agreements established in the 1950s with the private stockholders of SER). Prior to the first sale of packages of SER stock to PRISA, the socialist government blocked participation of Grupo 16 and other media groups, including the employees of SER who sought 15 percent of the shares at one point.

The PRISA buyout of SER, to the exclusion of both commercial and noncommercial media groups, set off a storm of controversy. The transfer of ownership of the most lucrative radio network to the largest multimedia company sent strong indications that one private TV promoter held extraordinary sway over the socialist government. That promoter was then called SOGETEL, a partnership formed by SER and PRISA and joined by Grupo March (whose head was Carlos March, a media and financial mogul who controlled the Banca March and the *Diario de Mallorca*). Most non-PRISA media outlets reported at the time that the licensing of SOGETEL for private TV was essentially a done deal.

Two years earlier, Felipe González had said in a SER interview that there would be no private TV. Now Jesús de Polanco, the president of the board of directors of PRISA, suggested that there would be no PSOE without private TV. Polanco was rumored to have said that there were only two truly important powers in Spain, "the government and PRISA," adding with hubris that "we [PRISA] appointed the government and it will last as long as we want."[33] The financial power of PRISA was undoubted; it was now one of the most highly capitalized media firms in Spain. Moreover, the popularity of *El País* was growing. PRISA's ability to influence government action seemed indisputable.

Francisco Virseda verified much of this newfound symmetry between the multimedia company and the government. When asked about the role of some of the lead pretenders to private TV licenses, Virseda was quick to praise SOGETEL for its patience and cooperation.[34] SOGETEL was in a position privileged by its solvency and cash reserves, according to *Mercado,* but also enjoyed the added asset of being in a partnership with the socialist government through the SER radio network.[35] The corporatist strategy of the PSOE, in this case, blurred any distinction between public and private media. All hyperbole about God, technology, or strong leaders aside, the state was making private TV a reality through deals like those with PRISA. In addition, by creating a legal situation in which only highly capitalized firms could provide universal service, the government encouraged other partnerships to form among multimedia groups. Thus the PSOE found a way to mitigate against a chaotic scramble of speculators.

10
Politics of Diminishing Returns

In May 1985, the Spanish government admitted that lingering suspicions about its plans for private TV were true. There was no explicit plan to license private TV within the quasi-confidential draft of LOC.[1] A familiar legal problem recalling the 1982 decision of the constitutional tribunal kept LOC split between technical issues and cultural policy. Felipe González confessed that private TV was not effectively a part of LOC, which mostly addressed the elimination of state control and furnished only a few generic statements on private ownership. He did make clear at this time, however, that a separate law was going to be developed, though no legislation for private TV would be discussed until after the elections of October 1986. The cynics were vindicated.[2]

Two political problems arose in June that further altered the direction of LOC and television reform. The first followed the change of hands of LOC from the minister of Transport, Tourism, and Communication, Enrique Barón, to the vice president of the government, Alfonso Guerra. This led to a well-publicized rift between the executive office and the ministry over items of social policy, but in particular private TV, that the presidency wanted included in LOC.[3] The overtly technical LOC generally had received little support from the president's office. In addition, the Ministry of Finance had opposed the current draft of LOC because of a provision that created a private holding company with state participation to handle capital flows for the telecommunication sector. It was thought that such a company would create unfair competition for other financial institutions and lead eventually to the weakening of the central bank, which had traditionally regulated capital flows through the telecommunications sector.[4] The Ministry of Transport, Tourism, and Communication had fallen from favor in this moment. González's impatience was clear months prior when he said, "In the end, the only one who is going to know what to do with private TV is me."[5] Shortly thereafter he handed the project over to his vice president.

Midway through September 1985, LOC was discarded and the new minister of Transport, Tourism, and Communication, Abel Caballero, offered three laws to replace it under the umbrella of the new project called the Ley de Ordenación de las Telecomunicaciones, or LOT. LOT promised to carry out telecommunications liberalization, integration and modernization of the infrastructure, and reorganization of the postal service. In addition, LOT would create a legal and technical framework making a separate private TV law feasible.

The second political problem occurring in June 1985 followed from another scandal in RTVE, and brought attention back to the slow reform of the state TV. On the night of June 19, TVE-1 showed on its most popular news program a political biography of Manuel Fraga Iribarne. Fraga was the leader of the opposition, head of Alianza Popular, and had served as the minister of the interior under the first transition government of 1975–76 (prior to democratic elections and UCD's rise to power). Fraga was also the minister of Information and Tourism under Franco between 1962 and 1969, and has been credited with much of the liberalization of press and publishing freedom that came about in that period—although TVE became increasingly tied to government communication and censorship during that time (see chapter 3). As the TVE documentary explained, among other things Fraga was responsible for the violent repression of strikers and demonstrators while he was the minister of the interior. The most tragic incident took place in 1976 when police fired guns into a crowd of demonstrators in Vitoria (in the Basque province of Alava) and murdered five workers. In their chronicle of the transition, Carr and Fusi describe Fraga as a man who "saw strikes and demonstrations as a personal challenge."[6] The documentary was praised for being faithful to this psychohistory, but was attacked by the opposition for its "manipulation, lack of professionalism, absence of respect for citizens, submission to political power, and mismanagement of the official television."[7] In other words, despite its accuracy, the TVE piece should have been censored for the good of political peace.

Indeed, this documentary was perceived as a direct attack on Francoism, considered impolitic within the framework of compromise of the transition. A tacit agreement prohibited the aggravation of the past among public officials, and TVE was regarded as the most prominent voice of official publics.[8] Using TVE to criticize the opposition—regardless of the truth—went against the consensual spirit of the constitution and the mandated separation of RTVE from the ruling party as contained in the RTVE Statute. Without equal time to reply to the documentary, Alianza Popular, and Fraga, could argue that RTVE was not democratic, that the RTVE Statute was a joke, and that the PSOE was to blame. To its detriment, TVE at first denied reply time to Fraga. Once Fraga was allowed to go on the air to rectify matters, TVE refused to broadcast a counterdocumentary prepared by Alianza Popular, instead showing only a photograph of Fraga while a voice-over read a summary of the AP reply.

Alianza Popular then initiated a lawsuit against TVE and the socialists. AP continued to pressure the government throughout the summer, and at one point distributed over one million posters calling for the firing of the director general of RTVE. In the name of pluralism and freedom of expression on the airwaves, AP sought to make the PSOE media reform look miserly and undemocratic.[9] Consequently, the PSOE was forced to enter negotiations with AP to reform television, and in October 1985 the socialists agreed to work with the opposition to enforce the RTVE Statute and write the law of private TV.[10] Disharmonious compromises like this manifest what Vázquez Montalbán called a "historical pact of nonaggression between Fraga and González": a pact meant to conceal Fraga's Francoist past but one that instead damaged the critical memory that Spaniards held of their own past.[11]

A preliminary draft of a reform bill was circulated in September, and the text of discussions between the PSOE and AP finally appeared in January 1986. In April the council of ministers passed a bill on to parliament that proposed to authorize three new private channels and to develop a separate technical plan for them. The bill contained stipulations for licensing, production quotas, and advertising.

Except for the populist rhetoric calling for the end of RTVE and the rise of citizen responsibility for state TV, the biparty discussions led to no practical outcome, and the law of private TV did not reach debate in the parliament before the next elections were called. Nonetheless, the private TV bill would soon serve a purpose utterly distinct from that for which it was designed.

Obviously, the government had other things to do besides legalize private TV. If not for the Fraga debacle and the fight over LOC, the issue of telecommunications and TV reform might have been kept in low profile. Throughout the winter and spring of 1985, for instance, the PSOE was more concerned with its June date to sign the treaty of adherence to the European Community. This precipitated a major internal crisis in the socialist party apparatus that revealed a move to create a more conservative leadership. Important changes were to take place before Spain entered Europe and the world of liberal democracies. Ministers were reassigned and several significant resignations were announced in anticipation of the formation of the second socialist government in May.

A key resignation was that of Fernando Morán, who had been the minister of foreign affairs since the first socialist government was formed in 1982. Morán was a staunch opponent of Spain's participation in NATO; he once called for the complete withdrawal of U.S. troops from Spain; and he was a prominent critic of liberalization plans that opened Spain to transnational investments. Morán's resignation typified the general modification in PSOE behavior at this time. The timing was indeed telling—just one month before EC agreements were signed, less than a year before the NATO referendum, and seventeen months before the next elections. The replacement for Morán as foreign minister was none other than Francisco Fernández Ordóñez.

Needless to say, the ministerial changes of May 1985 attracted immediate approval from the United States. The *New York Times* would later recall this period in its eulogy for Fernández Ordóñez, who was described as "more pro-American than his predecessor, Fernando Morán"; Fernández Ordóñez "campaigned for NATO membership" and for "greater European integration, championing the Maastricht treaty on political and economic union."[12] Shortly after Morán's replacement, the Reagan administration gave security clearance for AT&T to begin construction of a microchip factory near Madrid. Subsequently, the Spanish government began to channel its energies into the national referendum on Spain's continued membership in NATO.

While becoming more conservative in international relations, the PSOE was simultaneously charged with a rightward turn on the domestic front by Nicolas Redondo, leader of the socialist-affiliated trade union, Unión General de Trabajadores (UGT). Redondo denounced the government's labor record, and, taking advantage of UGT's independence from party control, he publicly accused the PSOE of creating "greater unemployment, greater inequality, and greater poverty."[13] In May and June 1985, the UGT-PSOE dispute could be found sharing headlines with the already-mentioned revelations about LOC and private TV. The association is curious: the PSOE promised eight hundred thousand jobs, and instead delivered between six hundred thousand and eight hundred thousand more persons unemployed; the PSOE promised private TV, and delivered a blinkered draft of a technical law that failed to fulfill its brief.

Hence, the practical problems of consolidating the party's hegemony came at a time of reduced popularity—but this was precisely the context in which the PSOE's private TV bill realized its greatest social influence. Ironically, the mere existence of the bill served to consolidate media support, private and state, for the PSOE's hegemony. Villagrasa argues that the 1986 bill was "used" by the government "to manipulate the Spanish press" into supporting the PSOE campaign for membership in NATO and eventually the PSOE reelection.[14] He says that the media were encouraged to sway Spanish voters away from their significant, and well-documented, opposition to NATO. The quid pro quo for the press was the assurance that the private TV bill would not be rejected because of political caprice. (Remember that the largest dailies, *El País* and *La Vanguardia*, were tightly linked to two major private TV promoters, SOGETEL and TEVISA.) The press acquiesced.

The rhetoric of the PSOE and the press during the pro-NATO campaign relied on fear. The suggestion was that a no vote would lead Spain back into the political dark ages dominated by military types like those who had led the coup attempt in 1981. A no vote also meant the end to modernization of the information, telecommunications, and computer industries that the socialists promised would spark new prosperity in Spain.[15]

The PSOE, the government-controlled RTVE, and the private press together won a pro-NATO victory in the popular referendum, by a notably narrow margin. Forty percent of the voters abstained, and another 13 percent were disqualified; of the eligible votes, 52.5 percent voted to stay in NATO, 40 percent voted to quit it. The vote occurred with polls still showing defeat on the eve of the referendum.[16]

The role of the press must be emphasized, given the widespread and false belief that the PSOE was able to win support for NATO because it controlled TVE.[17] The history of this period does not bear out such an argument. The government had used the private TV bill in such a way as to leverage the private press to the state's cause, and still the PSOE controlled TVE; this corporatist collaboration brought together a pro-NATO alliance of both state and private media. The role of the private press in both referendum and national election has too often been underestimated.

The government saw the NATO vote as a confidence vote and very quickly called for early elections. A media machine was on its side, as Polanco indicated it would be as long as the press got what it wanted, namely, licenses for private TV. By June 1986, the PSOE and González were back in power. The private TV bill was finally approved by the government, after six amendments from the opposition, in April 1987. González postponed enactment of the law until 1989, although this postponement was really meaningless: all major institutional players and all major points of the law were the same as they were prior to the NATO vote and the general election in 1986.

The technical steps to these resolutions followed within a few months. The most important of these, the new telecommunications law, LOT, was passed in December 1987 (Law 31/1987, December 18) and furnished the macrolegal and macrotechnical framework that gave the private TV legislation the means to be enacted. A law of private TV was finally enacted on May 3, 1988 (Law 10/1988, of Private TV), followed by a national technical plan for private TV in November.[18] The Ministry of Transport, Tourism, and Communication created a public company to extend and manage the technical infrastructure; RTVE infrastructure was finally absorbed into this entity, which served all TV signals for all systems.[19] All that remained was licensing, a resolution for which was announced at the end of January 1989. Twelve months later, test broadcasts of three new channels began, and the power for commercial media investors to make a ton of money had at last been unleashed.

Chomping at the Bit

Some races are prone to false starts, especially when an anxious competitor jumps prematurely from the post. The race for private channels had one such false start. Canal 10 appeared on Spanish screens sometime in January 1988. Word got out in November that this mystery company thought it had found a way to circumvent the existing legal barriers to private broadcasts—it would simply send the signal in from beyond the borders of Spain. After all, Spaniards enjoyed the right to buy and put up antennas to receive any signal that would reach them. This right to antenna, as it was called in Spain, did not include the right to broadcast within Spain, and in 1987 a company was formed with capital from a number of French, British, and Spanish investors. A holding company was set up in Panama, studios were hired in London, and a contract with British Telecom provided the linkup to a Greenwich transmitter.

Canal 10 broadcast from the Molinare Studios, near Carnaby Street in London. The area devoted to Canal 10 operations included a small studio and a cramped control room. The shelves along the narrow hallway between these two spaces were lined with telefilms and series with mostly English titles. For the price of the hire, Molinare provided one engineer, one technical director, a makeup artist (who was German), but no lighting technician; all were nonunion, an outcome of Thatcherism welcomed by the investors. The equipment, a mix of Japanese and American technology, was minimal: two cameras, a switcher, two videotape recorders, and a portable lighting kit. The Spanish company provided a managing director, whose training had been with TVE, and program directors, one of whom trained with TVE's regional office in La Rioja, Spain. It also subcontracted out for dubbing services in Madrid. Of the five writers, two were located in London and three in Madrid, where the main company office was also located. The primary task of the crew was to produce continuity segments that linked the prepurchased telefilms, serials, sports, and light entertainment programs in a nonstop, twenty-four-hours-a-day flow. The on-air talent announced upcoming amusements; otherwise there was no in-house production to speak of.

The Spanish crew at Canal 10 in London marked its third week without pay on July 21, 1988.[20] The reason for the delay, the staff was told, had to do with cash flow problems of one of the investors, Robert Maxwell. Two weeks later, the majority ownership (43 percent) of Canal 10 was sold by its founder, Enrique Talarewitz, to French investor Jacques Hachuel. Maxwell, Hachuel, the Basque investment group Noara, and Canal Plus France became the primary owners.[21] By the end of August, it was clear that the company was a loser, more of a front for a quick speculative run than a serious investment in TV broadcasting. The bill from Molinare Studios had not been paid, and the plug was finally pulled on Canal 10 in late August 1988.

The basic reason for the failure of Canal 10 is that it was a speculative venture that was seriously mismanaged and undercapitalized. Its main promoters—the most notorious being the former head of RTVE, José María Calviño—had misled investors into thinking that a market existed for satellite subscription television; they circulated figures that showed between 160,000 and 170,000 subscribers. This was an absurd financial bubble, although at three thousand pesetas (about twenty-four dollars at that time) per month per subscription, it was a bubble that was irresistible to the likes of Maxwell and Hachuel.

In Madrid, one ingenuous subscriber confessed that she had been paying but hadn't received any signal. Later she was informed by the company that she had to buy a satellite dish. Not being previously informed of this requirement, she quit paying. In truth, she simply didn't comprehend the technology, and had thought that getting private TV would be as convenient as switching a channel.[22] Countless similar stories surfaced after August. In the end, Canal 10 had installed only 654 aerials, and not all were in service. The idea that Canal 10 would create a parallel business in Spain for satellite-dish sales was patently idiotic, especially given its corrupt hard-sell style. Finally, the dubbing companies it used went bankrupt; its program supplier sued for payment; new shareholders sued former shareholders; and Canal Plus France withdrew. By January 1989, Canal 10 no longer existed, not even on paper.[23]

Villagrasa suggests that for some commentators, the whole project of Canal 10 was a conspiracy, designed from the Spanish president's office to discredit private TV.[24] After all, the former director of RTVE, Calviño, had been an important asset in convincing investors that a window of opportunity existed between passage of the private TV bill and its enactment. It was his interpretation of the law that argued the distinction between right of antenna and right of broadcast—a distinction that dressed up the satellite-dish business in the attractive clothes that only a few investors could see. The political conspiracy notwithstanding, Canal 10 is best thought of as an invention of financial speculators, an asset builder typical of paper empires made famous by the late, and shadowy, Robert Maxwell.

Back in 1983, González suggested that the main obstacle to private TV was the indifference of Spanish voters. He showed respect for that obstacle then. At some point, hard to register in this history, the Spanish voters changed heart. What is indisputable, however, is that in 1990 the Spanish people no longer stood in the way of private TV.

11
Private TV Now and Forever

It can be argued that political opportunism is pursued with a clear con-
science as long as what's at stake is winning elections.[1] But short-term
gains are often won at the expense of the long-term social effects. The
rhetorical claims for fast-track reform in Spanish media verged on the
aphoristic: the glass was neither half full nor half empty, just too big.
Can this banner pragmatism hold true when it signifies the reduction of
participation in the democratic process? Can the field of participation
in cultural policy ever be too big when a society is deciding on issues
that shape its cultural horizon? Regarding national policy for television,
the Spanish socialists answered affirmatively — but then, what European
government in the 1980s did not?

The very least that can be said about the socialists' pragmatism is
that it helped stabilize a political process that previously had made TV
reform the product of chance and caprice. In its first six years as the
ruling party in government, the PSOE led decision making through three
major media reform laws (the Third Channel Law, the telecommunications law, and the private TV law) without damaging the party's cohe-
siveness. Only the impending liberalization of the market and the state,
which was packaged with adherence to the EC and NATO, caused any
stirring. Dissent was handled quickly — the socialist left was excused;
ministers were shuffled about, dismissed, or resigned — and the identity
of the party was consolidated.

Tied to the EC and NATO, the socialists developed frameworks to
modernize the telecommunications system, trying to bring it up to Euro-

pean business and military standards. In addition, they managed the op-position with greater success than their predecessors. As with most of its reforms, the PSOE skillfully normalized private TV legislation by exploit-ing its hegemony in a political process defined by liberal corporatism.

The PSOE's corporatist arrangements created a situation where nei-ther private nor public agents could pursue an independent strategy. Needless to say, the influence wielded by state and market was often (and indisputably) protagonized by agents of one or the other. This does not always directly translate into power of a distinctly political or eco-nomic sort, however. No matter how it's sliced, the categorical division assigning decisive powers to either the state or private agencies are, after the Spanish case, purely theoretical. Market forces obviously circulated through the state, as the political class was itself constituted with eco-nomic actors. The notion that the state and the market are separate spheres—a notion still dominant among communication policy special-ists—does not hold true in the political economy of Spanish television. This interdependence was clear in the character of the PSOE leadership. It is also reflected in key aspects of the constitution (especially article 38) and has influenced the policy formulation of private TV since the UCD era.

The best example of the class nature of politics and the political char-acter of economics concerns the penultimate episode of television priva-tization in Spain. The PSOE encouraged higher levels of capitalization of television by extending restrictions with the stipulation for national territorial coverage. Public service principles aside, this action created a situation where only a few partnerships were able to show fiscal respon-sibility to back up their promotions. The less reliable and largely unco-operative media speculators were weeded out, a result that many would applaud. The Canal 10 debacle might be the best metaphor for the sup-posed ineptitude of the unregulated, but clipped in the process (albeit not for long) were the grassroots TV adventures.

The government had displayed strength and leadership through these big-money institutional arrangements. An even more direct demonstra-tion of strength was the PRISA-SER deal. The series of approved SER buyouts by PRISA showed how the government actually determined the capitalization necessary for the kind of private TV it had in mind. The head of PRISA, Jesús de Polanco, might argue in response that the buy-outs showed how PRISA could make or break a government to create the kind of state the press had in mind. But who had the economic power in this case, market or state? As for political power, whose inter-ests did the PRISA-SER deal serve, business or political classes? In light

of the press performance during the NATO referendum and general election, and recalling the quick passage of the private TV law, the distinctions might be considered superfluous.

Three social processes were accelerated by PSOE media policy. The
private TV law created conditions that increased conglomeration and
transnational influence in the television industry. The technical plan for
private TV structured new regional and national interconnections, effectively speeding up the diffusion of TV to the territorial periphery. This
regionalization of television from above curbed the centralist momentum inherited from Francoism, yet managed to reassert a centralist orientation. These three processes of conglomeration, transnationalization, and
regionalization promise to have lasting effects on the political economy
of television in Spain.

Conglomeration and the Transnational Presence

No single company bidding for a private TV license was allowed to be
wholly owned by a single Spanish media firm or individual. The private
TV law stipulated that no person (defined as a physical person or an
entity claiming rights as such, i.e., a nonnatural person or corporation)
can own, directly or indirectly, more than 25 percent of a company. Nor
can a single "person" own, directly or indirectly, more than one private
TV company.

Individual investors were present, but minor; after licensing, they held
only about 8 percent of total interests in private TV. The banks, in contrast, were encouraged to hold a big part of private TV. The law added
that at no time must total foreign ownership, direct or indirect, surpass
25 percent of the capital of the company. In addition, the private TV
law stated that there can be no hidden partners or hidden patterns of
ownership, and specified that the company must be headquartered in
Spain and have a Spanish nationality (articles 18 and 19). In principle,
monopoly ownership was outlawed, public accountability was required,
and transnational corporate control was restricted.

In practice the story unraveled differently. Among the firms that played
a part in the bidding for private TV were the familiar protagonists and
secondary characters introduced in the preceding chapters: PRISA (now
full owner of SER), Canal Plus France, *La Vanguardia* (along with the
most important regional dailies), Antena-3, Banca March, Berlusconi's
Fininvest, and Grupo 16.[2] The TV companies that actually won a license
were Antena-3 de Televisión (with *La Vanguardia* and Antena-3 together
holding 25 percent); La Sociedad Española de Televisión Canal Plus (with
PRISA and Canal Plus France each holding 25 percent); and Gestevisión-

Telecinco [with Fininvest (i.e., Berlusconi), ONCE (the national association of the blind), and Grupo Anaya (a publisher) each holding 25
percent].[3]

According to these percentages of individual holdings, no one company was controlled by a single interest. Taken together and grouped
by sector, however, the businesses owning private TV in Spain showed a
remarkable likeness. Total bank holdings of the Canal Plus group (whose
name was changed to Canal +) was 40 percent by 1993. Add this figure
to the foreign bank holdings of other private TV firms, divide by three
(the number of private firms), and the total control over private TV
directly related to financial institutions adds up to between 19 and 21
percent. Even this is deceptive, given the existence of interlocking direc-
torates in Spain, which have bank representatives sitting on boards, and
influencing the actions, of cultural industries as diverse as newsprint,
publishing, and publicity.[4]

The issue of interlocking interests also complicates the following figures. Thirty-nine percent of Antena-3 is controlled by the commercial
press; 50 percent of Canal Plus is held by national and foreign multimedia firms, as was also the case with Telecinco until 1990. This put the
commercial media (with outside holdings in press, publishing, publicity,
radio, and television) directly in charge of about 46 percent of the private TV industry in Spain. Indirectly, this control easily surpassed 50
percent if we consider the portfolios of companies like ONCE (which
owned 33 percent of Publiespaña, part of the Fininvest group, a major
holder of Telecinco stocks). Even with a conservative estimate that accounts for direct and indirect ownership, the banks, commercial media,
and publicists together held about 60 percent of private TV in Spain in
the early 1990s, giving them more clearance than any other group to
control the direction of the "independent" television industry.

Some banks, for instance, began in 1991 to sponsor entire television
programs in order to increase public awareness of their services in Spain.
This came on the heels of a surge in mergers and acquisitions that increased concentration of the industry, leading to greater competition
among a reduced number of large national banks.[5] Having both direct
and indirect control over television is an obvious asset for the big banks
in these circumstances.

In 1990, the Anaya publishing group left Telecinco over a dispute with
Berlusconi, selling 20 percent of its holdings to the Spanish representative
of the Kuwaiti Investment Office, Javier de la Rosa.[6] Berlusconi orchestrated this purge to get control of the company, which he did by extending ownership of Fininvest's Publiespaña in Spain to other Telecinco
shareholders. The Italian Berlusconi thus guaranteed his Fininvest would

be the dominant contractor for advertising on the Telecinco network —
a direct amplification of his influence.[7] In November 1991, Jacques
Hachuel of Canal 10 fame reappeared to buy 72 percent of the newspaper *El Independiente,* which was owned by ONCE. In the deal, Hachuel
acquired a 10 percent stake in Telecinco. Also at that time the financial
group Banesto bought 10.5 percent of Antena-3. These transactions put
nearly a quarter of the total direct holdings of private TV in the hands
of banks; with indirect holdings added, the figure would rise.[8]

A decisive level of ownership of private TV belongs to banks, advertising agencies, and the commercial media (press and radio). Obvious
too is the symmetry of interests and worldviews among these groups —
the bottom line of profits, business-as-usual. It becomes somewhat triv-
ial, therefore, to recognize that, taken together, the convergence of interests within the three companies reflects a clear class alliance.

This would not be important if the rhetoric of democratic reform
had not insisted that the transition of Spain beyond Francoism lead to
greater freedoms of civil society. Civil society was defined in the negative, i.e., it was not Francoism, it was not dictatorship, it was not the
state. This had been the case in relation to democratic TV as well, until
the last UCD proposal for private TV. After that, TV's end point in civil
society took on the added association of freedom of enterprise. The
evolution of the UCD/PSOE television policy helped make the elision of
expression and enterprise possible. But the PSOE was able to give substance to one last slippage of definition: namely, political freedoms of
civil society (of speech and thought and action) would be guaranteed by
the existence of commercial media. Given the ownership patterns already
discussed, the responsibility of television to support Spanish civil society can be said to have devolved to the banks, publicists, and multinational, multimedia firms.

Against this observation stands the private TV law. Yet even according the law's best intentions, it represents a mere paper fragmentation of
the dominant bloc of investors. Some commentators have found hope, ar-
guing that the three private TV firms are truly distinct in their orientation,
and so pluralism can be discerned in Spanish TV culture. Discernment
boils down to nuances between center-right and center-left, differences
in programming more news or more entertainment, or Canal Plus's subscription programs that include nudity, pornography, and so on.[9]

The less obvious outcome of privatization concerns the response of
future governments. Violations of the antimonopoly and nationalist spirit
of the law are already evident. Contrary to González's fantasy, the threat
to national cultural sovereignty brought by new TV channels in Spain
has been entirely Western and capitalistic, without a Soviet in sight. The

population (and most of the provincial capitals) by 1991. Phase two set for 1993 the completion of coverage to all demographic centers with populations over one hundred thousand, in order to reach 60 percent of the total population, including the rest of the provincial capitals. Phase three finished planting the relays, amplifiers, and other interconnections (including satellite links, when necessary) to reach another 20 percent of the population by 1995. Retevisión was already ahead of schedule in 1990, surpassing the 50 percent margin. The remaining population (about 20 percent by estimates) would eventually receive transmissions via satellite.

This time frame was linked to the spatial frame by the economics of audience demographics. That is, stages of national coverage were set to follow the national stratification of television viewers. Audiences were stratified according to population density and community status; at the same time, the infrastructure inherited by Retevisión was already fashioned after the same territorial bias. The major urban zones (all provincial capitals) were the focal point for the diffusion of these new communications services; all the sites of high per capita income could be reached from these installations after the first phase. With phase two, the medium-sized cities were included, followed by the small communities. Eventually, the privileging of locations would be eliminated, given that the entire territory was promised by law to receive the signals of the private firms — government insurance against the vicissitudes of commercial media economics. In the meantime, lower-status communities were forced to wait for private TV.

The zoning of private TV that the technical plan projects, once the equality of antenna is achieved, looks durable. Ten TV regions were created by the plan (see map 4). Each of these "territorial zones" was assigned a central production center for the reception and distribution of signals within the zone. Technical quality of each zone's network was guaranteed by law to be the same and to be developed and innovated simultaneously. No broadcaster was to have a competitive edge in terms of signal quality in separate zones.

The plan identified Madrid and Barcelona as the "principal production centers," and provided these cities with the greatest capacity for bidirectional flows between their studios, their regional transmission center, and the central transmission tower in Madrid, the Centro Nodal de Torrespaña.[14] The plan stipulated that the infrastructure permit the ten remaining production sites to "contribute" programs to the principal centers in Madrid and Barcelona. The regional centers were assigned a smaller capacity for bidirectional flows, because their primary relation

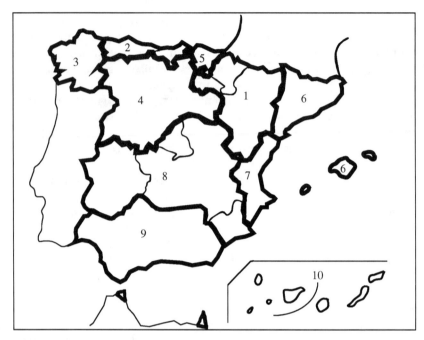

Map 4. The electronic regions of Spain according to the central government, 1988. The zones are assigned as follows: 1, Aragón, La Rioja, Navarre; 2, Asturias, Cantabria; 3, Galicia; 4, Castile-León; 5, Basque Country; 6, Catalonia, Balearic Islands; 7, Valencia; 8, Castile-La Mancha, Madrid, Extremadura, Murcia; 9, Andalusia, Ceuta, Melilla (the latter two are Spanish enclaves in North Africa); 10, Canary Islands.

to the national audience was seen as intermediary, that is, the regional centers were not designed to broadcast beyond their territorial zones. The regional centers were granted secondary status within the national linkup, being only distribution points, although they were to obtain primary status during schedules limited to regional broadcasts.

Thus, on a national scale, the regional centers act only to relay to the territorial zone the national programs received from the principal centers in Madrid and Barcelona through the central tower in Madrid. On a regional scale, they are the center, but their fortunes are limited, for the private TV law stipulated that the number of regional broadcast hours must never surpass that of national broadcast hours.[15]

The technical plan created a new level of regional consolidation and difference. It consolidated the flows of signals through the infrastructure so that all points in the territory could be connected. In addition, the plan reasserted the centralized control over the regional spectrum: every signal with a national audience must pass through Madrid, and every regional frequency allocation must fit the national plan. The technical plan differentiated and stratified points of reception, relay, and transmission. Principal and regional centers of production were distinguished, some more vital to the system than others. Barcelona and Madrid inherited the territorial bias of the old RTVE network; they remained the dynamic core of production and transmission (see chapter 12). In fact, the last point of the plan gave instructions that transmission facilities in Madrid and Barcelona must be ready for private broadcasts six months after licensing was finished.

In short, the Retevisión infrastructure regionalized technology, and in the process created technologized regions. The technological regions have their own logic and geographical identity; they can be mapped out to show the discrete electronic space they produce.

Yet the plan identifies parts of Spain with these electronic regions. This is deceptive, because the political regions of Spain (provinces, Autonomous Communities, and municipalities) are the product of a different history. The relations between electronic space and political space (not to mention economic geography), between centralized planning and regional realities, are messy and conflict-ridden. The expression of law in the electronic space of the technical plan moved the mess and conflict into the realm of regional politics.

The new technological regions instituted by the various laws and by the technical plan bring the story of privatization to an end. Chronologically, the national reform of television in Spain has evolved through the early chaos of the UCD government to the corporatist normalization under the socialists. The institutional evolution that parallels this policy began in the maverick days when hundreds of speculators staked claims to promises of private TV. After the dust settled, the PSOE had assured proprietorship to three highly capitalized conglomerates, eliminating most other pretenders. The law sanctioned by the socialists ended the battle over licenses and reasserted centralist control over the national space of a now-privatized and decentralized television system.

The state's regional policy for private TV closes the chapter on privatization and opens onto the clash between centralism and regionalism. The conflicts that have shaped the manner in which the Spanish government has chosen to organize television have until now been dealt with in linear time. If this story has not always followed a straight line, it is, in part, because of the unruly disruptions from the regions. Until the technical plan for private TV captured the spectrum, only the Third Channel Law had been regulating spectrum use in the regions.

The political and cultural conflicts expressed in the organization of Spanish television also, and very significantly, manifest themselves in spatial processes. Just as the transition to democracy in Spain can be understood only in the context of autonomy for the regions, the transformation of the TV industry in Spain cannot be understood without taking into account its spatial dimension.

Part III

The Geography of Television in Spain

It is scarcely any longer possible to tell a straight story sequentially un-folding in time. . . . Prophesy now involves a geographical rather than his-torical projection; it is space, not time, that hides consequences from us. . . . Any contemporary narrative which ignores the urgency of this di-mension is incomplete and acquires the oversimplified character of a fable.
John Berger, The Moment of Cubism and Other Essays *(46)*

Nothing much happens, bar angels dancing, on the head of a pin.
Doreen Massey, Spatial Divisions of Labor *(52)*

In a study conducted for the Barcelona County Council in 1988, the Catalan media sociologists Miquel de Moragas and María Corominas Piulats argued that it was a mistake for the New World Information and Communication Order to be defined primarily in terms of the nation-state. They said such definitions were inadequate given the existence of "minority nations or cultures which lack the infrastructure of a state on which to organize their communication policies."[1] This observation about small nations issues a warrant to investigate the local dynamics of cultural development within the modern nation-state. It asks international media research to readjust to a world that is no longer composed solely of Wilsonian or Leninist political regions. It calls for models that can account for regional cultures that aspire to the status of sovereign nation but, for historical reasons, remain without state power. Finally, the statement insists that regionalized communication policies be put into practice in order to make this cultural regionalism more than wishful thinking.

But where there is political will there may not be economic substance to back up this regionalism. Uneven regional development inhibits the potential for universal economic autonomy for small nations seeking to put policies into practice. Communications institutions of small nations may overcome the lack of state support, but not all regions enjoy the same level of economic development nor do they occupy equally advantageous positions within the economic space of the nation or the international economy. There are limitations to what the state and local authorities can do, especially when faced with the inconstant geography of services, resources, know-how, capital, and so on. Part III of this book examines this inconstant geography in terms of three distinct regionalizations: the electronic, the political, and the economic.

12
Electronic Regions of Spain

Experiments in radiowave communication started early in the twentieth century, and in 1921 Radio Castilla, a venture of the Compañía Ibérica de Telecomunicación, began regular broadcasts of concerts from the Royal Theater of Madrid after receiving special authorization from the government.[1] The Spanish government had created legislation in 1908 to establish state control over all broadcast technology. A royal decree of January of that year gave the central state the right to establish and exploit "all systems and apparatuses related to the so-called Hertzian telegraph, ethereal telegraph, radiotelegraph, and other similar procedures that are already invented or *that will be invented in the future.*"[2] The first official license was not granted until 1924, when all experimental stations were ordered to cease broadcasting and request state authorization. This first "legal" radio broadcast began in Barcelona and, like most pre-civil-war radio stations, was started up by private interests in order to make a profit.[3]

In the law on radio broadcasting of 1934, the Second Republic reaffirmed that "the service of national radio broadcasting is an essential and exclusive function of the state"; again, in 1935, "sounds *and images* already in use *or to be invented in the future*" would be established and exploited by the state.[4] The Republic, however, demonstrated little interest in centralizing more than the management of spectrum allocation and of distribution of transmitters. In one of its first decrees, the government of the Second Republic authorized the installation of low-power transmitters to promote the growth of radio with a distinctly local character.[5]

Despite such localism, radio was not attached in any systematic way to the regionalist projects that emerged under the Second Republic. The political projects in Catalonia, the Basque Country, and Galicia were entangled in other problems, such as fights over the purview of their charters and financing for the independent governments.[6] Throughout the rest of the Spanish territory, political authorities had little influence over the sites of investment in radio or the nature of the programming. The early development of radio instead followed a pattern of market-oriented investment, with multiplication of stations in urban zones, and only one private chain of any significance, Unión Radio, showing signs of concentration.

Some urban radio stations operated with wider regionalist intentions, like Radio Emisora Bilbaina, a private station in Bilbao. In the 1930s, Radio Emisora Bilbaina broadcast Basque language lessons as part of an educational program that included English and French lessons. Apart from commercial messages, music, and notices of general interest, the programming on Radio Emisora Bilbaina explicitly served as a public voice of regional concerns.[7] Independent radio of this nature was stopped, however, by the conditions of the Spanish civil war (1936–39). During the war, all stations were transformed into voices of military propaganda on both sides of the front.

Franco ordered the nationalization of all radio stations under the direction of the new state and the National Movement. The technical network of transmitters that the Republic had established within a rather laissez-faire framework was integrated into a new state-controlled network called Radio Nacional de España. Franco forced Spanish cultural-informational institutions back into the centralist mold, which shaped the form in which broadcasting finally grew in Spain. Use of the distinct idioms of Basque, Catalan, and Galician was suppressed within the Spanish territory. The national community imagined by broadcasting became monolingual, speaking only Castilian, and purposefully singular in its propagation of Francoist state-nationalism. New laws aimed at the press gave the fascist Ministry of the Interior full power to suppress communication that "directly, or indirectly, may tend to reduce the prestige of the Nation or Regime, to obstruct the work of the government of the new State, or sow pernicious ideas among the intellectually weak."[8]

The first public demonstration of television took place in Barcelona in 1948 as part of a promotion by the multinational communications firm Philips. Experiments continued until the autumn of 1956. On October 28, 1956, transmitted from a building in Madrid, Spain's first TV broadcast was a mass conducted by Franco's chaplain. The mass was followed by a speech from the minister of Information and Tourism,

Gabriel Arias-Salgado, who commemorated the regime's twenty years. These nationalist blessings reached nearly three thousand television receivers in the capital,[9] and occurred one year before Franco formed his sixth government with Opus Dei technocrats and three years after the military base agreement with the United States.

Most of the early programming came from the U.S. embassy, but there were also live transmissions of variety and children's shows, and a news program was started in 1957. By 1958 there were approximately thirty thousand TV sets in Madrid. From the beginning, Televisión Española (TVE) was supported by advertising, although it also received subsidies derived from a luxury tax on ownership and use of television receivers. In the late 1950s, TVE was extended to Barcelona via terrestrial lines, and parts of Castile, Extremadura, and Cantabria soon received the signal as well. At the end of the decade, fifty thousand sets were in use.[10]

As Spain moved timidly from its isolation, so did its television system. In 1959, through the Eurovision satellite system, Spanish viewers joined European viewers in an audience of some fifty million. One of the first images they shared was the historic meeting in Madrid between Franco and Eisenhower. This event symbolically marked the beginning of the Spanish "economic miracle" and the takeoff of Spanish TV.[11]

The regionalization of the television system proceeded much like the regional hierarchy established by the development plans of the sixties: a growth-pole model of developed TV towns, followed by trickle-down growth into the provinces. Television was a strictly urban phenomenon at this time, and Madrid was the supreme TV center. Except for Barcelona, total peripheralization characterized all regional TV development from the beginning.

By 1962, TVE claimed coverage of 65 percent of the Spanish territory with its one VHF channel. At that time there were only two production centers, one in Madrid and one in Barcelona. All transmission originated from Madrid, relayed in one direction to the rest of the territory. Despite these elements, television was then reaching only about 1 percent of the population. In 1964, a modern studio and office building were erected in Madrid to commemorate the twenty-eighth anniversary of the fascist uprising; the administrative center of the dictatorship became the indisputable center of electronic regions of Spain. A year later, TVE-2, a second channel (UHF) with production studios located in Madrid and Barcelona, began testing. Apart from the Barcelona and Madrid centers, which initiated a kind of rivalry in the late 1960s that persists to the present, the Canary Islands also had a small production center.

Also in 1965, the luxury tax on the purchase and use of television sets was eliminated, making advertising the major resource for TVE-1 and TVE-2.[12] Estimates put yearly advertising investment in television around one million dollars by the early 1960s. Weekly hours of programming increased from 28 to 70 between 1958 and 1964, rising to 110 hours in 1972. Advertising income for TVE multiplied one hundred times between 1961 and 1973, reaching estimated totals of over 100.5 million dollars.[13]

In the early 1970s, new regional centers were constructed in Bilbao, Oviedo (Asturias), Santiago de Compostela (Galicia), Valencia, and Seville (Andalusia). The entire system was finally brought together, with radio, under the management of one state-held corporation (RTVE) in 1973. The regional circuit was wired into a highly centralized network in which all regional broadcasts were obliged to pass through Madrid. The only regional centers with the capacity to produce programs of any length were those in Barcelona and the Canary Islands. At the beginning of the transition to democracy, the centralist domination of television was unquestioned.

The numbers reflect this centralism. Though the records of RTVE management are notoriously patchy and unreliable, a technical report for 1976 registered the portions of total airtime transmitted by the regional circuits on both TVE-1 and TVE-2. Out of approximately 5,348 transmission hours for all of 1976, the Barcelona center contributed about 161 hours, or 3 percent of the total, followed by the center at Las Palmas in the Canary Islands at 154 hours (2.9 percent). The rest transmitted a negligible amount of 1.8 to 1.85 percent of the total.[14] Another study conducted in 1982 showed little improvement, as estimates of news production for the TVE network showed that only 7.2 percent of total news transmitted came from all of the regional centers combined, and most of this was made up of local clips of soccer matches.[15]

The one-way flow from the center to the regions was an effect of the technical bias of the infrastructure. The regional centers (other than Barcelona and Las Palmas) were simply prohibited from connecting with Madrid. In the north, for instance, when TVE-1 and TVE-2 were both transmitting, there was no third line for the regional centers to use; only the images from Madrid could be transmitted. Because the local material for local broadcast had to be sent to and from Madrid electronically, the lack of a third line meant that the regional centers were sometimes forced to deliver recordings by hand or by post. The technical bias of the infrastructure put a veritable gag on the regional centers in their own regions. The northern zone finally got a third line in the late 1970s, but "it took a trip to Galicia by the president of the French Republic, Valéry Giscard d'Estaing, before the problem was solved."[16]

In the early eighties, eleven centers were associated with the RTVE regional circuit, and by 1988 there were sixteen. None of these centers respected political regions as defined by the State of the Autonomies, except, perhaps, those of Barcelona and the Canary Islands.[17] In the words of García Jiménez, "The activity of the regional centers conformed to the unitary structure of the central decision-making powers, ignoring altogether the cultural identity of the towns and *comarcas.*"[18]

The exception of the Barcelona center is worth noting. Reflecting certain liberalizations in the communications law of the late 1960s, all Barcelona productions (apart from one news program) were broadcast in the Catalan language. According to available figures, however, monthly transmission hours did not surpass the single-digit mark until after 1976 (figures for this year totaled about 3 percent of all TVE transmissions, as already noted). By 1980, Barcelona was contributing to TVE between 45 and 83 hours per month of Catalan-language programming. The average for 1982 was about 70 hours per month.[19] At this time the Barcelona center was in a state of disrepair relative to the highly modern Madrid center, and some equipment was said to have been acquired from North American universities (which had rejected the equipment because of its obsolescence).[20]

The Barcelona center furnished a foundation for the growth of regional talent within the culture industries—as a very distant second in comparison to the Madrid facilities—while the centers in other regions played no such role. The almost-total destitution of the infrastructure granted to other regional centers was reflected in a comment by an associate of the center in Santiago de Compostela: "There isn't even enough money here to build a small wooden stage."[21] This extremely uneven development would prove to be a decisive factor stratifying future regional broadcasting projects.

Efforts aimed at alleviating some of the inequities of this electronic regionalization began with the promulgation of the RTVE Statute, enacted in 1980. The statute initially envisioned the expansion of the regional circuits with a view to their becoming the basis for the creation of television stations operated by the regional communities under the jurisdiction of RTVE. This mandate reflected the constitutional stipulation to respect cultural and linguistic pluralism within the Spanish nation-state. In terms of regional television policy, however, the statute was a pale imitation of French legislation: it aimed to retain central control over regional television while dismantling centralism.

The statute called for RTVE to include increased participation of "territorial delegates" on the decision-making board of the corporation;

however, the explicit participation of official representatives of the Autonomous Communities was not stipulated and never really sought.[22] In addition, the statute implied that the Autonomous Communities must wait for their own regional TV until after the central administration of RTVE judged that the existing regional circuits were sufficiently expanded. Although the wording of the statute guarantees the existence of regional TV, it does so under the stipulation that RTVE and the central administration would control the semiautonomous regional systems.

Needless to say, the RTVE Statute would not be welcomed as the final option by the Basques and Catalans, given that it promised to keep regional industries dependent on the center. This recalled the old tensions between centralism and regionalism, and aggravated historic disputes that the transitional government could not ignore. The unruly presence of Basque and Catalan TV erupted on the scene to challenge the planned regionalization of RTVE. The unexpected disruption determined the central government's next move—the passing and enactment of the Third Channel Law, which opened the way for media systems to develop in the regions, but under the supervision of the central government.

The Emergence of Autonomous Regional Television

The Basques rejected the RTVE Statute because it lacked respect for their own statute of autonomy. The Basques included a mandate unique among autonomy statutes that called for the building of a radio and television system beyond the control of the Spanish state. As a result the Basque parliament initiated the construction of a "fourth channel" television. The Catalans, in contrast, rejected the statute on legal grounds, centering the problem on the inadequacy of the statute to define the Catalan government's legal competence over the regional administrative counsels of RTVE. The Catalans disputed the constitutionality of RTVE control over the subsequent construction of the third channel network within their region.

A pattern of different strategies to combat centralism was established. The Basques appeared to prefer action outside of the laws of the Spanish state, or at least to exploit the legal incoherences in the constitution and RTVE Statute (that they exploited legal polysemy was a view shared by both the central government and Basque authorities, in respectively reactive and proactive interpretations). For the Basques, their statute of autonomy furnished regional authorities with sovereignty over cultural materials, and they claimed exclusivity for their laws over those of the state.

The background to this battle over jurisdictional exclusivity is worth explaining. In 1979, the Basque and Catalan authorities negotiated the first full autonomy granted under article 151, known as the immediate route to autonomy; the Basque Country and Navarre later regained control over tax collection under a historical charter, or *fueros*.[23] Besides greater autonomous control over the regional economy, article 151 also included provisions that guarantee rights to an autonomous education system, to a separate police force, and to *an independent television network*.[24] Against these provisions for regional autonomy, the central state maintained powers and policy functions under article 149, which included foreign affairs, constitutional enforcement, defense, industrial relations, and monetary policy. The constitution also reserved for the central state *basic regulation of the press, radio, and television*.[25] This obvious and confusing overlap of powers was further compounded by a final clause in article 149 that gives the Autonomous Communities "exclusive" policy domains in which regional laws prevail over the national norms.[26] The statutes of autonomy empowered regional authorities' claim to exclusivity in areas that seem to contravene the laws at the national level, which were also granted "exclusivity." One significant area is broadcasting; hence, Basque intransigence and Catalan litigiousness.

In contrast to the Basques, the Catalans preferred the courts to challenge the constitutionality of centralist control over television in the region.[27] The Catalan delegation to the Spanish parliament eventually proposed the project of a third channel for Catalonia in the summer of 1981. It was approved by the central government with the concrete concession remaining to be legislated. The process was interrupted by the crisis of the central government in 1981–82, and efforts to renew it were postponed until after the national elections. The Catalan authorities nonetheless went ahead and established the legal and administrative framework for the creation of an autonomous regional television.

The Basques meanwhile implemented the mandate of their statute of autonomy for the creation of a television free of the technical and administrative jurisdictions of RTVE. In May 1982, the Basque government created the corporate entity Euskal Irrati Telebista (EITB), or Basque Radio and Television. EITB was founded as "an essential instrument for the informational and political participation of Basque citizens, and as a fundamental medium of cooperation with our own education system to foment and diffuse Basque culture, keeping very much in mind the fomentation and development of *euskara*."[28]

The Catalan parliament (Generalitat) was more circumspect, but still moved ahead with plans for the region's television before the legal framework had been approved. The Generalitat formed the Corporació

Catalana de Ràdio i Televisió (CCRTV), or Catalan Corporation of Radio
and Television, in May 1983. A regular schedule of TV programs was
finally broadcast in January 1984 on Televisió de Catalunya (TV-3), the
television subsidiary of the corporation.

In July 1984, the Xunta de Galicia (Galician government) founded
Compañía de Radiotelevisión de Galicia (CRTVG), or Galician Radio
and Television Company. CRTVG began television broadcasts on TV
de Galicia (TVG) in 1985, albeit in a much less contentious political environment than that of the Basque Country or Catalonia.

The three autonomous channels broadcast programs of national, international, and widely regional interest, although they paradoxically left
most of the strictly local coverage to the regional circuit of TVE. As
with the process of devolution of powers to the regions, the historic nationalities (Euskadi, Catalunya, Galicia) were the first to create autonomous television networks within their territories. Historic precedent
aside, political control over the regional parliaments was an important
factor guaranteeing the creation of media in those national languages.
Prior to TV, the only all-Basque-language medium was the newspaper
Deia, which was controlled by the Basque Nationalist Party (PNV). In
Catalonia, the nationalist party Convergencia i Unió (CiU) controlled
Avui. Both regional dailies served as ideological supports for the conservative nationalist parties. The Basques could begin broadcasting in
January 1983 because the Basque government, which was controlled by
the Basque Nationalist Party, was not beholden to the plans of the PSOE.
The vice president of the PSOE government, Alfonso Guerra, was still
saying months later that "it is not on the agenda of the government to
legislate any independent television."[29]

The PSOE government could not control events where it did not hold
a majority—Guerra's threats were meaningless in Euskadi. Where the
PSOE did control regional politics, it was able to keep the television
systems under the strict guidelines of the Third Channel Law. This was
the case in the communities of Andalusia, Valencia, and Madrid, where
the PSOE placed limits on the development of regional TV. The PSOE
preempted the regional start-ups until 1989, even though Telemadrid
was incorporated in June 1984, Valencia's Canal 9 in July 1984, and
Andalusia's Canal Sur in 1987.

The central authorities attempted, but failed, to stop the earlier, accelerated efforts of the Basques and Catalans. These efforts foretold of the
general thrust of the Third Channel Law. For example, the director general of RTVE, José María Calviño, along with the director general of
social communication in the office of the presidency, Francisco Virseda,
refused to acknowledge Basque and Catalan authority. They insisted

that the RTVE Statute prohibited the construction of "third channels" without dependence on, and the express permission of, RTVE and the central government.[30] They urged that a general law corresponding to regional autonomous networks must be passed prior to any construction and that, in any case, the infrastructure to be used remained under the jurisdiction of the central broadcasting corporation.

Calviño proposed that future television systems be constructed in the regions to complement the programming philosophy of RTVE. In the eyes of Catalan and Basque intellectuals, such a proposal submitted the autonomous channels to a kind of folklorization of their cultures, an anthropological appendage of RTVE programming.[31] In other words, Calviño sought to impose a multicultural curriculum on Spanish television by having regional talent provide diversity through—in his version—small-scale regional subsidiaries of the national network.

The Third Channel Law ultimately reflected Calviño's position: the regional networks were to depend on the RTVE infrastructure as well as on RTVE program purchasing structures. From the point of view of the regionalists, the Third Channel Law aimed to deny autonomy of new regional institutions. Still, when compared to the centralism of the previous regime, the Third Channel Law signaled near-revolutionary change.

In contrast, absolute autonomy for Basque, Catalan, and Galician TV was simply de rigueur for the regional authorities. Their self-determination rested on two crucial points: (i) using transmitters, relays/amplifiers, and interconnections of their own, which ran parallel to those of RTVE; and (ii) managing their own program purchasing. The only dependency of any consequence (and controversy) was the central state's control over universal frequency allocation within the Spanish territory.

Frequencies were assigned in bulk by the central government with regional allocations left to regional authorities, but the regional authorities ignored strict adherence to the central government's allocations. A sovereign state, after all, controls the spectrum of frequencies within its territory. Efforts in fact were made to codify the regional sovereignty over spectrum allocations even further, as the Basques and Catalans applied for independent status within the European Broadcasting Union. Membership of the Autonomous Communities was blocked, however, by the Spanish delegation because the communities lacked international recognition as sovereign states. They may have been nations without states, but the Basque Country and Catalonia still had their own broadcast networks. In the territory of electronic regions, if nowhere else, the Basques and Catalans enjoyed sovereign status—at least for the time being.

On August 4, 1988, the phone was ringing in the office of Julián Pérez, managing director of Euskal Irrati Telebista. His assistant informed him that an official from Madrid was on the line. Pérez smiled and told his assistant to respond that he was out. That day EITB started broadcasting on a new radio channel, but the central authorities had not been told about it. From the Basque point of view, it was none of Madrid's business. Julián Pérez winked. "Let them call. I know what they'll say and I don't care. We have another radio channel, and that's all that matters."[32]

13
In the Region of Electronic and Political Conflicts

Before the technical plan of the private TV law was enacted, the Basque, Catalan, and Galician communities had taken over a place within the electronic regions of Spain. These electronic regions became a territory lost to the central administration—or, at least when entered, a place of disrespect and harassment for the government of Madrid. With many of its calls going unanswered, management from the center was often frustrated by the resistance of regional broadcasters. In the summer of 1988, the chief technician in charge of monitoring frequency use in Spain put it this way: "We know which frequencies we've assigned, but we don't know which ones they're using. It appears that they use whichever ones they find most convenient."[1]

Julián Pérez of Euskal Irrati Telebista explained EITB's actions as part of "the traditional fight—or traditional point of difference—between the central government and the Basque government." He said that this battle boiled down to a disagreement over the nature of broadcasting in Euskadi. The central government says Basque Television (Euskaltelebista) is merely a third channel like that of the other regions, but Basques didn't see it that way. Euskadi is unique, Pérez said. "The infrastructure here exists because of a mandate in the statute of autonomy and not because of the Third Channel Law, which, in any case, was promulgated after Euskaltelebista was constructed. The law here states that Euskadi has the right to construct and maintain its own television system."

Pérez reiterated that the central government's only responsibility is to perform its duties as a signatory of the conventions of the International Telecommunications Union, i.e., to assign frequencies. Indeed, the central government is obliged by law to provide allocations once regional broadcasters decide to build new systems. "What has happened in the five years that EITB has been on the air," he said, "is that the central government has not fulfilled this obligation. As a consequence, our radio and television systems have to this day 'occupied,' as it were, the frequencies." "In other words," he concluded, "there is no legalization for Basque radio and TV from the point of view of the central government. From our point of view, Euskaltelebista functions 'alegally' because only the administrative concessions are lacking while the constitutional and statutory frameworks are active."[2]

This conflict over jurisdiction in the electronic region reflected a historic, and seemingly intractable, political schism between the central powers of the Spanish state and the historic nationalities. These conflicts converged in the space where electronic and political regions overlap. After the failure to rein in the Basques and Catalans with the Third Channel Law, the next indication that Madrid was out to retake the regional airwaves came with the passing of the national telecommunications law, or LOT. "Nationalization of the autonomous infrastructure is the spirit of LOT," commented Julián Pérez. The private TV law and its technical plan would bear this out with the stipulation that all existing networks be integrated into Retevisión. The reassertion of centralist control over the regional autonomous broadcasters was clear.

Agustí Gallart, head of the Cabinet of Radio and Television of the Catalan government, ventured that LOT would "create great conflicts." Gallart observed that although the technical aspects of the law require "unification of all the broadcast networks into a single structure, this is independent of the management or exercise of control." He added, however, that "it does mean the loss of a great investment within the region; someone will have to pay." At any rate, none of the technical aspects of LOT or of the private TV law was explicit about how the autonomous networks would be integrated. In the end, Gallart was convinced that "control will remain in the hands of those public companies that produce and/or distribute programs."[3]

Asked what the technical plan and Retevisión would mean for regional broadcasting, Jaime Souza, economic director of TV de Galicia, sighed as if to say "business as usual." As he drove from his office at TVG to downtown Santiago de Compostela, Souza looked up at the mountaintop where two relay towers stood—one belonged to RTVE, the other to TVG. He thought a little longer about the technical plan and then said, "Habrá guerra"—there will be a war.[4]

Meanwhile in Madrid, Francisco Virseda, director general of social communication under the presidency, considered the battle won. "Until now," he said, "they used whatever frequencies they wanted. When private television begins, all of this will have to be ..." — he paused to find the right word — "readjusted."[5]

Back in 1987, during the parliamentary debates over the private TV law, the Catalan and Basque opposition within the national parliament attempted to block the regional structure proposed in the law.[6] On July 26, 1988, the Generalitat de Catalunya approved legislation that actually sought to repeal the private TV law on the basis of its unconstitutional infringement upon the Catalan government's control over regional airwaves. The position of the Generalitat was that there are essentially two electronic regions in Spain, the national and the one defined by the borders of the Autonomous Communities. Agustí Gallart stated:

> When one channel with a national character — that is, within the territorial limits of the Spanish state — does not transmit in the national Spanish circuit, it has to transmit through peripheral circuits that correspond to the constitutional character of the Spanish state, that is, within the Autonomous Communities. In other words, the coverage has to correspond to the map of the State of the Autonomies.[7]

Gallart added that "the statute of autonomy guarantees the legal competence of Catalonia over television within the region." This echoed the position of all three systems belonging to the historic nationalities. The object of resistance was the centrally defined electronic regions, which were charted for a national circuit, Retevisión, and for control by an authority outside the regions.

Half of the political regions defined by the State of the Autonomies corresponded to the zones of Retevisión, but the other half did not. In addition, as chapter 11 demonstrated, the electronic zones of the technical plan of private TV were integrated into the national network in a hierarchical structure inherited from the RTVE system. At best the apparent spatial bias of Retevisión looked in the main similar to the political regions of the State of the Autonomies, yet the underlying interconnections reasserted centralist control.

Moreover, anticentralist stakes were higher for regional broadcasters by the time the private TV law was passed. The Basques and the Catalans each had started a second television channel. In May 1986, Basque television set up its second channel, ETB-2, as a broadcast service in the Castilian language. ETB-2 was meant to attract a very significant portion

of the regional population that did not speak Basque. (Basque government estimates for 1986 put the figure for total non-Euskara speakers
at 64 percent; of the remainder who understood Euskara, only 21 percent claimed to speak it. In contrast, a study in Catalonia in 1986 showed
that 90 percent of the population understood Catalan, 64 percent spoke
it, and about 60 percent read it.)[8] The Catalans started their second
channel, Canal 33, in September 1988, though its plans were well known
months before. A so-called minority-interest/high-quality channel, Canal
33 (like TV-3) broadcast in Catalan.

These channels not only contravened LOT but occupied frequencies that were eventually allocated to private channels in the 1988 technical plan. Occupying channels, however, was still the rule of the day.
"The central government is not going to give a new channel to TV-3,"
said Agustí Gallart. "So what does TV-3 do? It looks at the spectrum
and sees a frequency not in use and says, 'This one is free, we'll take
it!'"[9] Julián Pérez of EITB was less bold and ventured that the central government would win the day in the regional airwaves "because it
has won in the past and because, in the literal reading of the law, it
maintains the principal jurisdiction over the universal allocation of
frequencies."[10]

Indeed, the constitution protects laws created by the central government even while challenges to their constitutionality are appealed. In
this situation, the Basque and Catalan appeal against the private TV law
was powerless. The regional authorities had no control. Nonetheless,
respect for the regions was still "indissolubly tied" to democracy in Spain.
For this reason, Gallart was convinced that new channels could not be
stopped by the central government, even if the PSOE did not approve.
Beyond the legal battles over new channels, he said, lies "a major institutional conflict" between regional and central authority. The central
government must negotiate when "all of the political forces of the region — right and left, nationalist and not, monarchist and republicans —
are asking for another TV channel." With the regional forces united in
this way, centralist belligerency "would mean a great political loss. To
deny a new channel would be understood as denying the democratic
process."[11]

Though the PSOE government had proclaimed the end of the transition from dictatorship long before this time, the disputes of 1988 in this
electronic region of conflict showed no finality to transition politics and
processes. Julián Pérez attributed the problem to the PSOE's "botched
job" of reform. "If things had been done right," he complained, "then
none of these tremendous suspicions would be circulating among the
Basques, Galicians, and Catalans." The private TV law and LOT were

created out of a corporatist mix; with electoral opportunism (please the press) and political pragmatism (they *had* to do it) shaping fast-track reforms. The result was a new technical plan that aggravated the tension between centralism and regionalism. "It's the same old dog," Pérez concluded, "only with a new collar—it may have new administrators and a new central communications network, but nobody knows who it will protect."[12] Historical odds were in Madrid's favor.

Today the technical structure of transmitters, relay-amplifiers, and other equipment belonging to the autonomous systems remains intact and independent from Retevisión. However, infrastructural autonomy may be abandoned for guarantees of technical maintenance from Retevisión, which would lessen the costs of operation for the regional broadcasters. Villagrasa describes the continued separation of networks as "an absurd and much criticized duplication of public expenditure."[13] Still, political independence afforded by autonomous access to airwaves has been a powerful tool for the regionalist movements. Even Villagrasa admits that "in these conditions the governments of the Basque Country and Catalonia were able to establish second channels, since the necessary network for new signal transmissions had already been built."[14] Why then would the regional governments give up control over the technical infrastructure?

In the zone of conflict where electronic and political regions converged, the political region set decisive limits on the scale and use of electronic regions, yet not always in ways plotted by political intention. The political region was created by law, through constitutional and statutory order. Regional political authority was deployed to protect investments, the built environment, and cultural institutions within its territorial purview—which included electronic media. An infringement on this legal authority promised to lead to political conflict, interregional rivalry, and negotiated exchanges. According to the law, the regional broadcasters could not establish relays outside of their borders. That is still the logic of the political region; to do otherwise would constitute an infringement.

Yet the signals of the electronic regions of Spain spilled over the borders of the political region, legal restrictions notwithstanding. Three causes were basically responsible for this spillover. First, electromagnetic waves, by their nature, trespass borders—nowhere on this planet can radio signals be expected to stay within boundaries of political regions. Second, felt alliances of viewers do not necessarily correspond to borders; regional sentiment anchored to same-language programming, for example, might not share a political region. Finally, the commercial imperative of broadcasting seeks to maximize audience size, and this inherent expansionism rarely retreats from spatial containments of politics, sentiment, or technology.

The tension between centralism and regionalism also gave rise to trespassing among electronic regions. The complaints of Pérez and Gallart about the technical plan of LOT and private TV might be understood in this light. The central state was seen as trespassing beyond the statutory limits of its power. Centralism motivated this trespass, regionalism its containment (the values of containment and trespass can dress up whichever sovereign you want to privilege). In general, the play of trespass and containment defined the electronic turf wars over television in Spain.

One kind of trespass among political regions came from radiowave spillover. Map 5 illustrates the electronic regions of autonomous broadcasters based on 1988 reports. Basque technicians reported that beyond the three provinces of the Autonomous Community, signal coverage reached north to the three provinces of the French Basque Country, or Euskadi Norte, which Basques call Laburdi, Benabarra, and Zuberoa — that is, from Hendaya to Bayonne, Saint Palais, and Mauleon. Coverage reached south to Burgos (Castile-León), Logroño (La Rioja), and parts of La Ribera del Ebro in the south of Navarre; reached east into Navarre as far as Pamplona; and reached west to Santander (Cantabria). Containment of these signals is next to impossible, though no guarantee of broadcast quality exists beyond the ring of relays on the borders of the Basque Country. There have been reports of signal jamming in the western provinces of Navarre, which has an old rivalry with its Basque cousins to the west.[15]

Signals of TVG, Galician television, reached into northern Portugal and east into parts of Asturias and the provinces of León and Palencia (Castile-León).[16] The Catalan TV-3 easily reached into zones bordering Catalonia: southern France, eastern Aragón, northern Valencia, and the Balearic Islands. TV-3 even included some of the attached viewership numbers in its rate card for advertising. In addition, TV-3 recorded a surprising number of viewers throughout Valencia and as far south as Murcia.[17] Again, containment was difficult, and there were no reports of jamming — in fact, the opposite of jamming occurred.

The extensive reach of TV-3 was caused not by the intentions of the regional broadcaster, but by people in outlying regions who installed the relays themselves. In Valencia, the terrestrial system that allowed the signal of TV-3 to reach into the north of Murcia was built by an independent cultural group that desired to watch Catalan language programming (Valencian and Catalan are linguistic cousins). The alliance of language also applies to the efforts of consumer groups in the north

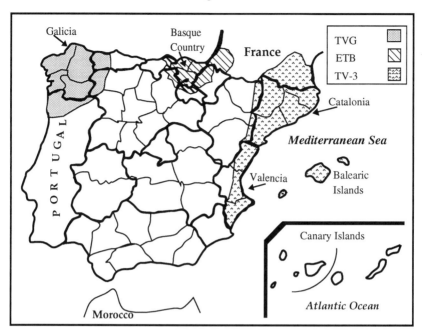

Map 5. The electronic regions of Spain according to TVG, ETB, and TV-3, 1988. This image of electronic regions is based on reports of engineers at the three regional broadcast companies; these electronic regions are not recognized by the central government. The coverage reported for TVG and TV-3 reflected the efforts of viewers in Portugal and Valencia, respectively, to extend the electronic region to fit zones of linguistic and cultural commonality. The coverage reported by ETB reflects the broadcasters' attempts to reach audiences in the French Basque Country (Euskadi Norte) and Navarre. Officially, the signals do not reach this far beyond the political borders of each region.

of Portugal who put in the relays to get the signal of TVG. In these cases, the electronic region was widened beyond the reach of the political region in order to fit the language zone of viewers.

The "right to antenna," however, was not a strong enough principle to keep these relays working—after all, the user groups were enabling transmission of the television signal. As a result, political authority could be deployed, at least within the Spanish territory, that is, to contain TV-3. Containment of the electronic region, which had been extended to fit a language zone of viewers in Valencia, fell back into the hands of official politics. Under these circumstances, in the region of political and electronic conflicts, politics proved to be more decisive than viewer choice.

Containment of TV-3's signal became the basis for a political tradeoff between the Catalan government and the central government. Recall that the second Catalan channel, Canal 33, went on the air in September

1988. In the midst of the battle over the assignment of regional frequencies, however, the Madrid authorities stopped Canal 33 almost immediately. Behind this preemption was a negotiated exchange. The story is that the conservative nationalist coalition, Convergència i Unió (CiU), bargained with the central government to let the Catalan radio-TV corporation have Canal 33 in exchange for the containment of TV-3 in Valencia. This involved holding off Canal 33 until the Valencian user groups could be cut off from TV-3. The Catalan government was said to have cooperated to garner political capital. Whatever the case, the result was that the control over interconnections in the Valencian Community returned to the regional authorities and to Canal 9, the Valencian television. The "alegal" system of relays was thereafter legalized within the framework of the Third Channel Law.[18]

In September 1989, Canal 33 returned to the regional airwaves. One month later, Canal 9 started broadcasting throughout Valencia. While the system erected by the user group was effectively expropriated, rumors were that extralegal systems were once again capturing transregional signals. Apparently, the felt alliance in language created a zone of viewers that endures without a political region to legitimate it.[19] By 1990, the number of Valencian TV households still reporting regular viewing of TV-3 was about 3 percent, which was triple the next highest figure in any region for audiences of spillover TV.[20]

The third trespass of political regions was the hardest to contain or control with political power. Commercial imperatives of growth inherently require border crossings. Of course, the most convenient kind of viewership beyond political borders, and the rarest, was that furnished by user groups. Without user groups outside the political regions, few options existed for increasing the scale of viewership. One option was to amplify the power of transmissions, which seems to have been the rule defining the play of trespass and containment among the regions (although figures for spillover reception are always negligible). Another option was the multiplication of audience volume, which was achieved in one way by starting second channels, especially the Castilian language channel in the Basque Country, which tripled the audience for ETB to a little over 16 percent of the regional population in 1990. The third option was production/organization innovation, such as the federation of regional companies, FORTA, initiated in meetings in the fall of 1988.

No matter which strategy or circumstance was appealed to, all expansion existed to protect the investment in the political region. The contradiction is obvious—these investments in the regions were made in order to safeguard the language and culture of those places, yet the necessity to reach and maximize audiences, or to cut costs, pushed the regional firms beyond political and linguistic boundaries to expand their audience or make transregional bargains. This can be interpreted as the basis for a healthy cultural exchange, but such an interpretation does not account for the imperative to capitalize on differences of regional economy, sentiment, politics, and technology. In other words, the extensions of the electronic region beyond the official borders of the Basque Country, Catalonia, or Galicia were more than just incidental to nationalist political claims over the irredenta of these small nations. The PNV fantasized about its dominion over Euskal Herria — that place that includes three southwestern French provinces and Navarre — and ETB extended this fantasy electronically beyond the political region of Euskadi. With greater success than in the Basque case, TV-3 projected for the Catalan nationalist government of CiU the imagined community of "els paisos catalans," a territory that would include the four official provinces of Catalonia, parts of southeastern France (Roussillón) and eastern Aragón, the three provinces of Valencia, and the Balearic Islands. The Xunta de Galicia dreamed less ambitiously, perhaps, but was still happy to welcome home TVG's viewers from northern Portugal. To be sure, the invitation to identify with small-nation nationalism that these regional broadcasters proffered served (and continues to serve) the politics of the nationalist parties. Nevertheless, these television projects have been, from their inception, industries of electronic communication, and as such have been anchored to the political economy in which they function.

14

The Distant Space of Political Economy

Regionalist television was decidedly anticentralist and anti-Francoist, but not anti-imperialist in the supranational sense. Nor, it might be argued, was it anti-imperialist in an infranational sense, although in respect to the political regions, containment of expansion has been highly regulated. Nonetheless, once the demands for territorialized cultural sovereignty were given substance as a commercial cultural institution, regionalism became part of a system that out of necessity seeks to trespass sovereign cultural borders (of the political region).

The extent of electronic trespass may have varied among the television projects, but the imperative to maximize audiences does not. In practice, then, a truly autonomous regional broadcast system would seem an impossibility (of course, this may be viewed by some as a dispute over the semantics of autonomy, that is, over whether it is imperious or defensive). At the very least, the regional systems maintain an institutional orientation that can be called selective autonomy (or selective dependence). The factors that have determined regionalist autonomy are related to economic development, linguistic and cultural alliances, and the territorial hierarchy of political authority.

This chapter explores these themes to reveal a view of cultural imperialism where the frontiers defining national and regional sovereignty are blurred. The analysis demonstrates how modern communications plays a dual role in extending the cultural project of a national movement; television can engage a regionalized audience for the cultural project of regionalism and also link this regional public to a transregional system of audience commodification. The paradox is that the transregional exchange of regionalized audiences favors those communication firms that are not bound politically or economically to the region; transregionalism (and ultimately transnationalism) is thus encouraged. The economic causes of this problem are examined and identified as limits to autonomy within the economic geography of television in Spain.

The Infranational Scale

By the late 1980s the American trade press was calling Spain "Europe's sleeping giant" precisely because of the hyperexpansion of its TV program and advertising markets.[1] The growth potential was attributed to the regional autonomous networks and to the regionalized markets these created for advertising and program sales and distribution. In the location and identification of the nonmass (or niche) market, American marketers saw in Spain what almost every market researcher or consulting firm would now speak of as business as usual: efficient strategies for communicating with culturally diverse consumers.[2]

Behind this market rhetoric was the expectation of a surge in the volume of audience attention to the commercial messages of advertisers: "The 'war of audiences,' as it has become known, has led to across-theboard studies by all parties of the tastes and habits of the Spanish viewer."[3] The groundwork for this battle over viewer attention had already been laid by TVE's national financing structure prior to the startup of regional television (see chapter 3). In 1984, in reaction to the establishment of regional autonomous television, TVE reconstituted the finance structure of its regional circuit, fragmenting its advertising contracts by region. The commercial media promoters reeled with excitement after this reorganization. Revenues in the regional circuit of TVE rose from about 1.1 million dollars to 14.6 million dollars in a brief three-year period.[4] In all, as noted in chapter 3, the difference in advertising income between 1975 and 1985 — the first decade after dictatorship — marked an increase in advertising billings of over 1,200 percent for TVE, an increase that surpassed that of any other European television firm.[5] After the initial euphoria subsided, the yearly average spending increment on all TV advertising in Spain was about 27 percent between 1985 and 1990.[6]

Total TV advertising in Spain was minuscule in comparison to global advertising revenues (less than 1 percent of the estimated 252 billion dollars of global ad trade in 1989). The growth of Spain's regionalized ad market after 1985, however, proved to be one of the more profitable examples of the international marketing strategy of localization. In market terms, the sale is always local. The ideal communication system from a market standpoint therefore positions advertisers equidistantly to all key customers.[7] A regionalized television audience makes this goal of localization much easier to attain.

For the regional autonomous networks, the defense of investments in their political region constituted the material basis for the localization of audiences. At the same time the same defense of investments for trans-regional firms has led to a universal factional struggle over regionalized audience attention. This war over audiences was manifest in the geography of Spanish television on three fronts. The first was expressed as an attempt by regional public television to take over an institutional space, and media territory, once the province of the central state. This was the frontal assault posed by political regionalism. The second battle over audiences was an effect of the national public television's reasserting its claim over this institutional space, a fragment of a national media territory. This was akin to a rearguard attempt by the central powers to retake the regions, the imperative of political centralism. The third front was opened by what can be called metropolitan capital: an attack on the regional media market by all owners of money capital, media assets, and other global properties.

The particular position of metropolitan capital in the war over audiences was not anchored to place by sentiment or politics. Regional investments of metropolitan capital were anchored to place on the basis of a logic of accumulation. That is, investments of metropolitan capital were made on the promise of profit, and only in that framework did national or regional alliances become expedient. This bottom-line imperative united the regional bourgeoisie with national and transnational capital in the battle to capture regional audiences. Recall the metropolitanism of investments in national media properties by Basque banks or the Catalan speculator Javier de la Rosa.

This war over audiences would pose neither moral nor pragmatic problems if access to the imaginations of people was not decisively linked to the structures of power in society. In other words, if left to microeconomic or technical problem-solving, the multiplication of the regional firms and the regionalization of the audience can be seen positively to encourage growth of the TV industry in Spain. Regional and national public firms compete among each other and with firms whose brief is written in the portfolio logic of metropolitan capital. In this scenario, competition for viewer attention gives rise to a healthy public culture (i.e., one that is growth-oriented, technologically innovatory, creatively vigorous, and so on).

But once the power structure of this market economy is revealed, the three approaches to regional audiences prove to be stratified in a manner that harms regionalist firms and favors metropolitan capital. The remainder of this section on infranational media space examines the causes of this hierarchical structure, with emphasis on a contradictory effect of regionalist television: namely, that the regionalist cultural enterprises have, of necessity, generated forms of external dependence through their television industries. Such dependent relations have made them unwitting partners in the extension of the dominance of metropolitan capital in the national media space. Paradoxically, these same dependencies were previously the object of regional resistance — that is, the object of autonomy.

In the previous chapter, audience maximization was introduced as one of the systemic forces mitigating against autonomy. Although the regional autonomous networks are advertising funded, not-for-profit companies, they, like other cultural industries, depend on maximizing their audience in order to cope with the increasing costs of production and distribution of their services. These firms thus protect their investment by capturing larger audiences and selling them to advertisers; public subsidy and bank loans make up the difference.

Like any other industry, without income these firms obviously risk losing their investment altogether. In order to protect these investments in their locales, these companies must be able to realize growth of their initial investment within their region — as they put it, they seek to become self-financing. The situation gets tougher given that the regional authorities can afford very little subsidy, which is also kept to yearly limits by law. Telemadrid, in fact, receives no subsidy but instead relies on a line of bank credit for its survival.

The ideal scenario would be a regionally restricted turnover of invested capital that would be self-expanding without transregional exchange. In material terms, this scenario suggests that a regional firm would have exclusive access to audiences in its region, access that could be capitalized through exclusive exchange of this audience for competing advertiser money. In other words, only the regional firm would tap into and increase the supply of commodified audiences, allowing the firm to be truly autonomous, and self-determination in political, cultural, and economic projects could be expanded.

In reality, this was of course impossible. The politically defined region remains a porous economic zone. Competition over audience volume, moreover, is already a transregional game. It tends to be a zero-sum game at that — winning larger audiences is always done at the expense of reducing audiences of other firms that operate in a particular electronic region. A structural condition affects the operations of regional broadcasters, as demonstrated in chapter 13, where the political limits to trans-

regional electronic space are rigid. For the regional firm, audience volume is restricted to its political region; for national firms, audience volume expands to include all political regions; and for transnational firms,
the sky seems to be the only limit. Each expanded scale of audience
space represents a market closed off to some participants at a smaller,
politically defined, spatial scale. In contrast, capital investors can participate at all spatial scales where there is no state regulation curtailing
investment or prescribing economic boundaries. Metropolitan capital
can thereby duplicate efforts to expand audience attention at all spatial
scales at its disposal; that is, holders of money capital (e.g., banks and
private investors) can be local, national, and transnational all at once,
given the fungibility of the currency in use.

Sticking to the national scale, then, open participation in a transregional market improves a firm's ability to maximize its audience; restricted activity at the national scale discourages this ability. The numbers bear this out, reflecting the clear domination of TVE and private
television at the infranational scale.[8] Moving in for a closer look at the
regional scale, the numbers demonstrate how transregional competition
over audiences tends to disfavor regional firms, though inconsistent preferences among the regional audiences for national channels are shown
(for example, residents of Madrid tend to watch more commercial TV,
while Basques and Galicians prefer TVE).[9]

Consider the premise that if an audience is not produced for a firm
located in a political region (say, for instance, in the Basque Country),
then it is possible that such an audience can be produced for a firm
located outside that region (say, a national network headquartered in
Madrid). In theory, when this occurs, it then becomes feasible for the
advertising value of a regional audience to be realized outside that audience's home region. In this scenario, a regionalized audience does not
necessarily contribute income to the regional firm. Obviously, again,
the nationwide broadcasts (public and private) are the primary beneficiaries of the transregional system in Spain. Basque television, to use
the same example, is thus constrained by the institutional logic of the
political region; private TV and TVE are not. In this political and economic framework, a regionalized audience does not necessarily offer a
better money value to a regional firm, at least as long as transregional
participants are operating in the same electronic space. But who said
the regional firms were in it for the money?

Though nobody claims to be making a profit in the Spanish TV
industry, the register of state and private TV revenues far outweighs that
of any regional firm.[10] To offset this imbalance, the political authorities

in the Autonomous Communities have provided subsidies to regional TV. In the absence of sufficient subsidy, as chapter 13 showed, aside from starting up second channels, regional TV firms were forced to reach across their borders for exchange of the sort that either reduced costs through strategic alliances or increased the scale and status of their audience (e.g., by establishing FORTA and by spillover, respectively).

Private broadcasters have accused the regional broadcast corporations of unfair competition because of their subsidy, but the politico-economic geography of broadcasting in Spain shows this charge to be groundless. It is prohibitive financially, and prohibited politically, for the regional broadcasters to participate in the national commercial environment on a par with TVE and the private TV companies.

The regional federation FORTA (Federation of Autonomous Radio and Television Organizations) is a very significant institutional creation. The federation has enabled the smaller regional firms to pool resources for program purchases and for coproductions. As a de facto network linking diverse regional audiences, FORTA also enjoys a unitary structure for advertising sales and contracts.[11] The objective rationale for FORTA is clear. Though programming strategies might be appealed to for increasing audience ratings, a basic systemic barrier to regional TV growth exists. A federation, in short, was an economic necessity for the protection of regional broadcasters in a transregional system.

At the same time, while the regional firms sought to regionalize the audience and make it their own, both national and private firms have followed the localization marketing strategy — with the appeal to regional markets, everyone is going local. Obverse to this trend of localization, the regional federation has tilted the spatial scales in a different way: with FORTA, firms restricted to local markets can also go national. Thus economic imperatives push expansion against spatial barriers erected by politics and culture. As the presence of Catalan and Basque investors in private TV demonstrates, moreover, regional capitalists have no qualms with their position as media merchants among nationalities other than their own. Here again, the analysis of economic classes behind localization strategies reveals the intertwined relations between regional capital's metropolitanism and metropolitan capital's "regionalism."[12]

Economic history has left its mark on the geography of television in Spain. Up to this point, the analysis here has focused on three distinct strategies of gaining access to regionalized audiences. The argument thus far pits regional TV against national businesses belonging to the state and private investors. A clear spatial hierarchy among these firms has been identified. Another enduring spatial hierarchy needs to be revisited, however. Despite the objective rationale for a federation, the regional systems do not, in fact, share the same resource endowments. Persistent geographical inequalities directly and indirectly stratify the regional broadcasters within the federation.

"We may be brothers," reflected Jaime Souza of TVG, "but the Catalans are much, much bigger." Souza observed that Basque and Galician economies are more traditional: "We have much less buying power and fewer possibilities in the advertising market, while the Catalans have many more means at their disposal."[13] Julián Pérez of ETB agreed: "Basque, Galician, and Catalan systems all share the same institutional reason for existing—to safeguard our distinct idioms and cultures. But the Catalans have been much more serious about making money than we have."[14]

The power held by the Catalan radio and television network is based in large part on the spatial bias toward Barcelona carried over from the past TV regime. Though this hierarchy privileged Madrid, the experience inherited by the regional management in Catalonia gave the Catalans a head start as a regional industry. Perhaps more decisive, however, have been the demographic differences that arise from the concentration of wealth in the electronic region of TV-3/Canal 33. Catalonia lies at the core of what Alcaide has identified as "the Spain on the rise" (see chapter 2 and map 3). Anchored to the axis of economic prosperity of Spain, Catalonia enjoys relatively high levels of per capita consumption, employment, and general social well-being.

The same cannot be said of Galicia. With Galician television, for example, economic vicissitudes of the traditional small agricultural economy place limits on the potential for consumer advertising. Self-financed television cannot be achieved easily in this "economy of self-sufficient farming and consumption." Jaime Souza explained: "You have to understand that the small farmer who produces only for himself and family produces no income that is measured as part of the national indices. Of course, city folks must buy everything, but the small farm economy that dominates this region requires that very little money be in circulation."

With less dependence on money capital, in a land where only 27 percent of the population lived in cities in the late 1980s, commercial advertising has a limited basis for expansion. And though "people with money" are obviously living and making purchases in Galicia, Souza points out that "they rarely need to shop in stores. They have their pigs, cows, their plots of land, potatoes, their legumes, vegetables ... they have everything. This doesn't produce commercial exchange. And this is not registered in statistics." What has been registered is zero macroeconomic growth, which led Alcaide to identify Galicia as a "survivor" region. Souza concludes, "Unless the structure of this region, of this nationality, changes, it will be very difficult to achieve advertising support of any consequence." Nonetheless, there have been bright moments for this economist. "Once in a while," he said, "with special programming events like the celebration of the patron saint of Galicia, we are able to achieve some outstanding sales."[15]

The advertising portions of the budgets for both the Basque and Galician channels were never projected to reach beyond 50 percent.[16] In fact, advertising income for CRTVG, the corporation of Galician radio and television, has yet to surpass 25 percent of the budget. For EITB, the Basque corporation, the advertising portion of the budget also remains below the 25 percent margin. Dependence on official subsidy has not alleviated the budgetary woes of CRTVG and EITB, both of which have had yearly deficits of between 3 million and 5 million dollars.[17]

In contrast, already in 1988 Catalonia's TV-3 was funded by 70 percent advertising income. One year later, advertising income covered 95 percent of its budget — in fact, with the public subsidy the Catalan channel showed a surplus of about 47 million dollars. By 1991 advertising income was back down to a little more than 70 percent, although as a portion of a much fatter budget — triple the size of Galicia's and about two and three-quarters bigger than that of the Basque Country.[18]

Jaime Souza nonetheless measures the humble budget of TVG against a cultural rather than economic standard. "Compared to the Catalans," he notes, "we are working on a much more institutional level." TV de Galicia "was not created as a business, but with the goal of normalizing and extending Galician culture and language throughout this territory." For Souza, "if TVG achieves that, it achieves its goal." In this sense, television for Galicia is a public good, a loss leader promoting social well-being. "Of course," he added, "it is better if it costs the Xunta de Galicia less to achieve its goal. But if it costs more, well, it's like maintaining the roads: though we won't ever profit from it, there is still a social need for it."[19]

Francisco Virseda concurred on the decisiveness of economic regionalization in Spain. "The possibilities for each autonomous regional TV are effectively linked with the economy of the region," he said. He notes that the three new competitors of Madrid, Valencia, and Andalusia — whose "fundamental reason for existing is economic, though they emerged for ostensibly political reasons" — have very different chances of succeeding. "Take Madrid, for example, where the smallest investment will create a TV that has the possibility of reaching the majority of people in this country."[20] Such coverage would be the result of spillover into Castile-León and Castile-La Mancha, though today this is not officially recorded in Telemadrid's ratings.[21]

Though Telemadrid has the lowest ratings in FORTA, its advertising income covers between 50 and 70 percent of its budget; the rest is paid for by bank loans.[22] Its budget is the third largest among regional broadcasters, after Catalonia and Andalusia respectively. In contrast, the network that covers Andalusia (a land area the size of Portugal) has not been able to garner more than the equivalent of two-thirds of Telemadrid's advertising income. Although the costs for coverage are much greater than for Madrid, Canal Sur has much higher reported ratings and reaches a population almost twice the size of that of Madrid (at least officially). Still, Canal Sur's income from advertising has supplied only about one-third of its annual budget.

In short, the demographic weight of the capital city is undeniable. That "Madrid is a nucleus of professionals" makes a major difference, and is a fact that Virseda links to the uneven historical fortunes of center and periphery. The demographic outcome is also, as Virseda observes, reproduced in commercial messages. "Luxury products appear in the pages of the Sunday edition of the newspaper in the capital, but not in the provincial press, where the more utilitarian products appear." It makes sense, then, that television marketing strategy follow "the same localized advertising as in the print medium."[23]

With the establishment of FORTA, some of these differences were mitigated, but none was eliminated. FORTA was first conceived in meetings held in Seville in the fall of 1988. Today the Catalan company TV-3 holds the leading position in FORTA, serving as the principal force among autonomous regional broadcasters, mostly for the reasons just explained. Ironically, FORTA was born out of the rivalry (perhaps envy) felt toward the Catalans by some regional broadcasters. When it was originally organized, FORTA was seen as a way to reduce Catalonia's power by excluding TV-3 from federation agreements. Suspicions have fallen on the Andalusians, who have the largest potential viewing population after the Catalans. Executives of Radiotelevisión de Andalucía (RTVA) saw their chance to springboard to preeminence among autonomous broadcasters by using the federation. It was later revealed that this design for FORTA relied on beating out the Catalans, a plot that failed after executives of RTVA were dismissed on charges of corruption.[24]

Although Andalusians and Catalans do not share an electronic region, the fight over the commanding position within the national federation was won by a company whose advertising income was almost four times greater than that of RTVA, despite the potential audience of the Andalusian company. The Catalans are simply much better placed politically, economically, and organizationally than all the rest.

Thus in the region of political economy of television in Spain, Madrid and Barcelona retain their privileged place. They have inherited key positions as the core electronic regions in Spain. They lie in the heart of the economic region of "the Spain on the rise." And they enjoy the protection of regional political authority derived from the historical regionalizations of the Spanish state. Finally, it should be emphasized that their position within the infranational hierarchy helps offset the inherent spatial bias favoring those broadcasters who operate transregionally at the national scale.

Nonetheless, it is the transregional political economy that is decisive; for the remaining regionalist projects, local protections have minimal effect—they survive, for the most part, because of expansion across their borders. Border crossings, however, are not the province of infranational forces alone. The imperious logic of capital, whether embodied by its regional, national, or transnational proprietors, is not as a rule anchored by the sentiments of place, i.e., by cultural regionalism. In the wake of privatization of global communications, the border crossings of capital flows have multiplied exponentially, released from most of the spatial containments associated with political regionalizations of the modern nation-state.

The Supranational Scale

"Our reference is not just Spain, it's Europe," said Francisco Virseda. "It's logical that Berlusconi—and I believe that it is good—enters the Spanish market through the autonomous TV systems."[25] Virseda was referring to the advertising and program purchasing deals that the Italian monopolist made with TV-3. In May 1988, Berlusconi, through Fininvest, contracted with the Catalans to make a series of coproduced variety stage shows. The Catalans also managed to gain the broadcast rights for 180 episodes of *Dallas*; Berlusconi then owned the sole European rights for the popular American program.

At about the same time in Galicia and the Basque Country, Fininvest's advertising sales agency, Publitalia, negotiated to become the international sales representative for TVG and ETB. Obviously, the relatively small sales departments of the regionals could not supply the same consistent income from advertising as Publitalia through its centralized organization. Moreover, prior to the legalization of private channels, the regional systems were the most likely entry point for investments like Berlusconi's (i.e., from the grass roots to national dominance, as in

Italy). FORTA would come to inherit this relation with the Italian media giant, who eventually gained control of the private TV company Telecinco. This kind of postmodern, postnational alliance has come to typify the emerging European television economy.[26]

Virseda explained the open-door policy toward foreign investment: "In the framework of Europe, and more concretely the Common Market, everything that has to do with finding formulas of coproduction, or joint European productions, is good." Virseda recalled the EC directive *Television without Frontiers,* invoking notions of one big European fraternity. "If Europe doesn't realize that it has to produce a lot more audiovisual material than it is currently producing, faster and of higher quality, the U.S. market will finish the race ahead of us." The conclusion was clear. "So if tomorrow Berlusconi, TV-3, Telemadrid, whoever, wants to make coproductions, that's fine. Why not? With Televisión Española, RAI, Canal Plus . . . perfect. Let's see productions!"[27]

What about productions? Towns and villages that had only one of two channels to choose from in 1989 could choose up to six or seven in 1990. That year the regionals, private TV, and TVE together pushed the number of programming hours up to fifty-seven thousand, doubling the number from 1989. Without a doubt, this multiplication of channels enhanced Spanish TV culture; yet it also outpaced the production capacity of the Spanish TV economy. As it turned out, no one in Spain could fill the amplified schedule with in-house productions, and as a result no television company could resist the abundance of programs on the international market. Today, without exception, all TV firms in Spain depend on foreign production to meet the demand created by the multiplication of channels. Since 1985, statistics show a marked increase in the proportion of foreign productions on all TV systems in Spain, though the private companies have officially stuck to guidelines of a fifty-fifty mix.[28]

Moreover, in the "train of buy and sell" at Cannes or Monte Carlo, you discover in the apparent openness of the market, as one Spanish buyer put it, that "there are always classes." "There are concretely two classes," this buyer said, "North Americans and the rest. Practically all of the market for program sales is dominated by U.S. distributors. One-third of the hundreds of cassettes belong to them, along with a sizable portion of the entire business. They tend to operate with a certain degree of self-sufficiency, knowing that they—in contrast to the rest—only have to wait."[29]

Prominent among the "waiting class" of distributors in Spain are Time Warner, MCA, MGM, Disney, Paramount, Columbia, Mercury, Rank, Ealing, and ITC. RTVE has sole rights with Disney and has major deals with Time Warner; FORTA and Telecinco have negotiated sole film rights with Paramount and Columbia, and together they have deals with MGM as well.[30] The copurchasing agreements between Telecinco, which Berlusconi effectively controls, and FORTA can be explained by the ongoing relation of FORTA and Berlusconi's Fininvest (which holds a 25 percent share of the private network Telecinco).

The competitive structure of program purchasing that now obtains in the Spanish television industry was significantly transformed when TV-3 and ETB entered the scene in the mid-1980s. According to most accounts, when TV-3's program purchasers first attended the international program markets, their alacrity at scooping up the latest U.S. goods and foreign films shocked RTVE's buyers. Until that time, the state system was highly centralized, bureaucratized, and therefore slower in deal making. After all, the buyers for RTVE never actually had to worry about bids or timing before the decentralization of television. When the new competition hit the market, however, all complacency had to be abandoned. TV-3 and ETB thus initiated a new period of invigorated competition among Spanish firms.

But outflanking the competition in the international marketplace does not necessarily equal an advance. As Lluís Ferrando, a buyer for TV-3, said, "The biggest winners in this entire process have been the international program distributors."[31] In addition, the "unfortunate consequence" of private television, as Villagrasa says, has been to ensure that Spain become a seller's market for foreign productions, giving rise to higher prices.[32] As the conclusion of this book argues, import dependence and inflation, the unfortunate consequences of private TV, have in turn stricken the national independent film and video industry.

What about in-house production? So-called fictional programming (films, series, soaps, and *telenovelas*) took up the majority of both broadcast time and the number of imports on all channels. Grouped under the rubric "entertainment," game shows and variety shows constituted the second most important category on all production schedules. Entertainment was followed by sports, although in Catalonia and the Basque Country sports programming often dominated broadcast hours. Children's programs were also an important category, and Spain enjoyed a developed animation industry. In-house production dominated these categories and equally prominent ones like informational programming. Game shows, however, were often based on foreign shows, such as *El precio justo* (*The Price Is Right*) or *La rueda de la fortuna* (*Wheel of Fortune*).

TV-3 is the only regional broadcaster to have achieved any significant in-house production in the fictional category. In addition, according to Lluís Ferrando, TV-3 initially sought to support local independent filmmakers and video artists, but the audience was not interested. The productions "were too abstract," he said, "and people didn't understand them."[33] As a consequence, generic formulas were relied on to build the audience, and programs like *Dallas* and comedies from the BBC began to be more prominent on the Catalan channel. Nonetheless, TV-3 managed to gain some high ratings for its own productions, some of which were eventually sold on the international market. One in-house production was a comedy series done in mime, obviating the linguistic barrier.

Other successes involved informational and variety programs coproduced by Canal Sur, Telemadrid, Canal 9, and ETB. The most popular of the private TV channels is Telecinco, and among the most popular programs it shows are imported films, *Benny Hill*, and the game show *Su media naranja* (*The Newlywed Game*). *Twin Peaks*, the American series, was one of Telecinco's biggest hits. In short, where in-house production has made some headway, formal and generic similarities with imported programming seem to blur much of the national distinction.

In the end, the scale of coverage/distribution and the capacity to realize the money value of transregional audiences, more than production, have defied the limits to autonomy. These two decisive, related aspects of the Spanish TV industry highlight once again a key lesson from critical international communication research: namely, that the unregulated interregional/international struggle over audience attention enhances the position of media owners who are situated in a nexus connecting local to global economic (and media) spaces. In other words, cultural autonomy (national or regional) appears to be a structural impossibility in the context of a deregulated and globalized communication industry. Moreover, political compromises with this structure, of the kind that hinge on what might be called selective association/selective autonomy, have tended to improve the business of highly capitalized, transnational firms. As the conclusion proposes, these structural realities have economic causes beyond the reach of present-day cultural politics of difference.

At any rate, Francisco Virseda got his wish. By 1992, Spaniards were seeing plenty of productions. Curiously, when Virseda made that wish in 1988 he could not conceal a latent pessimism in his subsequent words. Worried about the future, especially about the dominance of aggressive global businesses within the international media market, Virseda observed that "within the framework of European TV," regulation of the transnational phenomenon is weak. He asked aloud, "What will happen?" A moment later he offered this guess: "Europeans will end up in the hands of a few magnates of television who will have enormous power over social communication on the margin of government and nation." He paused again before continuing, apparently caught up in his own contradictory position. Finally he said: "Who'll control that?"[34]

It's not surprising that this director general of social communication under the presidency of Spain would make those words sound merely academic. After all the liberalizations on the continent, it must have seemed to him already too late for public intervention. Nevertheless, the question of social control at the margin of government and nation was then, as it is now, the most important one to ask.

Conclusion
The End of National Mass Media?

In February 1992, as part of the alignment of the Spanish economy with the economic and monetary union of the European Community, the Spanish government lifted all restrictions on capital movements in and out of its territory. In March the Spanish government approved the Convergence Program, which stipulated for a four-year period strict fiscal monetary controls, slower wage increases, and a brutally stratified labor contract system (also called labor flexibility), and stronger incentives for market competition. Interest rates were already among the highest in Europe, and they continued to rise monthly in small increments (reaching as high as 18 percent in 1993).[1] As part of the economic and monetary union, the Spanish government had agreed to keep the peseta tied to the exchange rate mechanism (ERM), meaning that the Bank of Spain (the central bank) would intervene if the peseta could not maintain a margin of 6 percent between its value and the value of other currencies participating in the ERM. The bank agreed to stand ready to buy or sell currencies of the participating states in order to maintain this relative parity and, if necessary, sacrifice part of the value of the peseta to fix the system.[2]

In June 1992, Danish voters rejected the treaty of economic union. After Denmark's doubts were expressed, European financial markets became increasingly unstable. The costs of German reunification were pushing prices in that country up, and the Bundesbank (Germany's central bank) responded to the general malaise within and among ERM participants by increasing the cost of its currency, i.e., by raising interest rates. By raising the interest rates on the strongest currency participating in the ERM, Germany caused massive readjustments throughout the system. In September, after the Italian lira lost 20 percent of its value against the deutsche mark, Italy withdrew from the ERM. The British also withdrew the pound sterling. One day later, on September 17, 1992, the Spanish central bank devalued the peseta by 5 percent, but chose to stay in the ERM. Still, some controls on capital movements were reintroduced to discourage speculators from buying too much of the cheaper money.[3]

The devaluation of the national currency brought Spain back within ERM controls, and helped Spain retain its competitiveness by cheapening the cost of its products. The only trouble with this kind of competitiveness is that it is always a short-term boost, for, if successful, low-cost competition can only lead to more inflation. To offset inflation, a central bank will tend to raise interest rates. For political reasons, the Spanish government was unwilling to raise already-high interest rates; instead, the Bank of Spain chose to devalue the peseta by another 6 percent in November, at which time it lifted all temporary restrictions on capital movements. After the first devaluation, the foreign reserves that the central bank was forced to spend to support Spain in the ERM totaled 23.5 billion dollars. By the end of 1992, the value of the peseta had fallen 15 percent against the value of the deutsche mark.[4]

The two-tiered monetary system of the EC had crystallized, and as Spain could not defend its currency against the events in northern Europe, it was pushed into a secondary role. On May 13, 1993, the peseta was devalued another 8 percent within the ERM. The argument to justify further devaluations was that trade within Europe had to be facilitated, no matter the costs. In other words, the ERM adjustments would ensure a reprieve for Spain on international markets.[5] Once again, the internal market was passed over for foreign trade—the historic key to the "Spanish miracle." Compare the response of Britain, just to take one example. There the monetarist adjustment was focused on the internal national economy. The British lowered interest rates, and despite the weak pound the internal market was reliable enough to recover (at least for the time being) from the near collapse that followed September's financial crisis.

Spain's dependence on transnational finance and European monetary policy was clear. Such dependence has far-reaching impact on the already-extreme regional disparities, political intervention notwithstanding, and on the spatial hierarchy of the Spanish TV industry identified in chapter 14. In the TV industry, economic dependence played an important role in the latest episode of consolidation in the commercial media market. One basic fact stands out: foreign investment in Spanish media marked the most prominent growth in the internal market, while the only substantial external Spanish investment in foreign media was restricted to one company, PRISA. This conclusion analyzes the general significance that economic dependence has for the social and media transitions described in this book.

Consolidation

In the summer of 1992, about the same time the Danes rejected the Maastricht treaty, Rupert Murdoch and the Spanish media company Grupo Zeta took over a 25 percent stake in Antena-3 television. Also at that time the industrial arm of the bank Banesto increased its holdings of Antena-3 TV to 25 percent. Mario Conde, the head of Banesto, arranged the one hundred million dollar financing for Murdoch's Grupo Zeta hostile takeover, which ousted the owner of *La Vanguardia* and Antena-3 radio, Javier de Godó. In July 1993, Javier de Godó sold just over 10 percent of his individual holdings in Antena-3 TV to Banco Central Hispano. Before this, Banco Central Hispano had provided loans to Grupo Zeta for its expansion.[6] Nevertheless, by June 1992, Antena-3 TV was effectively under the control of Mario Conde and Rupert Murdoch.[7]

Two important changes in the ownership structure of Antena-3 TV took place in 1993–94. Rupert Murdoch sold his 12.5 percent share in Grupo Zeta, holder of 25 percent of Antena-3 TV shares, to the Banco Central Hispano in order to raise cash for other global ventures. Mario Conde was arrested after the central bank intervened to put Banesto under state guardianship. In the first months of 1994, Banesto's holdings were being investigated and where possible divested, leading to the following restructuring of the capital in Antena-3 TV: Grupo Zeta (25 percent), Renvir (25 percent), Banesto (10 percent), Bouygues (15 percent), and Invacor and Corpoban (25 percent). Banco Central Hispano and Banesto are the loan guarantors of Renvir, a company owned by Antonio Asensio (given Banesto's weakening, this makes Banco Central Hispano a powerful controller in this firm). Bouygues, one of the biggest construction companies in France, bought its shares from Banesto, and Invacor and Corpoban are investment vehicles of Asensio. Asensio also controlled nearly 70 percent of Grupo Zeta, Ediciones Primera Plana owned 5 percent, and Banco Central Hispano and Banesto each controlled 12.5 percent. In short, by early 1994, Asensio held indisputable, direct control over Antena-3 TV (at illegal levels), and Banco Central Hispano increased not just its direct ownership but also its indirect control as the guarantor of long-term loans to Asensio's ventures. As Banesto was brought down to size, Banco Central Hispano increased its media power.[8]

When Catalan financier Javier de la Rosa bought 25 percent of Telecinco from the publishing group Anaya in 1991, he became the individual Spanish investor with the largest share of any private TV company in Spain.[9] Yet this was later revealed to be a speculative fancy of regional capital's metropolitanism, nothing else. In December 1992—one month after the second devaluation and uncaging of capital movements—de la Rosa sold this property to the Kirch Group of Munich, a multimedia firm with holdings in commercial cable/satellite TV and film libraries in Germany. When the sale was approved in early 1993, Telecinco became the first private TV company to be controlled directly by foreign investors. The alliance of Berlusconi's Fininvest and the Kirch Group gave them a controlling interest of over 50 percent of the firm.[10] In August 1993, the Compaigne Luxembourgeoise de Telediffusion, through its Radiotelevision Luxembourg, entered into negotiations with ONCE for the purchase of a majority of its remaining stake in Telecinco. By early 1994, the ownership of Telecinco broke down as follows: Kirch, 25 percent; Berlusconi, 25 percent; Radiotelevision Luxembourg, 19 percent; Jacques Hachuel, 10 percent; Bank of Luxembourg, 8 percent; the commercial builder Angel Medrano, 7 percent; and ONCE, 6 percent. The shares held by the Bank of Luxembourg were reportedly sold by Medrano to Kirch, who was forced to stash them in the name of the bank in order to abide by the letter of the ownership restrictions stipulated by the private TV law. Regardless, the "Spanish firm" Telecinco is clearly controlled by non-Spanish interests.[11]

The ownership structure of Canal Plus remains much as it was in 1989. Canal Plus broke even in 1992, and expected a profit of two billion pesetas in 1993. Today it ranks third among pay TV channels in Europe for audience and turnover. The difference between this and other commercial TV ventures is that its one major Spanish media investor has not retreated from the field. On the contrary, PRISA has moved beyond the internal market, using the internal market as a staging ground for global expansion. After surpassing circulation records at home, after buying into all major national media, and after raising profits over 28 percent between 1991 and 1992, PRISA was ready to apply its unquestioned dominance of the internal Spanish market to become a global media company.[12]

For PRISA the gold lay in the liberal policy of media acquisition created by the Spanish government. In no other country in Europe can a media company hold as much property in so many different media sectors. Recall that PRISA runs the largest daily newspaper, El País, and now Canal Plus is about to make massive profits on the heels of its rising subscription rates.[13] Moreover, PRISA has added to its potential fortunes by starting up the first Spanish satellite television channels, Cinemania and Documania.[14]

The public systems, for their part, have been slipping nonstop into crisis since 1991. In midyear 1992, the regional firms together registered a deficit of two billion dollars, quadrupling the figure of 1991. FORTA's red ink made some politicians put forward plans to sell the regional systems to private investors.[15] This seems unlikely, given the political and cultural importance of TV to the regional governments, but it is not altogether out of the question, especially among the poorer regions.

Other strategies besides full privatization have emerged. Among the most surprising was the cooperation agreement signed between RTVE and ETB, the Basque television system, in June 1993. That these two bitter rivals should come to a truce highlights the force of external economic conditions. The deal was designed to eliminate the duplication of resources, encourage joint production, share transmission rights (especially for sports), and exchange information.[16]

Ten years ago when ETB was being created, many Basque politicians treated Spain as an external state, an imperial ruler. Rather than turn to that state for help, the Basques looked elsewhere for advice and expertise to create their new TV system. Although there are conflicting reports about who turned down whom, RTVE was not involved in the design of ETB; instead, the Basque government called upon Media Consult International, a subsidiary of Studio Hamburg.[17] For a decade, as part III of this book indicates, the tensions between RTVE and ETB persisted, reflecting historic conflicts between centralism and regionalism. The cooperation agreement of 1993 is perhaps a small sign that this conflict has lost some of its defining force.

In addition, the regional TV system in Aragón has contracted with Antena-3 TV, giving the commercial firm full management of the region's television. Though by late 1993 this was pending the approval of the regional government—and was complicated by a lawsuit brought by the leftist parties of the Aragonese government—it suggested a new trend in organizing regional systems.[18] No other region had pursued this option at that time. Finally, there is still the reliance on bank loans rather than public subsidy. Telemadrid continues to follow this strategy, and in August 1993 the regional government of Madrid backed a loan of ten billion pesetas for the broadcaster.[19]

RTVE has followed the trends discussed in earlier chapters. In January 1994 the market share of the broadcast audience was 33.1 percent for TVE-1, 20.5 percent for Telecinco, 14.5 percent for TVE-2, and 13 percent for Antena-3 TV.[20] Though its share of audience attention is still shrinking, and its demand for in-house production has declined sharply, at the expense of national film and video producers, it retains a privileged, if extremely tarnished, position within the industry and among political classes. Except for its decline within the internal TV market structure, RTVE holds on to this significant presence by virtue of being the national state broadcaster. As such, it continues to be the preferred target of reform, liberalization projects, or basic outrage from the opposition. It is not surprising to discover that in 1993 the Partido Popular (formerly Alianza Popular) was still bringing lawsuits against RTVE and the government, this time concerning the manner in which the latest director general of RTVE was appointed. The democracy of the state system is perpetually in question — and so it should be. The fact that it is open to such questioning at all is perhaps the single most important attribute of a democratic public system, one that a privately held company cannot claim.

The newest players in 1993 are the satellite channels. Before the Hispasat 1A satellite was launched in September 1992, broadcasters used the Astra, Intelsat, and Eutelsat systems. Among the major broadcasters were Galavisión, from Mexico's Televisa, Eurosport, TVE International, Super Channel, and the SOGECABLE venture managed by PRISA. Extending Spain's economic problems, the Hispasat 1A was found to be damaged a few months after its launch. None of the DBS transponders could be used as planned, because of a bent antenna, though in February 1993 the spot beams to Spain were working well enough to relay transmission to the terrestrial network of the three private television channels.[21]

Finally, to make up for the estimated loss of thirty-five billion pesetas in rental income from the Hispasat 1A system, the Spanish government launched Hispasat 1B in July 1993. All three commercial TV channels have applied for use of Hispasat 1B transponders, despite some worries that the satellite service is not going to succeed.[22] Apart from the debacle of the 1A system, Hispasat has been criticized by private companies. Antonio Asensio said Hispasat had "very doubtful profitability" because the law on satellite broadcasting is "very restrictive."[23]

With the addition of satellite services, the Spanish television industry achieved the infrastructural expansion stipulated by the telecommunications law (LOT). The year 1993 thus closes the chapter on the transformation of TV in Spain, although new questions have arisen that concern competition for audience attention, new liberalizations (with or without government sanction), program production, and the general financial bust.

Audience Merchants

When the Murdoch group took over management of Antena-3 TV, the company had the lowest audience share of the two commercial broadcasters and the lowest earnings of the three commercial TV firms (including the subscription service Canal Plus). By the following summer it was making a profit and regularly gaining audience shares equivalent or superior to Telecinco, which had been the most popular until then. This appears to be the result of the radical move away from the former emphasis on news, investigative reports, and talk shows (recall that principal ownership was in the hands of *La Vanguardia* and the regional press).[24] Shifting to film and entertainment, Antena-3 TV managed to increase revenues by 90 percent in its first year, to eighty-six billion pesetas by June 1993.[25] Topping the programming was an in-house comedy series called *Farmacia en Guardia,* followed by the U.S. import *The Fresh Prince.*

Telecinco has consistently been the most successful of all of the private channels. According to Nielsen Repress, Telecinco's earnings for 1992 rose 78 percent over the previous year. (In 1992, overall spending on TV advertising had grown 4.5 percent to reach 508 billion pesetas, of which Telecinco took more than one-third.) Programming is dominated by game shows, films, and gala variety shows. On average, Telecinco grabs about 20 percent of the audience, and figures indicate that two-thirds of that measure are women—a fact that led Proctor and Gamble, the biggest TV advertiser in Spain for 1992, to spend half of its Spanish TV advertising budget on Telecinco.[26]

The subscriptions for Canal Plus surpassed 630,000 in 1992, when combined satellite services were estimated to reach about one million homes.[27] Though this is small in real terms of audience attention (about 3 percent), projections for satellite subscription suggest the number will triple in the next few years. One commentator has observed that "PRISA's 25 percent stake in Canal Plus now looks like the proverbial license to print money."[28] Competition in satellite services may soon increase, as Antena-3 and Telecinco start up new channels. RTVE is also bidding for two satellite channels and one international service.

Advertisers have benefited greatly from all this expansion of commercial airtime. In 1992, the number of TV advertisements broadcast daily increased 30 percent over 1991. By 1993, the level of viewer attention given to televised commercial messages was up 36 percent over 1992 (according to estimates of Central Media), though the cost of reaching viewers was also rising. About one-third of all advertising investment in Spain went to TV in 1992.[29]

Some twenty-nine million TV viewers were accounted for in the national register of audience shares in 1992. In the 1980s, TVE could count on up to twenty-seven million viewers for its top-ranked shows. In 1993, however, it could rarely get more than eight million people to watch even its most popular program—and TVE was still attracting more viewers than any of its competitors.[30] By 1993, the combined shares of private broadcasters, including Canal Plus's estimated 2.2 percent, regularly surpassed the combined shares of TVE-1 and TVE-2. The trend indicates equalization of audience attention among TVE-1, Telecinco, and Antena-3, with the greatest loss in TVE-2 (leading inevitably to talk of privatizing the second state channel). Despite this equalization among the national scale broadcasters, FORTA has kept its combined average of 14 to 15 percent of the national audience through 1993. Equalization, combined with the stable differentiation represented by FORTA, parallels a trend toward homogenous programming strategies that are "ratings-led and advertiser sensitive," as one trade magazine described.[31]

The push to guarantee viewership levels, which RTVE did before the others, also resulted in the extension of audience measurement techniques, thus putting a premium on ratings data and increasing the scope of social surveillance in Spain.[32]

Finally, as all Spanish TV operators are beholden to advertisers without apology, Spain has been witness to continued violations of EC and Spanish government directives that limit commercial messages on TV. The most controversial instance occurred when the Spanish government attempted to restrain Telecinco and Antena-3 from too many product endorsements on their game shows. The resistance of the commercial channels was apparently so fierce that the government had to request an extension from the EC to bring Spanish advertising in line with the 1989 directive, *Television without Frontiers*. Telecinco representatives said that to reduce product advertising "would ruin our viability," and Antena-3 TV objected that it "would have to close down in a matter of days."[33]

Of course, there is very little likelihood that either of these businesses will shut down. With the government's ignoring its own laws that limit ownership packages of commercial firms to 25 percent, it is also unlikely that investors in the Spanish TV economy will opt for good citizenship. Wishfully hoped-for transformations of commercial banks, media barons, and global financiers is the stuff of Capra movies, not the political economy of television.

The Collapse of Independent National Production

In 1991, the euphoria in the TV industry that came with the start-up of private TV was especially prominent in the film and video production sector. As chapter 14 showed, the tripling of demand between 1988 and 1990 created great new opportunities for suppliers, even though no one could fill the order. Still, production companies that had until then only served clients for advertising and corporate communications were, as one excited trade writer put it, "springing up all over the country, keen to satisfy the demand for programs."[34]

At first a number of start-ups allowed large film processing and editing companies to move out of the declining film industry and into video. But as Spain's economic geography would have it, these were all based in Madrid and Barcelona.[35] Madrid has traditionally been strong in post-production because of its links to TV, while Barcelona has been the capital of the print industry and commercial communications—not to mention its status as the second TV production city in Spain. The only significant regional production facilities to spring up after the liberalizations of the 1980s were dubbing companies. As one observer noted, "Local industries compare with Barcelona and Madrid much as the independent facility bases in Manchester and Bristol compare with London."[36]

Worries that overexpansion would lead to a crisis in Spanish production facilities were borne out in 1993. The collapse was caused by conditions similar to that obtained in Paris in the mid-1980s and in London in 1991. Demand was increasing, but the independent producers were not being hired. Spain suffered the "European paradox of more television hours, but less work."[37] Films and teleseries bought on the international market tended to take the place of job orders. In Spain, "the champion of indigenous production" was RTVE, but by 1991 the cash crisis of the state company was already bringing commissions (and its own production) to a standstill. RTVE commissioned no new projects in 1991 or 1992, and finished only 157 hours of old orders (recall that demand in the Spanish TV economy had risen to fifty-seven thousand hours by 1990). Despite all the euphoria in 1991, the share of television hours filled by independent producers barely reached 2 percent. One telling symptom of the collapse was the rising percentage of repeats of dramatic broadcasts on TVE: 54 percent in 1991, double the figure for 1989 and triple that for 1982.[38]

In 1993, private broadcasters were obliged by law to produce 15 percent of their programs in house, after a two-year grace period prior to enforcement of the law. No set rules have been established about commissioned work, but standards basically require a fifty-fifty mix of import and national programs. Antena-3 has been the most active in this area, promising to meet its obligation and having already commissioned small but numerous low-budget drama series. Telecinco has not been as open to the independent sector, but it is being pressured to comply with regulations.[39]

The cash crisis throughout the system of buying, commissioning, and production has forced the independent producers back into commercial and corporate communications. Some have sought out foreign coproduction partners, while others have been lucky enough to get work in the rare telefilm drama. As long as the international media operators are scheduling their films and teleseries against each other's commercial stations, little room will be made for national independent productions. In the end, with the collapse of commissions in the state system, coupled to RTVE's general financial turmoil, it appears as though independent program production in Spain has been abandoned without significant institutional support.

Doctor, Heal Thyself

There's a very apt, if macabre, story about a doctor who collapsed and died from a heart attack while appearing on a live broadcast, about healing, on Valencia's Canal 9. The multiplication of channels was also about healing: it was supposed to invigorate the TV economy. Moreover, it was part of a larger program to make telecommunications the fount of recovery for the ailing national economy. But like the poor doctor, new channels and extended schedules came on the air in a weakened condition. The Spanish TV economy could not withstand the demand placed on it.

Except for the internationalized companies, the Spanish TV industry risks collapse. In large part, this has to do with the failure to recognize the subordinance of the Spanish economy to what Hobsbawm called the supranational restructuring of the globe. An argument could be made that Spain had to submit itself to these changes, that the Spanish government had no choice but to liberalize the system. After all, what else could come from the mix of EC directives to open markets, socialist modernization of the communications infrastructure, and social pressures to reform broadcasting?

Nevertheless, the history of the political decision to release RTVE to market competition showed that a rather different mix of options was also available (see part II). Indeed, the resistance to full privatization, and the critique of the tendency toward monopolization, informed the laws governing TV ownership. Recall that on paper, television was to be held by a plural and diverse group of investors, communications firms, and interested others; it was obliged to promote national production, and to keep commercial messages within tolerable limits. What happened in the few years of consolidation of the private TV business, however, was obviously something else altogether.

In 1993, ownership of the private TV industry in Spain, as a whole, belonged directly to banks (about 26 percent, at least) and to foreign investors (about 38 percent). With indirect control of banks through the debt structure of some of the commercial firms, the first figure is actually much larger, though this is difficult to track. Equally difficult to track is the current spate of acquisitions within the wide open, deregulated European market. As previously noted, foreign ownership of Telecinco, for example, surpassed 85 percent. Once combined, foreign ownership of the commercial TV industry in Spain added up to about 50 percent with capital from major French, Italian, Luxembourgian, and German media investors in 1994.

Further speculation concerns the banking interests in Spanish TV. Banesto was a powerful bank within Spain, but since markets collapsed during the Gulf War it had been vulnerable to takeovers. Though in 1994 it entered receivership under the central bank, it never ranked among the world's top hundred banks. Its industrial holdings in Spain, however, (including Antena-3 TV, *Ya,* and a major video production facility, Telson), were estimated to account for a full 1 percent of the Spanish economy. Compared to the largest national bank (Ban-co de Bilbao-Vizcaya), Banesto succumbed to major problems in the 1990s, both financially and politically. First, it was not strong enough to withstand the market liberalizations of 1993, which gave EC banks full and unfettered access to Spain's financial market. Then, as a result of the enmity between the Spanish government and Mario Conde, the socialists encouraged the central bank to take over Banesto—which relieved Conde, the presidential pretender, of his financial and media influence.

Before liberalizations, the presence of foreign direct investment in the financial sector was 30 percent greater in 1991 than in 1981.[40] With the complete opening of the financial market to EC banks, there is a great likelihood that smaller Spanish banks will not be able to hold off foreign buyers. The current advantage of small banks over European institutions—i.e., their extensive branch networks in Spain—is also the most attractive feature to foreign investors. Rather than start from scratch, foreign banks will more than likely buy into Spain's commercial bank system. This is already the case for Banca March (of Canal Plus), which formed a joint venture with National Westminster Bank.[41] Banco de Bilbao-Vizcaya and Banesto both have expanded into foreign markets as well, the first with an important partnership with Banque Nationale de Paris, the second with stakes in Portuguese banks.[42]

Though a complete account of foreign direct investment and the indirect holdings through interlocking bank relationships is difficult to construct, there is no doubt about the trend to extend ownership of Spain's commercial television industry to the internationalized sector of finance and to global media proprietors (prominent in Banesto are J. P. Morgan and Bank of America). In other words, the only national media currently skirting the cash crisis in Spain are in the main not national media at all; rather, they are actively seeking to denationalize the television industry and the laws regulating that industry.

This does not mean that banks and transnational corporations are immune to buyouts, cash shortages, investment crises, and other anarchies in the international economy. On the contrary. Still, they possess the greater financial power to survive these effects of structural crises. Such power is both a cause of their politico-economic strength in the currently stricken national media and the reason why they are not beholden, in the last instance, to the politics and culture of the national society. Paradoxically, it was their appeal to "regionalism" (through localization strategies) and the demands for a plural television culture that helped them establish a foothold in the Spanish television industry. Today, that television industry is just one among many properties, invested with hopes of deepening pockets but with little sentiment for the place.

In contrast, the public television system (that is, the ensemble of central state and the regional televisions) is running up debts totaling billions of dollars.[43] The central state is not providing subsidy to RTVE, and the shortfalls for the regional system are increasing. The state and regional authorities are looking to long-term credit arrangements to overcome this problem, but pressure to privatize at least part of the public system of national and regional broadcasters is mounting. In the end, who else will step forward to provide the loans or hard-cash investments if not those who already control the private television business? Where does this leave regional TV?

The Financial Bust

Regional finance on the whole depends on resources from the central government. With the exception of the Basque Country and Navarre, which retain the right to collect taxes within their regions, all remaining regions receive a percentage of public monies that reflect their contributions to the national tax base. Two programs exist that are designed to redistribute a portion of this public funding to less-developed regions to adjust for the inherent inequalities of the national tax base.[44] The redistributive aims of these projects have not been fulfilled, however, and some changes have been made to entitle only the poorest regions to these benefits. Nonetheless, the regions have a high degree of discretionary power and are basically "free to dispose of more than 80 percent of their [tax] revenues as they wish."[45]

Given the spatial hierarchy of the tax base, the inadequacy of the redistributive programs, and the persistent economic geography of Spain,
the poorest regions have accumulated the highest debt percentage of the
regional gross domestic product. Table 1 and map 3 (both in chapter 2)
help illustrate this point. In the core of economic growth in Spain, regional governments are better able to protect their investments in their
political region. Again, this means that Catalonia, Madrid, and also
Navarre (which in continental terms is situated between the EC and the
Ebro River Valley) are particularly well positioned to keep public projects from collapsing. After the boom of 1985–90, these three regions
(holding 30 percent of the population) improved their economic positions relative to the rest of Spain. Meanwhile, Extremadura, Galicia,
and Andalusia (with another 30 percent of the population) suffered further impoverishment. The rest of Spain achieved some minor revenue
growth before the crisis set in in 1991.[46]

Two outcomes affecting the regional TV industry can be noted. One
is that capital flows continue to concentrate in Catalonia and Madrid.
Moreover, the Organization for Economic Cooperation and Development estimates that between one-half and two-thirds of all foreign investment into Spain went to Madrid and Catalonia (in 1992, foreign investment accounted for 20 percent of all private investment in Spain).
In places like Galicia, where agriculture remains less capitalized and
traditional industries are declining, the redistributive programs have been
decisive causes of survival.[47]

For the public TV industry, this means greater available public resources are anchored to the same old places, with one important difference. Because the Autonomous Community of Madrid was established
under articles 143 and 148 of the constitution, it does not retain direct
control over television, whereas under the principles of article 151 the
authorities in Catalonia do.[48] Hence, Telemadrid is forced to take out
bank loans of ten billion pesetas, while TV-3/Canal 33 receives a subsidy
from the Generalitat three times that amount. Despite the general decline
throughout the public system, the Catalans are still much bigger than
the rest.

The other, more basic outcome of the financial bust concerns the
global cheapening of the peseta. Against the dollar, the deutsche mark,
the franc, and currencies close to them, the peseta was worth a lot less
in 1993 than in 1991 (nearly 40 percent less compared to the dollar).[49]
The Spanish government is adverse to raising the already-high interest
rates — which, if raised, would have the effect of increasing the cost of
the peseta and discouraging capital flight. A weak peseta encourages
export, however, which might bring further foreign reserves to boost

the peseta in the future. Monetary scenarios aside, the importance of currency weakness to the TV industry is that the program market in Spain is import-oriented. As such, purchases made by firms must at some point or another be convertible into cash; the cash must, at some time, be exchanged into the national currency of the seller. This affects more than any others those firms that have no ties or agreements with the international partners in commercial television.

Internally, a weak peseta therefore positions the three commercial television systems in the most privileged place in the TV industry. Externally, program sellers get more pesetas for the same goods; even if sales volume declines, program sellers will not get hurt — that is, as long as the declining volume stays within a range offset by devaluation. The decisiveness of global finance in this one, relatively small sector reflects the broader pattern in the balance of Spain's assets and liabilities in the foreign market: between 1987 and 1991, foreign liabilities outgrew foreign assets by 45 percent.[50]

What to Expect

The public firms have followed strategies (some of which have been described here) that have increased their solidarity but have not improved their programming budgets. There is a good chance that further efforts to enhance their position in the face of commercial hegemony might create conditions for a legitimation crisis of the public firms. Strategies that have been floated include a license fee, privatization, or subcontracting to commercial firms. All tend to portray public services as burdensome, private organizations as efficient.

The decline of one territorial imperative for the television industry in Spain continues. The regionalization of television, the first challenge to the national configuration, appears to be following an inherited spatial order that keeps Catalonia and Madrid at the core of the industry. The national state system will probably survive, although it's not clear how. Meanwhile, the growing private, commercial television businesses have bullied their way beyond the legal norms in existence. The last time that happened the norms changed.

Overall, the trends analyzed here indicate a convergence of regional, national, and transnational dimensions of the Spanish TV industry. Coordinating this convergence is capital accumulation — the proverbial bottom-line — which has reiterated the conditions of its own international regime of self-defense: monopolization and the overthrow of spatial barriers. Under these conditions, national mass media are being absorbed into a global estate and organized to fit a transnational logic.

Will the state continue to retreat? Probably. Alternative policies would perhaps have to examine the viability of smaller public works. This is not to suggest that small will be beautiful: it probably won't be, compared to the central presence of Hollywood in whatever spectacular guise. Yet in the internationalized TV economy of Spain, small may be the only way to nurture and protect those people who want to make TV and film.

One Summary

The nation, by the end of the nineteenth century, was for European states the natural zone of electronic communication. As the weight of public opinion became a real force to reckon with in modern democracies, modern state administrations drew more heavily on terms and symbolic assets that had until then only reigned among nationalist intellectuals and protonational affiliations. A national zone of alignments was a necessary condition for the extension of a state perspective that envisioned a new region of experience for the people under its administration.

All nationalisms imagine a communication system fit for a nation. Electronic mass media were fancied as great connectors of peoples to the project of nations—even today, the rhetoric attached to new nationalisms invariably includes independent electronic media tied to a national project, which in turn is anchored to a territory. The ideology of nation building was, in its heyday between 1870 and 1914, the banner under which conventional thinking about mass media systems was established. Its screens on the world were language, race, ethnicity, citizenship, and modernization. What these ideological screens concealed were the social and cultural imperialisms that formed the conditions of universality of the modern nation-state. What they repressed were the particularities and differences among the populations mobilized under the banner of one big common people, the national community.

Electronic culture inherited this past as a world divided among particular models of commercial, of public-service, of development, and, to a much less degree, of state-centered broadcasting. In the West the tension between state-supported public services and private, for-profit commercial broadcasting marked out the battle lines across the Atlantic. These were the dominant models of broadcasting fit for nations where liberal democracy defined the polity. The global expansion of commercial and public-service logics defined cultural imperialism: the postwar penetration of cultural organizations from the former empires into newly independent states in the less-developed regions witnessed on-the-ground reproductions of the colonizers' media systems.

What emerged were conflicts between the geopolitical alignments of the North-North divide, expressed in national mass media by commercial versus public-service principles, and a North-South divide, expressed in cultural terms as mass consumption versus dependent development. This axis intersected with the rivalry of East and West, of socialism and capitalism. These conflicts among "macrosubjects" formed the key axes of research on international communication for most of the twentieth century.[51]

In media markets and national cultures this was, so to speak, the old world where private versus public, or dependent versus imperialist, media actually meant something; a world where the flows and absorption (or injections) of foreign modes of cultural production could be stemmed, argued over, regulated, denounced; and where alliances existed to maintain these boundaries. This was the world where political regions could still contain very different economic regions.

In the course of the past twenty-five years (that is, practically the life of the notion of cultural imperialism), privatization has won the Atlantic battle, the state sector in all regions has relinquished (whole or in part) the sovereignty of national economies of culture, and new regional alliances and cultural interpenetrations have emerged in the less-developed zones of the globe. These cultural shifts occurred in a context in which exports had surged from East Asia; democracy had been restored with a notable absence of violence in Southern Europe, Latin America, and the Pacific; and most recently—and perhaps most decisive—the East-West coordinates of the cold war have vanished.[52]

A decade ago, Cees Hamelink observed how the global cultural landscape was undergoing what he called "cultural synchronization," a process not so much about impositions of foreign cultures as of canny reorientations of national cultural industries in line with (on-line with?) the core of capitalist cultural production.[53] Although these incipient "cultural shocks" may have led finally to the "decline of the imperial model," as Mattelart suggests, the crucial change surely must be the end of the Soviet Union.[54] Sentiments regularly echoed throughout the 1980s that "Americanisation has metabolised into ... 'world modernity,' "[55] but this was not certified until the failed coup of August 1991 in the USSR.

Thus the old certainties of the international relations perspective on global communication are replaced by a new kind of geosubjectivity defined largely by global cultural industries; one that resignedly accepts the extensive regime of transnational capitalism, "the socialization of 'universal' norms and matrices" across the globe, as Armand and Michèle Mattelart put it.[56] These norms have been metabolized, to use Mattelart's apt metaphor, and are therefore less perceptibly about impositions and invasions.

The state no longer provides traditional political safeguards for the national culture, but acts as manager of the spreading transnational phenomenon "in the best interests" of the nation—usually listed as jobs, foreign investment, growth, and trade (look at the latest OECD survey on Spain for an example of this rhetoric). Today, pleas that were heard ten years ago for dissociation from international communications markets sound distantly romantic.[57] More generally, economic "delinking," though supported theoretically and by historical precedent, attracts fewer national leaders willing or able to listen today than it did thirty years ago.[58]

At the same time, the state has relinquished its tutelage over the culture of the national community, most significantly in Europe, where centralizing tendencies of various state nationalisms can no longer suppress old regionalisms and new diasporas. As a result, even within the most centralized Jacobin state cultures, decentralized, socially multinational, and interregional forms of cultural production and organization are now emerging. In turn, new social actors have begun to participate in international relations, with a prominence of demands from ethnic/linguistic groups for greater recognition and self-reliance.

As these political tensions regain prominence, the smaller political regions also start to show their porousness. The infranational and supranational economic regions have their own boundaries despite political nationalisms of whatever size. And as argued here, capital produces its own media geography on its march for environments of the highest return—some areas remain in a periphery and some in weighty centers of demographic history. The economic region has no provincial, regional, or national borders.

The electronic regions produced by TV signals are still beholden to the boundaries formed by politics. The signals, no matter how they come to reach a greater proportion of the audience, are still tied in many ways to place. First, they are a mechanism that protects the investments in space. Within a commercialized television culture, the signals can reach across borders, mark receivers as numbers in the ratings game, and draw them in as the price of airtime to be sold to advertisers. For broadcasters tied to place, signal trespass and audience capture remain a strong political, economic, and cultural link.

Regional firms like those in Spain are media industries with crossbred functions of identity politics and audience maximization. As such they are forced to risk autonomy of the regional community in order to defend the cultural industry of the region. In a sense, they had to capitalize their nationality, selling distinction of language and custom in the form of culturally diverse TV audiences, and they were followed by RTVE and private TV, whose marketing logic of localization was part of a wider transnational logic of consumer marketing.

Stated flatly, regional TV made a difference by selling difference. In addition, it encouraged more competitive program purchasing, bidding wars, and ultimately greater presence of foreign programming. In this way, the regional firms made another decisive difference by extending an international cultural exchange. Yet at the same time they encouraged the further immersion of their own TV economy into an internationalized market within which they have little control.

For the Basques, Catalans, and Galicians the stakes were high—the revival and survival of the nationality. Their cultural politics were defined in opposition to the centralist culture of the national state. At the point where supranational and infranational processes intertwined, the question was whether and in what manner capital would reassert its power to coordinate the geocultural disruption. At this juncture, the public was no longer addressed simply as Basque, or Catalan, or Galician. The use of distinct languages in TV advertisements and imported programming might attach the illusion of national identity, but the idioms are inflected with a decidedly American accent of marketing and television genres. In the end, nationality became the costume worn by cosmopolitan agents of the transnational phenomenon.

Aijaz Ahmad argues that nationalism is not the "determinate, dialectical opposite of imperialism." In Ahmad's caution, we are also asked to understand that "some nationalist practices are progressive; others are not."[59] I would add a historical dimension to this dialectic: some that appear progressive today will reveal tomorrow that they are not. The last part of this book supports Ahmad's first caution. Yet distinct from Ahmad's project, the book emphasized the historical role of nationalism in relation to the development of electronic media during the early phase of a transition to democracy. Some nationalist practices were identified in reference to anti-Francoism as truly progressive. (Obviously, and with justification, the whole story of regional politics did not come out in this book.) Later the same cultural practices were shown to be articulated to transregional and transnational media economies; in that exchange, nationalist practices were identified as extensions of the imperialism of global media proprietors. The transition to democracy was, in this sense, also a transition of the historical role of nationalism—today progressive, tomorrow not. That change was perhaps foretold already in the deterritorialization of the media in the era of transnationals. After all, several decades of liberalizations of public controls in European media should have cautioned Spanish reformers. No longer fit for a nation, except on paper, national mass media have been absorbed into processes of privatization of communication around the world, and Spain has been just one more stomping ground of this global juggernaut. I still don't think this was inevitable: politics matter. The problem was that media for Spanish democracy were dreamed up in a market imaginary ... and the dream came true.

Notes

Introduction

1. Radio liberalizations had taken place in the 1960s, followed by further licensing to commercial stations in the late 1970s. However, the actions of the Basques and Catalans were to have more far-reaching consequences than radio reform, as part II of this book reveals.

2. Rather than abide by the letter of the Third Channel Law, which established the norm of one network within each autonomous region, the authorities in these three regions built independent networks that function, in their words, "alegally"; transmission for which there is no explicit law is considered alegal, rather than illegal, unregulated, or pirated. That is, the regional authorities contend that the Third Channel Law only pertains to the central state allotments and not to their own independent allotments, which have been guaranteed by their statutes of autonomy and the national constitution but which correspond to no existing regulation. The result is that the Basques and Catalans operate two channels, but argue, along with the Galician parliament (which operates only one channel), that these are independent of existing law. They maintain that they are still guaranteed one additional channel within the framework of the Third Channel Law, raising the potential number of land-based channels to eight (three private, two state, and three regional). See part III for further discussion.

3. See Clemencia Rodriguez, "Media for Participation and Social Change: Local Television in Catalonia."

4. The six were in the Basque Country, Catalonia, Galicia, Madrid, Valencia, and Andalusia; the remaining autonomous broadcasters were in the Canary and Balearic Islands, Navarra, Aragon, and Murcia.

5. See Justino Sinova, *La gran mentira.*

6. The regional companies that developed parallel infrastructures — Galician, Basque, and Catalan — had not relinquished control to Retevisión at the time of this writing.

7. All figures for 1989 from José María Villagrasa, "Spain: The Emergence of Commercial Television," 425.

8. Figures from Villagrasa, "Spain," 351–57, and M. Castells et al., *Nuevas tecnologías, economía, y sociedad en España*, 2:826–27.

9. The absence of hierarchical judgments or elitist frameworks to inform readers of Spanish media talents is intentional. That I like Spanish TV is irrelevant. Its worth is a question of taste, tradition, closed markets, and cultural translation.

10. Armand Mattelart and Michèle Mattelart, *Rethinking Media Theory*, 125.

11. Eric J. Hobsbawm, *Nations and Nationalism since 1780: Programme, Myth, Reality*; A. G. Kenwood and A. L. Lougheed, *The Growth of the International Economy, 1820–1990*.

12. Mattelart and Mattelart, *Rethinking Media Theory*, 126.

13. H. I. Schiller, *Culture Inc.*, 5. Dallas Smythe is another central figure among Western scholars who developed the cultural imperialism thesis; see, for example, Smythe, *Dependency Road: Communications, Capitalism, Consciousness and Canada*. Also, see J. Wasko, V. Mosco, and M. Pendakur, *Illuminating the Blindspots: Essays Honoring Dallas W. Smythe*.

14. Schiller, *Culture Inc.*, 4.

15. Annabelle Sreberny-Mohammadi, "The Global and the Local in International Communications."

16. See Schiller, *Culture Inc.*, 111–34.

17. Perhaps a historico-geographical review of the literature would reveal a path of theoretical conversion similar to that followed by the process of deregulation—the removal of political barriers to global trade and domestic competition in telecommunications and mass media, which spread from the United States to Europe and Japan. Such reflective research has yet to be carried out, however. For political history related to this point, see Dan Schiller, *Telematics and Government*. For general exceptions to this trend, see the work of H. I. Schiller, Rafael Roncagliolo, and Armand Mattelart; also, especially see the latest volume edited by Karle Nordenstreng and H. I. Schiller, *Beyond National Sovereignty: International Communication in the 1990s*. For a liberal discursive account, see John Tomlinson, *Cultural Imperialism*.

18. Andre Gunder Frank, "No End to History! History to No End?," 15–16; all emphasis in the original.

19. Mattelart and Mattelart, *Rethinking Media Theory*, 134–35; see also Schiller, *Culture Inc.*, chap. 6.

20. Mattelart and Mattelart, *Rethinking Media Theory*, 135.

21. On the narrow forms of action chosen by European states, see Kenneth Dyson, "Western European States and the Communications Revolution," in K. Dyson and P. Humphreys, *Broadcasting and New Media Policies in Western Europe*, 10–55.

22. Hobsbawm, *Nations and Nationalism*, 187.

23. See Nordenstreng and Schiller, eds., *Beyond National Sovereignty*, passim; Armand Mattelart, *Advertising International*, 37–38.

24. Examples that illustrate this trend include the domination of the Bertelsmann group in magazine publishing; the control of large audiovisual production studios and of television advertising sales by the Italian Silvio Berlusconi; the influential interests in private television represented by Jacques Hachuel, Canal Plus France, and Berlusconi; and the dominance of British and U.S. advertising firms within the national market. The convergence of broadcast and telecommunications infrastructures—linking post, computer systems, telephony, and television—was the fulcrum of socialist reform. Public broadcast and telecommunication systems were pulled into a process of "informatization" and "privatization."

25. Hobsbawm, *Nations and Nationalism*, 187–91; see also Mattelart and Mattelart, *Rethinking Media Theory*, p.134.
26. Hobsbawm, *Nations and Nationalism*, 191
27. Mattelart and Mattelart, *Rethinking Media Theory*, 134.
28. Armand Mattelart, Xavier Delcourt, and Michèle Mattelart, *International Image Markets*.
29. Mattelart, *Advertising International*, 37. This is a point regularly missed by model builders in instrumentalist or functionalist style. Still, the charge of instrumentalism (spiced with accusations of conspiracy) is often unfairly brought against analysts of U.S. deregulation who have shown that the restructuring of the U.S. information economy in the 1970s and early 1980s caused irreversible changes in global telecommunications (cf. Schiller, *Culture Inc.*, 113–15). This history is well documented and does not require further comment. See Schiller, *Telematics and Government*.
30. Mattelart and Mattelart, *Rethinking Media Theory*, 135–36. See also David Morley and Kevin Robins, "Spaces of Identity: Communications Technologies and the Reconfiguration of Europe"; and Kevin Robins, "Global Times" and "Reimagined Communities? European Image Spaces, Beyond Fordism."
31. This phrase belongs to the political theorist William Connolly; the context and its associations are my doing.
32. Fredric Jameson, "Cognitive Mapping." See also Anthony Giddens, *The Consequences of Modernity* and *Modernity and Self-Identity*.
33. Stuart Hall, "The Emergence of Cultural Studies and the Crisis of the Humanities"; cf. Schiller, *Culture Inc.*, chap. 7. Amid this din of pleasure, Schiller's remarks (echoing Hobsbawm) are hushed (or footnoted, as in this case): "Whatever the unique experiential history of each of the many subgroups in the nation, they are all subject to the rule of market forces and the domination of capital over those forces" (*Culture Inc.*, 153).
34. Mattelart and Mattelart, *Rethinking Media Theory*, 177.
35. Sreberny-Mohammadi, "The Global and the Local," 121.
36. Ien Ang, *Desperately Seeking the Audience*, 158–60.
37. Ibid.; John Fiske, *Television Culture*.
38. Armand Mattelart has followed both lines of argument for several decades now; see especially "For a Class Analysis of Communication," "For a Class and Group Analysis of Popular Communication Practices," and Mattelart and Mattelart, *Rethinking Media Theory*, 39–83. See also Fiske, *Television Culture*.
39. Mattelart, "For a Class and Group Analysis"; Mattelart and Mattelart, *Rethinking Media Theory*, 175–76.
40. Mattelart and Mattelart, *Rethinking Media Theory*, 176; Herbert I. Schiller, *Mass Communication and American Empire*; "World Television: The Inexorable Spread" [anon.]; Kenwood and Lougheed, *Growth of the International Economy*, 245–73.
41. Ien Ang, "Culture and Communication: Towards an Ethnographic Critique of Media Consumption in the Transnational Media System."
42. Fred Fejes, "Media Imperialism: An Assessment," 287.
43. Phillip Schlesinger, "On National Identity: Some Conceptions and Misconceptions Criticized," 232.
44. Gerald Sussman and John A. Lent, eds., *Transnational Communications: Wiring the Third World*; Ben Bagdikian, *The Media Monopoly*, 4th ed.; Edward Herman and Noam Chomsky, *Manufacturing Consent*.
45. Manjunath Pendakur, "Political Economy and Ethnography: Transformations in an Indian Village"; Sreberny-Mohammadi, "The Global and the Local."

46. Hall, "The Emergence of Cultural Studies," 22; emphasis added.

47. There are many dialects and "unofficial" languages in Spain but only four officially recognized idioms: Castilian, Basque, Catalan, and Galician. For more general discussion, see Benedict Anderson, *Imagined Communities*; Hobsbawm, *Nations and Nationalism*.

48. These arguments, elaborated in part III and the conclusion, connect to a lively exchange between Fredric Jameson and Aijaz Ahmad (*Social Text* 15, Fall 1986, and *Social Text* 16, Fall 1987, respectively) in which Ahmad argues with Jameson that the nation is a poor allegorical basis for understanding the place of oppressed peoples within the structures of dominance in the world. Cf. Enrique Bustamante, "TV and Public Service in Spain: A Difficult Encounter." Also see J. Mac Laughlin, "Reflections on Nations as 'Imagined Communities.'"

Part I. Political Transitions, Media Transitions

1. Raymond Carr and Juan Pablo Fusi, *Spain: Dictatorship to Democracy.*

1. The Death of the Dictator and the Twilight of National Mass Media

1. Raymond Carr and Juan Pablo Fusi, *Spain: Dictatorship to Democracy,* 207.
2. Ibid., 1.
3. Ibid., 208.
4. Ibid.
5. Ibid., 6–7.
6. Ibid., 44.
7. The assassination was carried out by ETA (Euskadi Ta Askatasuna, or Basque Homeland and Liberty) after months of careful planning, and resulted in a spectacular detonation of a bomb under the jeep in which Carrero Blanco was traveling home from mass. The explosion was so well timed and highly directional that it launched Carrero Blanco's jeep high into the air, over a building, and onto an interior patio. This event was made into a film by Gillo Pontecorvo called *Operación Ogro,* after the book by the same name by Julián Aguirre. It inspired a political song, "Voló, voló, Carrero voló" (He flew, he flew, Carrero flew). The song was popular at demonstrations; after the song's last refrain people would jump up and shout a cheer, something like hooray.
8. Carr and Fusi, *Spain,* 218.
9. Enrique Bustamante, "Riesgos nacionales, retos internacionales," 1.
10. José María Maravall, *La política de la transición,* 74.
11. A law regulating regional radio and TV was passed in 1983 (see chapters 7 and 12). For general analysis of this period, see Enrique Bustamante, *Los amos de la información en España.*
12. A. Vazquez Barquero and M. Hebbert, "Spain: Economy and State in Transition," 285.
13. Sources for these figures are Richard Gunther, "The Spanish Socialist Party: From Clandestine Opposition to Party of Government," 33; and Vázquez Barquero and Hebbert, *Spain,* 287.
14. Carr and Fusi, *Spain,* 214.
15. Ibid.
16. John Hooper, *The Spaniards: A Portrait of the New Spain,* 42; Carr and Fusi, *Spain,* 233–34.

17. Hooper, *The Spaniards*, 43.

18. See Nicholas Garnham, *Capitalism and Communication: Global Culture and the Economics of Information*, part II; Graham Murdock, "Television and Citizenship: In Defense of Public Broadcasting"; Paddy Scannell, "Public Service Broadcasting: The History of a Concept"; Anthony Smith, *The Shadow in the Cave*.

19. Bernard Miege, *The Capitalization of Cultural Production*.

20. Todd Gitlin, *Inside Prime Time*.

21. Though commercially funded, ITV in Britain functions under a public service principle.

22. A logical paradox is that the system promoting individual sovereignty is more beholden to enhancing the business environment, while the system promoting general welfare is more beholden to the enhancement of individual citizens.

23. Enrique Bustamante, "TV and Public Service in Spain: A Difficult Encounter."

24. Ibid., 72.

25. See James Curran, "Mass Media and Democracy: A Reappraisal," 92–96.

2. The Regional Question

1. Raymond Carr, *Spain, 1808–1975*, 2d ed.; Ramón Tamames and T. Clegg, "Spain: Regional Autonomy and the Democratic Transition," 31–33. The periodization of Spain's administrative unity as a nation-state, although still a matter of historiographical debate, can reasonably be tied to the first national census under the reign of Felipe II in the latter part of the sixteenth century.

2. Pierre Vilar, *Spain: A Brief History*, 74; John Hooper, *The Spaniards*, 225.

3. Koldo Mitxelena, *La lengua vasca*.

4. Hooper, *The Spaniards*, 216–18.

5. Ibid., 225.

6. Robert P. Clark, *The Basques: The Franco Years and Beyond*, 43.

7. Ibid., 226.

8. Vilar, *Spain*, 74–75.

9. Ibid., 75.

10. Eric J. Hobsbawm, *Nations and Nationalism since 1780: Programme, Myth, Reality*.

11. Fernand Braudel, *The Perspective of the World: Civilization and Capitalism, 15th-18th Century*, 3:288.

12. Ibid.

13. Braudel, *Civilization and Capitalism*; J. Nadal, *El fracaso de la revolución industrial en España, 1814–1913*, 2d ed.; J. Vicens Vives, *An Economic History of Spain*; Immanuel Wallerstein, *The Modern World System*.

14. Nevertheless, the northern industrial zones grew as European capitalism developed, while the south became a reservoir for additional capital for the north—siphoned out of agriculture through a process of northward labor migration combined with undervaluation of southern products. See Ernest Mandel, "Capitalism and Regional Disparities"; J. Naylon, *Andalusia*; Costis Hadjimichalis, *Uneven Development and Regionalism: State, Territory and Class in Southern Europe*; S. Giner, "Political Economy, Legitimation and the State in Southern Europe"; and Nadal, *El fracaso*.

15. Tamames and Clegg, "Spain," 33; Carr, *Spain*, 433–35.

16. Tamames and Clegg, "Spain," 33.

17. Clark, *The Basques*, 49.

18. Carr, *Spain*, chap. 14.

19. Ibid.; Tamames and Clegg, "Spain," 34.
20. Vilar, *Spain*, 120–21.
21. Base agreement quoted in ibid., 121.
22. The model followed ideas of permanent disequilibrium and the necessity of state intervention developed by Myrdal and Perroux. See A. Vázquez Barquero and M. Hebbert, "Spain: Economy and State in Transition"; Raymond Carr and Juan Pablo Fusi, *Spain: Dictatorship to Democracy*, chap. 4; Tamames and Clegg, "Spain," 35–36; Hadjimichalis, *Uneven Development*, chap. 3.
23. Giovanni Arrighi, ed., *Semiperipheral Development*, chaps. 7 and 10.
24. Tamames and Clegg, "Spain," 35.
25. Vázquez Barquero and Hebbert, "Spain," 284.
26. The inability of older industrial sectors to innovate has led to a situation in Spain similar to that in the United States in which older pockets of capital accumulation have shifted not just within the country but, in its most dynamic forms, out of the country altogether, toward East Asia. See Alain Lipietz, *Mirages and Miracles: The Crisis of Global Fordism*; J. R. Cuadrado Roura, "Tendencias económico-regionales antes y después de la crisis en España."
27. The location of much economic activity has moved from Asturias, Cantabria, and the northern Spanish Basque provinces to the southern Basque province of Alava through La Rioja to southern Navarre, through Zaragoza to Tarragona (Catalonia). There was a slight but general trend toward equalization of regional per capita income prior to the crisis, but after 1979 there has been a notable reassertion of disequilibrium in interregional levels. Again, this shift follows the changes to the Ebro River Valley that resulted from the response to industrial crises, reconversion, and a more coherent structural mix of sectors in this zone. See Cuadrado Roura, "Tendencias económico-regionales"; and Julio Alcaide Inchausti, "Las cuatro Españas económicas y la solidaridad regional."
28. *El País Anuario 1988*.
29. Alcaide Inchausti, "Las cuatro Españas económicas."
30. Cf. Lipietz, *Mirages and Miracles*, chap. 5.
31. Goldie Shabad, "After Autonomy: The Dynamics of Regionalism in Spain," 119.
32. Ibid., 123.
33. Ibid., 119.
34. Quoted in ibid., 123.

3. Transnational Phenomena in Spanish Media

1. Herbert I. Schiller, *Mass Communication and American Empire*; Lawrence Lessing, "The Electronics Era."
2. Richard B. DuBoff, *Accumulation and Power: An Economic History of the United States*. National public policies that sought to manage expansion of communications infrastructures and regulate the flow of information have been typically patterned on state and business relations obtaining in each national state. In the United States, public policy had come late to the developments in transport and communication, preventing the state from participating as directly in the development of public communication systems as was typical among European nations. Until the late nineteenth century, as DuBoff shows, U.S. corporations intervened directly in a vacuum of national policy until state apparatuses were established that worked for U.S. business at home and abroad in the name of the national community. Since World War I, state agencies have been actively pursuing policies to serve business rather than public interests in communications material; this situation allows corporations to exert pressure on federal regulators to relax antitrust enforce-

ment, especially in regards to "cooperation and price fixing among firms in the export trade" (DuBoff, *Accumulation and Power*, 152). This expansionary "political capitalism" shaped the history of broadcasting in the United States, where, as Herbert I. Schiller shows, the "structure, character and direction of the domestic communications apparatus" did not develop as "entirely national concerns" (*Mass Communication*, 17).

3. Fred Fejes, "The U.S. in Third World Communications: Latin America, 1900–1945"; Manuel Castells et al., *Nuevas tecnologías, economia, y sociedad en España*, 1:124.

4. Castells et al., *Nuevas tecnologías*, 124.

5. Another "quid pro quo was that the United States would gain entry into formerly protected foreign and colonial markets (like those of the British Commonwealth) and would sacrifice 'declining industries' at home" to free trade with the contracting European empires (DuBoff, *Accumulation and Power*, 154).

6. Manuel Vázquez Montalbán, *La penetración americana en España*. Vázquez Montalbán is cited critically by Casanova as perhaps aiming his observation at disassociating later development from foreign investment; see José Casanova, "The Modernization of Spain."

7. Raymond Carr and Juan Pablo Fusi, *Spain: Dictatorship to Democracy*, define Opus Dei as follows: "A lay brotherhood of committed Catholics, aimed at influencing university and political life. Nursery of the 'technocrats' of the 1960s. Fell from influence in 1973" (xvi). Today the Opus is active throughout Latin America. Despite what some may see as the withering away of its influence in Spain, the Opus Dei has left a legacy of technocratic rationalism that marks the current behavior of policymakers, especially around issues concerning the so-called information society. See R. L. Fregoso, *The Information Society in Spain: The Confluence of Cultural and Economic Forces*.

8. Carr and Fusi, *Spain*, 53.

9. With Ericsson of Sweden holding 49 percent, Telefónica created INTELSA to produce switching technology; with Italy's Telettra holding 49 percent of Telettra Española, the national phone company built transmission equipment; with American Cable holding 51 percent, Telefónica created Cables de Comunicaciones (Castells et al., *Nuevas tecnologías*, 126).

10. Casanova, "The Modernization of Spain," 33. One marker of growth that most economists associate with Spain's "economic boom" in the 1960s was an annual average share of 9 percent of world trade for Spain's manufacturing exports (1962–73).

11. Carr and Fusi, *Spain*, 102.

12. Ibid. Newspaper readership was low in Spain (about half that of France).

13. José María Iñigo, quoted in ibid.

14. Ibid., 103.

15. J. R. Cuadrado Roura, V. Granados, and J. Aurioles, "Technological Dependency in a Mediterranean Economy: The Case of Spain," 118–24.

16. *El País, Anuario 1986*, 366.

17. I am indebted to Daniel Jones, of the Autonomous University of Barcelona, for this data. See also Castells et al., *Nuevas tecnologías*, 480–85.

18. The Opus technocrats were largely responsible for the economic policies of the last two decades of Franco's regime. Later, through the influence of Admiral Carrero Blanco, they were able to extend their power to TVE.

19. Figures vary because of an absence of documentation on many company holdings; see Enrique Bustamante, *Los amos de la información en España*, 64.

20. Ibid., 66. Foreign direct investment gives transnational corporations greater flexibility of control and more freedom to move among shifting locations of growth and investment in the global economy without too much attachment to national economies.

21. Enrique Bustamante and Ramón Zallo, coordinators, *Las industrias culturales en España: grupos multimedia y transnacionales,* 123.
22. Ibid., 152.
23. Figures from UNESCO, cited in ibid., 124–25.
24. Enrique Bustamante, "TV and Public Service in Spain: A Difficult Encounter," 71–72.
25. Castells et al., *Nuevas tecnologías,* 423–29.
26. Fregoso, *The Information Society in Spain.*
27. Castells et al., *Nuevas tecnologías,* 487; emphasis in the original.
28. R. L. Fregoso, "The PEIN in Spain: Telecommunications and Government Policy."

4. It's Private

1. Hooper, *The Spaniards,* 43
2. Enrique Bustamante, *Los amos de la información en España,* 182.
3. E. López Escobar and A. Faus Belau, "Broadcasting in Spain: A History of Heavy-handed State Control," 126–27.
4. Royal decree 2.664 was effected on October 6, 1977. See Emili Prado, "El movimiento por la libertad de emisión en España."
5. Royal decree 2.648, October 27, 1978; royal decree 1.433, June 8, 1979. Also in 1979, four hundred million pesetas (about four million dollars) were authorized for the construction of Spain's first broadcast monitoring center.
6. W. B. Emery, *National and International Systems of Broadcasting*; Bustamante, *Los amos de la información,* 159.
7. Miquel de Moragas i Spà, "Mass Communication and Political Change in Spain, 1975–1980."
8. See Bustamante, *Los amos de la información,* 182–85.
9. Quoted in Hooper, *The Spaniards,* 140.
10. Bustamante, *Los amos de la información,* 182–85.
11. Hooper, *The Spaniards,* 140.
12. Bustamante, *Los amos de la información,* 184; Moragas, "Mass Communication," 519.
13. Hooper, *The Spaniards,* 140–41.
14. Bustamante, *Los amos de la información,* 192; Moragas, "Mass Communication."
15. Moragas, "Mass Communication," 519.
16. N. Torrents, "Cinema and the Media after the Death of Franco," 108.
17. Carlos Elordi, "La televisión pronto llegará."

5. Unlikely Hegemony, Unfinished Party

1. Salustiano del Campo, J. F. Tezanos, and W. Santin, "La élite política española y la transición a la democracia," 32–33. The king, however, was so pleased with the accomplishments of "Suarism" that he bestowed a dukedom on Suárez.
2. R. Morodo, *La transición política*; Raymond Carr and Juan Pablo Fusi, *Spain: Dictatorship to Democracy*; José María Maravall, *La política de la transición*; J. Santamaría, ed., *Transición a la democracia en el sur de Europa y América Latina*; L. García San Miguel, *Teoría de la transición: un análisis del modelo español, 1973–1978.*
3. Maravall, *La política de la transición,* 25; C. Huneeus, "Transition to Democracy in Spain: Unión de Centro Democrático as a 'Consociational Party': An Exploratory Analysis."

4. Antonio Bar Cendon, "¿Normalidad o excepcionalidad?: para una tipología del sistema de partidos en España, 1977–1982."

5. Maravall, *La política de la transición*, 26.

6. Ibid.

7. Carr and Fusi, *Spain*, 254.

8. Ibid., 38.

9. Maravall, *La política de la transición*, 63.

10. Carr and Fusi, *Spain*, 248.

11. R. Gunther, "Constitutional Change in Contemporary Spain," 58.

12. Carr and Fusi, *Spain*, 252–55.

13. Ibid., 255.

14. *ABC*, September 23, 1979, quoted in ibid.

15. General Gutiérrez Mellado, Minister of Defense under the UCD government, quoted in Carr and Fusi, *Spain*, 255–56.

16. Ibid.

17. A. Vázquez Barquero and M. Hebbert, "Spain: Economy and State in Transition," 293.

18. Two of my neighbors, elderly sisters and staunch Francoists, knocked on my door to ask if they might use the phone to call their nephew to congratulate him, as he was a soldier of the Guardia Civil. What would you do?

19. *Correo Catalan*, June 16, 1981.

6. Political Failure, Broken Rules, and the Symbolic Advance of Private TV

1. Pere Oriol Costa, *La crisis de la televisión pública*, 95.

2. See Luca Pavolini, "Communicazioni di massa e democrazia: una nuova fase della reforma."

3. My reference here is to those who formed an early liberal movement within the last government of Franco, Pío Cabanillas being the most prominent of those involved.

4. *El País*, September 19, 1981; cf. Enrique Bustamante, *Los amos de la información en España*, 191.

5. *El País*, August 12, 1981.

6. Ibid.

7. The socialists denied these rumors (see *El Socialista*, August 8, 1981), although they were later confirmed by several members of the UCD (see *Baleares*, October 8, 1983).

8. *El País*, August 19, 1981.

9. Americans may remember hearing on network TV news a recording of the attack on the congress direct from the parliament building, accompanied by sketches and photos. Radio and TVE reporters in the upper levels continued to broadcast descriptions of the siege until threatened by the soldiers. The audio documented the sounds of gunfire and fear. One reporter's newscast was repeated over and over that night on Spanish radio as it ended with the words "I must turn off now, they're pointing their guns at me, I'm turning off now," followed by sounds of the microphone being wrested from his hands. Two press photographers from the news agency EFE, Manuel Hernández and M. Barriopedro, also acted courageously as they rapidly ran off a roll of film that captured the scene and then replaced it with a fresh roll. They quickly hid the used film in their clothes before the soldiers got to them and confiscated the cameras. When they were allowed to leave the building, they smuggled the film out with them.

10. Cabanillas had been Franco's minister of Information and Tourism in 1974. The Council of State was the supreme legal consultative organ of the government.

11. Miquel Moragas i Spà, "Mass Communication and Political Change in Spain 1975–1980," 505.

12. *El País*, August 12, 1981.

13. As reported later in *Diario de Barcelona*, September 9, 1981.

14. "Tensiones en el gobierno a causa de la TV privada," *Tiempo* (June 10, 1985): 33.

15. *El País*, September 18, 1981.

16. The constitutional tribunal is the supreme interpretative organ of the constitution, similar to the Supreme Court in the United States.

17. *El País*, April 2, 1982; emphasis added.

18. *El Periódico*, April 18, 1982.

19. *La Vanguardia*, April 2, 1982.

20. *La Vanguardia*, April 15, 1982.

21. Costa, *La crisis de la televisión pública*, 114.

22. *El País*, April 3, 1982.

23. *El País*, April 8, 1982.

24. *El Noticiero*, April 8, 1982.

25. A. Vázquez Barquero and M. Hebbert, "Spain: Economy and State in Transition," 290–91.

26. Ibid., 291.

27. Ibid.

28. Raymond Carr and Juan Pablo Fusi, *Spain: Dictatorship to Democracy*, 253.

29. Moragas, "Mass Communication."

30. José María Maravall, quoted in *La Vanguardia*, April 13, 1982.

31. *El Noticiero Universal*, May 1, 1982.

32. See José María Villagrasa, "Spain: The Emergence of Commercial Television," 346.

7. The PSOE

1. Quoted in E. López-Escobar, "Spain Waits for Private TV," 44.

2. Justo Villafañe, "Decentralización y servicio público"; Carmelo Garitaonaindía and J. V. Idoyaga, "La televisión en las regiones, nacionalidades, y naciones de Europa."

3. Carmelo Garitaonaindía, "La televisión y las comunidades autónomas."

4. Raymond Carr and Juan Pablo Fusi, *Spain: Dictatorship to Democracy*, 255.

5. *La Vanguardia*, December 13, 1983.

6. See *El País, Anuario 1985*, 376, 381.

7. B. Jessop, "Corporatism, Parliamentarism and Social Democracy."

8. *El País, Anuario 1985*, 385.

8. For the Few

1. *Tiempo*, February 7, 1983.

2. *El País*, February 24, 1984.

3. See A. Vázquez Barquero and M. Hebbert, "Spain: Economy and State in Transition."

4. *El País*, March 22, 1984.

5. *Diario 16,* August 21, 1984.
6. *Diario 16,* January 10, 1984.
7. *El País,* March 28, 1984.
8. *El País,* April 6, 1984.
9. Compare *El País,* April 6, 1984; *El Correo Catalan,* April 6, 1984; and *Cinco Días,* April 6, 1984.
10. *El País,* April 7, 1984; *Ya,* April 7, 1984.
11. *El País,* April 7, 1984.
12. *ABC,* April 27, 1984.
13. *Ya,* April 28, 1984.
14. *El País,* May 3, 1984.
15. *Ya,* May 19, 1984.
16. *ABC,* May 19, 1984.
17. *Ya,* November 30, 1984.
18. *Tiempo,* July 9, 1984.
19. Enrique Bustamante and Justo Villafañe, "La larga marcha de la televisión privada," 2.
20. See any number of polls conducted by the Center for Sociological Research; those that I have examined include Centro de Investigaciones Sociológicas survey studies numbers 1.403, 1.407, 1.414, 1.415, 1.419, 1.425, 1.437, 1.442, 1.450, 1.451, 1.462, 1.464, 1.475, 1.496, 1.512, 1.527, 1.544, 1.719. The goal of these tabulations was to acquire a sense of pre- and postelection sentiments toward political parties and the media in distinct regions. The Centro de Investigaciones Sociológicas is a publicly funded polling institute under the direction of the Spanish government; it was created toward the end of the Franco regime as the Instituto de la Opinión Pública (whose history and function has yet to be studied seriously). The agenda of its surveys is determined largely by the ruling party of the Spanish government, and starting in the early 1990s its operation came under increasing scrutiny by the minority parties in the central government.

9. Social Democracy, Modernization, and Corporatism in Action

1. *Diario 16,* February 10, 1985.
2. *El País,* February 5, 1985.
3. *Liberación,* January 18, 1985.
4. *Business America,* January 20, 1986.
5. *El País,* February 7, 1985.
6. See *Diario 16,* February 19, 1985.
7. In *Disorganized Capitalism,* Claus Offe remarks: "In order to achieve anything like that stimulation effect upon growth and employment (as was the case in the past, for instance, with automobiles, synthetic fibres, and other substances, as well as television and other entertainment electronics), new products would nowadays have to display some rather unlikely overall properties. Namely, they would have to be capable of mass consumption, their productions would need to be both labor-intensive and capital-intensive, while neither their raw materials nor their use or disposal could legitimately give rise to further economic, health, or ecological problems" (85).
8. *Diario 16,* February 18, 1985; *La Vanguardia,* February 19, 1985.
9. The Industrial Reconversion Program did not begin in earnest until 1983 with the new socialist administration (see U.S. Department of Commerce, "The Spanish Industrial Reconversion and Development Program"). This program was unique in comparative law,

according to A. Vázquez Barquero and M. Hebbert, "Spain: Economy and State in Transition."

10. *ABC,* March 20, 1984.

11. Enrique Bustamante and Justo Villafañe, "La larga marcha de la televisión privada," 2.

12. Interview of Francisco Virseda by the author, July 1985.

13. Interview of Emili Prado Pico, director of the Department of Audiovisual Communication, Publicity, and Research, Autonomous University of Barcelona, by the author, June 1985.

14. For more on local media at this time in Spain, see the Spanish magazines *Alfoz* 11 (December 1984) and *Arrel* 3 (April-September 1982); see also Emili Prado Pico, "La televisión comunitaria en Cataluña."

15. RTVE, *Anuario 1985.*

16. Gabriel Barrasa, "Condicionamientos y posibilidades de la tecnología para la televisión," 21.

17. See ibid., and also Gabriel Barrasa and Antonio López, "España: esfuerzos insuficientes e inconexos."

18. *Anuncios,* May 7, 1984.

19. Bustamante and Villafañe, "La larga marcha."

20. Compañía Telefónica Nacional de España, *Memoria 1984* (Telefónica's annual report); Organization for Economic Cooperation and Development, *Changing Market Structures in Telecommunications.*

21. Enrique Bustamante, *Los amos de la información en España.*

22. *El País,* June 12, 1985.

23. See Manuel Castells et al., *Nuevas tecnologías, economía, y sociedad en España,* 480–85; cf. R. L. Fregoso, "The PEIN in Spain: Telecommunications and Government Policy."

24. In 1972 Telefónica started an ill-fated cable TV venture in Madrid and Barcelona, CONESA, with investment from four of the largest banks in Spain.

25. Compañía Telefónica Nacional de España, *Memoria 1984.*

26. *El País, Edición Internacional,* September 23, 1985.

27. Bustamante and Villafañe, "La larga marcha," 2.

28. Enrique Bustamante, "TV and Public Service in Spain: A Difficult Encounter," 71–72.

29. *Tiempo,* March 25, 1985.

30. *Ya,* January 4, 1985.

31. *Mercado,* May 3, 1985.

32. This summary is composed of information from *El País,* January 30, June 11, and June 14, 1985, and July 31, 1986; *Diario 16,* January 30, 1985; *Liberación,* January 30 and March 2, 1985.

33. See *Epoca* 1 (March 18, 1985); *Cambio 16,* February 11, 1985.

34. Interview of Francisco Virseda by the author, July 1985.

35. *Mercado,* May 3, 1985.

10. Politics of Diminishing Returns

1. *El País,* May 22, 1985.

2. *El País,* May 24, 1985. A third element in these declarations betrayed most of the negative predictions: González announced that official investigations suggested that the

spectrum, the infrastructure, and the advertising market could stand the addition of more than one new channel with national coverage.

3. *Tiempo,* June 10, 1985.

4. Interview of Francisco Virseda by the author, July 1985.

5. *Tiempo,* June 10, 1985, 32.

6. Raymond Carr and Juan Pablo Fusi, *Spain: Dictatorship to Democracy,* 213.

7. *El País,* June 21, 1985.

8. These ideas were brought to my attention in my discussions with the Spanish political scientist Rafael Bañon Martínez, during his lecture "Spain in Transition" presented at the University of Wisconsin-Madison, October 23, 1985, and in an earlier interview, also on October 23, 1985.

9. *El País,* July 16, 1985; *El País, Edición Internacional,* August 5, 1985.

10. *El País, Edición Internacional,* November 11, 1985.

11. Manuel Vázquez Montalbán, "Año de consolidaciones."

12. *New York Times,* August 8, 1992.

13. Quoted in P. Camiller, "Spanish Socialism in the Atlantic," 28.

14. José María Villagrasa, "Spain: The Emergence of Commercial Television," 346.

15. See also the U.S. press support for NATO in Spain that employed these same themes. For contrast, compare *New York Times,* March 13, 1986, and Gabriel Jackson, "Socialists: Front and Center," *The Nation* (March 15, 1986): 854–56, both reasoning in NATO's favor.

16. Eusebio Mujal-Leon, "The Foreign Policy of the Spanish Government."

17. See ibid., as well as Stanley Payne, "The Elections of June 1986."

18. Royal decree 1362/1988, November 11, for the national technical plan of private TV.

19. The mandate for this technical network, Red Técnica Española de Televisión (Retevisión), was derived from LOT and the private TV law, with further elaboration in the Ley de Presupuestos/29 December 1988 (law for the federal budget of 1989).

20. This account of Canal 10 in London is based on interviews with personnel and on a visit to the Molinare Studios during the week of July 18, 1988.

21. *El País,* August 2, 1988.

22. This information I owe to Carmen Usobiaga, whose only wish was to watch sports and American movies.

23. Villagrasa, "Spain," 347.

24. Ibid.

11. Private TV Now and Forever

1. See Claus Offe, *Disorganized Capitalism,* 214–20.

2. Grupo 16 was eventually disqualified for a license after failing to provide the required deposit.

3. Regarding Antena-3 de Televisión, other shares besides those belonging to *La Vanguardia* and Antena-3 were distributed among twenty-three daily regional newspapers (10 percent), eight magazines (4 percent), various Spanish companies (35 percent), various individual managers and executives (10 percent), and the rest among foreign investors.

The rest of the shares of La Sociedad Española de Televisión Canal Plus went to Banca March (15 percent); Banco de Bilbao-Vizcaya (15 percent); Bankinter, Grucysa, Grupo Eventos, and Caja Madrid (each 5 percent).

The remaining shares of Gestevisión-Telecinco were owned by Juan Fernández Montreal (15 percent) and Angel Medrano (10 percent). All figures are from José María Villagrasa, "Spain: The Emergence of Commercial Television," 349.

4. See Enrique Bustamante, *Los Amos de la información en España*, 88–90; Enrique Bustamante and Ramón Zallo, coordinators, *Las industrias culturales en España: Grupos multimedia y transnacionales*, 152–55.

5. Ian Tucker, "Spain: Fierce Competition Forces Change."

6. Villagrasa, "Spain," 377. The London-based Kuwaiti Investment Office "began to invest in Spain in 1984 as part of a diversification policy adopted after its managers found they had accounted for 20 percent of the total turnover of the London Stock Exchange" (Justin Webster, "Kuwait Investment: Spanish Inquisition," 60–62). After 1984 the Kuwaiti Investment Office bought into industries as diverse as paper, chemical, banking, and food processing; penetration into the TV industry was part of its larger investment and conglomeration strategy. In the past few years the Kuwaiti Investment Office has suffered a partial collapse in Spain, losing about half of its holdings to illiquid investment (ibid.). At the time of this writing, it was in bankruptcy court, in arrears of 1.8 billion dollars in payments to Spanish banks. De la Rosa, however, managed to get rich off of commissions and fees. See *Wall Street Journal* (November 24, 1992): 1.

7. Villagrasa, "Spain," 377.

8. Ibid., 426.

9. See ibid.

10. See Nicholas Garnham, *Capitalism and Communication: Global Culture and the Economics of Information*, 64–69, 154–68.

11. This was a projected figure. A commercial satellite company called Hispasat was created in June 1989. Three satellites, built by MATRA and British Aerospace, have been planned, with one being a backup. The first, Hispasat 1A, was launched in 1992. It had five channels for Europe, one in reserve, and two for the Americas. Ownership broke down as follows: Telefónica (25 percent), Retevisión (25 percent), Caja Postal (22.5 percent), National Institute of Industry (10 percent), Spanish Aerospace Institute (15 percent), and Center for Development of Technology and Industry (2.5 percent). Those vying for one of the first five channels were RTVE, the regionals, the private firms, the Mexican Galavisión, and another commercial promoter. See Villagrasa, "Spain," 424. A bent antenna on the Hispasat 1A put a hold on the project. Loss of transponder rental income was estimated at thirty-five billion pesetas; no broadcast was possible (Justin Webster, "Eye on Europe: Spain-Hispasat Hitch Puts TV Project on Hold"). The technical problem did not affect the non-DBS transponders. The three private broadcasters have used this satellite since February 1993. Hispasat 1B was launched in July 1993; see conclusion of this book for further discussion.

12. C. Garitaonaindía, A. Gurrea, J. V. Idoyaga, J. A. Mingolarra, R. Zallo, and S. Zunzunegui, "Estructura y política de comunicación en Euskadi," 7.

13. Ley de Presupuestos/29 December 1988, article 124 (law for federal budget of 1989).

14. Article 11, royal decree 1362/1988, 11 November.

15. No continuity programming (slates, identification cards, black, and so on), repeated programs, or advertising will be considered part of this minimum broadcast time. The company's own production must make up at least 15 percent of the total; at least 40 percent must come from EC production companies (including Spanish firms); 55 percent must be original Spanish programming; and 40 percent of the commercial films broadcast should originate from EC sources, with 50 percent of that cinematographic transmission reserved for Spanish films. No film can be broadcast before two years have passed since its theatrical exhibition, except when said film was produced especially for TV. Advertising must not exceed 10 percent of annual programming. This is only a partial summary of Law 10 1988, May 3, of Private Television.

Part III. The Geography of Television in Spain

1. Miquel de Moragas i Spà and María Corominas Piulats, *Local Communication in Catalonia (1975–1988)*, 4.

12. Electronic Regions of Spain

1. Lluis Bassets, ed., *De las ondas rojas a las radios libres*, 266.
2. Justino Sinova, *La gran mentira*, 30; emphasis in the original.
3. E. López Escobar and A. Faus Belau, "Broadcasting in Spain: A History of Heavy-handed State Control," 122.
4. Ibid., 124; emphasis in the original.
5. Bassets, ed., *De las ondas rojas*, 266.
6. See John Hooper, *The Spaniards: A Portrait of the New Spain*, 204–51, for a general perspective on this period.
7. Alberto Díaz Mancisidor, *Historia de radio Bilbao: antecedentes y primeros años*, 75–93.
8. Article 18, Press Law of 22 April 1938, quoted in Henry F. Schulte, *The Spanish Press, 1470–1966: Print, Power, Politics*, 13–14.
9. R. De Mateo, J. M. Corbella, and D. E. Jones, "Structure, Property, and Control of Spanish Television (1956–1988)," 5.
10. Ibid., 5–6.
11. Ibid.
12. Ibid., 9.
13. Ibid., 7, 34–35.
14. The centers that showed this final percentage range were Bilbao, Santiago de Compostela, Seville, Valencia, and Madrid (the regional center of Castile). Oviedo was somewhat higher at 124 hours, or 2.3 percent. The study, from the Secretaria Técnica de Emisiones de TVE, is cited in J. V. Idoyaga, *Televisiones regionales en Europa*, 156.
15. Idoyaga, *Televisiones regionales en Europa*, 157–58.
16. Juanjo Mardones, "La televisión regional en España," quoted in Idoyaga, *Televisiones regionales en Europa*, 158.
17. Idoyaga, *Televisiones regionales en Europa*, 151.
18. Quoted in ibid., 152. *Comarcas* are historic local geographical boundaries, like cantons, departments, or parishes.
19. Ibid., 159–60.
20. Ibid., 165.
21. Quoted in ibid., 148.
22. Ibid., 173.
23. Article 143 of the Spanish constitution (with exact provisions in article 148) furnished what was known as the slow route to autonomy. Devolution under these articles limited statutes of autonomy, during the initial five-year period, to administrative and legislative powers in the areas of "regional interest" such as local government, housing, small roads and rail, noncommercial ports and airport, forestry, and so on. See Ramón Tamames and T. Clegg, "Spain: Regional Autonomy and the Democratic Transition," 38–43, for a good summary. In the Basque Country, the recuperation of the historic fiscal privileges under the *fueros* (charter), called the *concierto económico*, provided the right to collect all taxes within the territory (except custom duties and receipts of state-controlled businesses) and to make a lump-sum payment to the central government for national services.

24. In contrast, the provisions related to articles 143 and 148 left education, police, and mass communication to the central state.

25. The basic regulation of press, radio, and TV was included along with control over interregional flows of railway, roads, telecommunication, and post; see Tamames and Clegg, "Spain," 40.

26. Ibid., 41.

27. Idoyaga, *Televisiones regionales en Europa*, 173–74.

28. Article 45, Law 5/1982, May 20. *Euskara* (or *Euskera*) is the Basque word for the Basque language.

29. *La Vanguardia*, August 3, 1983.

30. Idoyaga, *Televisiones regionales en Europa*, 176; Francisco Virseda, "Los argumentos jurídicos de la Ley del Tercer Canal," 244–47.

31. Idoyaga, *Televisiones regionales en Europa*, 177–78.

32. Interview of Julián Pérez Delgado by the author, Durango, Vizcaya, August 4, 1988. The insistent ring disrupted the interview briefly but significantly.

13. In the Region of Electronic and Political Conflicts

1. Pasqual Menéndez, phone interview by author, Madrid, July 11, 1988.

2. Interview with Julián Pérez Delgado, managing director of Basque Radio and Television, by the author, Durango, Vizcaya, August 4, 1988.

3. Interview of Agustí Gallart i Teixidó, Secretaria General, Gabinet de Radiodifusió i Televisió, by the author, Barcelona, July 26, 1988.

4. Interview of Jaime Souza Porto by the author, Santiago de Compostela, August 3, 1988.

5. Interview by the author, Madrid, July 18, 1988.

6. A. Díez, "La oposición bloquea las 'mejoras' que el PSOE pretendía introducir en la ley de televisión privada."

7. Interview of Agustí Gallart, July 26, 1988.

8. Figures on Basque speakers are from *Anuario Estadístico del País Vasco*, 1986. The total of nonspeakers of Basque varied among the provinces: in Alava, 87 percent; Vizcaya, 73 percent; Guipuzcoa, 42 percent. In both the Basque Country and Catalonia, children and adolescents who were taught in the regional schools were more fluent. Indeed, education, more than media, seems to be the decisive element in language acquisition.

Figures on Catalan are from *Consorci d'Informació i Documentació de Catalunya*, 1986. The percentage of those who claimed to be writers of the language was 35 percent.

9. Interview of Agustí Gallart, July 26, 1988.

10. Interview of Julián Pérez, August 4, 1988.

11. Interview of Agustí Gallart, July 26, 1988.

12. Interview of Julián Pérez, August 4, 1988

13. José María Villagrasa, "Spain: The Emergence of Commercial Television," 361.

14. Ibid.

15. Technical information provided by engineering staff at Euskaltelebista to Julián Pérez, who gave me access to it.

16. Details provided by Antonio Posse Peña, director of engineering for TVG, in an interview with the author, August 3, 1988.

17. Details provided by Lluís F. Grau i Bruni, production and transmission engineer for TV-3. Interview of Grau conducted by the author, July 26, 1988. Further information from Jaume Pérez i Santos, director of administration for TV-3, interview with the author, July 26, 1988.

18. Conversation with Emili Prado Pico, March 16, 1990, Madison, Wisconsin.

19. There is a danger in overestimating the operational force of such a zone. Clubs, based in shared language or pleasures, are organizations of civil society. Regional politics, national politics, and the interregional operations of commerce can, and do, determine the territorial significance of organizations of civil society (such as clubs). In this case, as in others, a zone of viewers does not constitute anything approaching a sui generis electronic region. These viewers are in fact subordinate to the political and economic forces that overdetermine the play of trespass and containment of electronic regions. They can, nevertheless, help extend the scale of these regions, which makes them historically very important.

20. Villagrasa, "Spain," 391–92.

14. The Distant Space of Political Economy

1. *View Magazine* 9, no. 10 (June 6, 1988).

2. The Dow Jones publication *American Demographics* put it this way: "You'll know it's the twenty-first century when ... everyone belongs to a minority group." *American Demographics* promoted its eleventh annual conference in 1991 on consumer trends and markets with such slogans.

3. David Nogueira, "Unrelated Diversity," 9.

4. J. Walter Thompson, *La inversión publicitaria en España, 1987*. These figures exclude the Canary Islands, and are based on an exchange rate of one dollar to one hundred pesetas, the 1982 average.

5. Enrique Bustamante, "TV and Public Service in Spain: A Difficult Encounter," 71–72. Separate from the figures on TVE, total advertising investment in the Catalan network, TV-3, between 1984 and 1987 surged from 2.1 million dollars to 10.3 million dollars, while the Basque ETB earnings tripled after 1984 to nearly three-quarters of a million dollars in 1987 (0.73 million). The network of the Autonomous Community of Galicia, TVG, reported an increase from 0.31 million dollars in 1986 to 0.81 million dollars in 1987. By 1990, TV-3 was taking in over 170 million dollars in advertising income (an increase of 8.5 percent over 1989). In the same year, both channels of ETB registered about 23 million dollars (up 1.4 percent from 1989), and TVG shared with its radio company a total of 19.2 million dollars. Consider that until 1990 yearly growth in global advertising billings was somewhere around 10 percent. In contrast, a total increase of 156 percent in the Spanish market was recorded in 1985, the first full year of both regionalist TV and regionalized advertising for TVE. In 1986, this increase jumped 239 percent over 1985, and in 1987 advertising income jumped an additional 53 percent. Figures from J. Walter Thompson, *La inversión publicitaria en España, 1987*; "Regionals Play Wildcard," *Television Business International*, 46. Figures vary according to exchange rates applied. See also José María Villagrasa, "Spain: The Emergence of Commercial Television."

6. As a percentage of the gross domestic product, total advertising investment in Spain had grown from 0.7 percent to over 1.1 percent between 1975 and 1985; it reached levels in 1986 equal to the same index in the United States for 1979; in 1990, the total revenue for advertising in Spain grew to around 2.1 percent of the gross national product. See *Europe 2000*, July 1, 1991; Enrique Bustamante and Ramón Zallo, coordinators, *Las industrias culturales en España: grupos multimedia y transnacionales*, 155–56. Villagrasa, "Spain," 353, points out that TV revenues alone reached 0.49 percent of GNP in 1990.

7. Kevin Robins, "Global Times," 21.

8. In 1989, TVE's share of the national audience was 87.6 percent, while the regionals together registered 12.4 percent. In 1990, after Retevisión was able to take private TV

into half of Spain's TV households, private television moved from 8 percent to about 23 percent of the audience, while the average share for TVE dropped as far as 66 percent. The regionals held their own within the four-fifths of the territory they reached, with registered totals surpassing 18 percent in some rating periods. At the end of 1991, TVE's two channels continued downward, but still topped the ratings with over 55 percent of the total audience, and private broadcasters together came in a distant second (but still rising) at around 27 percent. Broadcasters in the regional federation, FORTA, were still holding averages of about 15 percent throughout the national electronic space. Nonetheless, the ability to capture transregional audiences clearly favored firms that operated at the national scale. Figures cited in Villagrasa, "Spain," 391–92, 425.

9. In 1990, Basque viewers preferred the two channels of TVE almost 72 percent of the time, while they watched ETB's channels 16.4 percent and private TV 11.6 percent of the time. Catalans, in contrast, preferred to watch private TV 41 percent of the time, their own TV-3/Canal 33 about 25 percent, and TVE channels about 43 percent. Galicians only watched private TV 7 percent of their viewing time, while TVG enjoyed a regular audience of almost 20 percent, with TVE's channels reaching a high of over 73 percent. By far the most avid viewers of private TV are those in the region of Madrid, who claimed that over 41 percent of their viewing time was devoted to commercial TV and only 45 percent to TVE's two channels. See Villagrasa, "Spain," 392. It should be noted that private TV was unevenly distributed at this time.

10. See ibid., 360–90.

11. A committee meets monthly to decide on the program purchases to be made, and on who the participants in the deal will be. One of the buyers of one of the firms makes the acquisition and signs contracts that include licensing for the other firms, who pay the acquiring firm their part of the purchase price once the deal is made. Dubbing is then done by local firms. In 1991, about 80 percent of acquisitions were shared by all FORTA firms, 10 percent by only some, and 10 percent were bought on an individual basis. See Susan Eardley, "Spain: Increased Competition at Home Is Forcing Broadcasters to Rethink Their International Strategy," 25.

12. I am grateful to Dan Schiller for urging me to highlight this aspect of my analysis and for the rhetorical parallelism used in this sentence.

13. Interview of Jaime Souza Porto by the author, August 3, 1988.

14. Interview of Julián Pérez Delgado by the author, August 4, 1988.

15. Interview with Jaime Souza Porto, August 3, 1988.

16. Interview with Jaime Souza Porto, August 3, 1988; interview with Julián Pérez Delgado, August 4, 1988.

17. Estimates based on Villagrasa, "Spain," 372. At 1980 exchange rates, these are probably underestimates.

18. Ibid.

19. Interview with Jaime Souza Porto, August 3, 1988.

20. Interview of Francisco Virseda Barca, director general of social communication in the presidency of the government (i.e., for the executive branch), by the author, July 18, 1988.

21. Spillover gives Telemadrid one-quarter of the entire viewing population over fourteen years of age within the Spanish territory.

22. Villagrasa, "Spain," 372–74.

23. Interview with Francisco Virseda Barca, July 18, 1988.

24. Villagrasa, "Spain," 374.

25. Interview with Francisco Virseda Barca, July 18, 1988.

26. See Armand Mattelart, Xavier Delcourt, and Michèle Mattelart, *International Image Markets.*

27. Interview with Francisco Virseda Barca, July 18, 1988.

28. On TVE-1, foreign purchases made up 28 percent of broadcasts in 1985, but rose to 40 percent in 1989. FORTA reported in 1990 that Canal Sur, the Andalusian channel, showed foreign programs in 33 percent of its schedule, following TV-3 at 34 percent, TVG at 35 percent, and ETB-1 at 39 percent. The highest level of imports was recorded by Telemadrid at 64 percent, followed by Canal 9, the Valencian channel, at 51 percent, and ETB-2 at 49 percent. See Villagrasa, "Spain," 382.

29. José Miguel Contreras at Monte Carlo's Television Program Market, reported in *El País Edición Internacional* (February 15, 1988): 23.

30. Villagrasa, "Spain," 383–84. FORTA renewed its licensing deal with Columbia Tristar (Sony) in 1993, giving it access to more than three thousand programs and Sony Picture's library of over 270 series; see "Spain: Columbia Tristar Renews Licensing Deal with FORTA," *Broadcast,* March 12, 1993.

31. Interview of Lluís Ferrando, program buyer for TV-3, by the author, July 26, 1988.

32. Villagrasa, "Spain," 383.

33. Interview with Lluis Ferrando, July 26, 1988.

34. Interview with Francisco Virseda Barca, July 18, 1988.

Conclusion

1. Richard W. Stevenson, "Spain and Portugal in Devaluations."

2. Organization of Economic Cooperation and Development (OECD), *Economic Surveys, Spain, 1993.*

3. "Finance: Torn beyond Repair?" *Economist,* 89–90; John Rossant, "One Day Panic, Next Day Sales," 49–50.

4. Alison Warner, "Down, but Not Out," 18; OECD, *Economic Surveys.*

5. Stevenson, "Spain and Portugal in Devaluations."

6. Murdoch's News Corporation International (News International) had previously bought a 25 percent stake of Grupo Zeta in 1989. Grupo Zeta is headed by Antonio Asensio, who held about 70 percent of the firm in 1993, with Jacques Hachuel holding another 5 percent (through a company called Servifilm, later sold). Prior to this, in order to increase cash reserves after losing miserably in the first two years of private TV competition, Godó arranged a cooperation agreement between Antena-3 radio and PRISA (which owns Radio El País and the newspaper *El País,* and is a principal shareholder of the rival commercial television company Canal Plus). Perhaps Godó sought new allies, but the result increased PRISA's control over commercial radio. The Godó group lost Antena-3 TV after it backed out of a deal—on the urging of the PSOE government—with Mario Conde, who wanted to buy part of *La Vanguardia* and Antena-3. It seems Conde had his eyes on establishing a conservative presidency in Spain, and the government thought it wise to keep him out of the media. The conservative triumvirate of Asensio, Conde, and Murdoch also obtained the national daily newspaper *Ya* in the deal. See Franco Mimmi, "Continue la radicale metamorfosi del sistema televisivo a Madrid."

7. See *Financial Times,* June 18 and 19, 1992.

8. Data compiled from reports in *El País* (January 30, 1994): 49; *El País* (February 12, 1994): 38; *La Vanguardia* (February 6, 1994): 83.

9. See note 6, chapter 11.

10. Recall, too, that publisher Jacques Hachuel gained control of 15 percent of Tele-cinco when he acquired the newspaper *El Independiente* from another institutional owner of Telecinco, ONCE (the national Spanish organization of the blind). See Mimmi, "Continue la radicale metamorfosi," and Katja Fischer, "Spain: *Marketing Week* Report on Spain."

11. *El País* (August 26, 1993): 36.

12. Twenty-five percent of Canal Plus belongs to PRISA, 25 percent to Canal Plus France, about 8 percent to Grupo Eventos, and the rest to major banks (about 16 percent to Banca March, 15 percent to Banco de Bilbao-Vizcaya, 5 percent to Bankinter, and 5 percent to Banco de Zaragoza). PRISA's international investment strategy began in earnest in 1991 with the purchase of an 18 percent stake in the British firm Newspaper Publishing, which publishes *The Independent*. By 1993, PRISA had increased its holdings in Britain, Portugal, France, and other European countries. The shares of Newspaper Publishing held by the Spanish conglomerate have been matched by *La Repubblica* of Italy. PRISA's expansion in the summer of 1993 took it to Mexico, where it joined a consortium of Mexican investors to buy *La Prensa*, the largest newspaper there. As a result of such expansion, PRISA's chairman, Jesús de Polanco, has become Spain's equivalent of Silvio Berlusconi. See *El País* (June 18, 1993): 52–53; "Spanish Media Consortium Buys Mexico's Largest Newspaper," *Business International-Business Latin America*, August 9, 1993.

13. Tom Burns, "Survey of Spain."

14. *Cinco Días,* May 8, 1993. The ownership of these cable/satellite ventures falls to a company called SOGECABLE, which has the same shareholders as Canal Plus. Prior to moving to PRISA, the general director of SOGECABLE worked as a legal consultant for Rupert Murdoch's News International. His name, coincidentally, is Pío Cabanillas, but he is not the former ex-Francoist, former ex-post-Francoist — that irony would be too fantastic.

15. *International TV and Video Almanac,* 655.

16. *El País* (June 5, 1993): 65.

17. John Howkins, "Basques Use TV to Speak Their Own Language"; Jill Fickling, "Spain: From Broadcast Backwater to One of the Most Exciting Markets in Europe," 4.

18. *El País,* August 15, 1993.

19. *El País,* August 4, 1993.

20. "Spain: TV Channels Consider Rate Hikes."

21. Since February 1993, however, SOGECABLE/Canal Plus has used the Astra system (against the preference of the government) to run its subscription services Cinemania and Documania (*Satellite TV Finance,* February 18, 1993). See note 11, chapter 11. In February 1994, the first cable regulation was passed, promising further advances for PRISA.

22. "Hispasat 1B Scoops the Spanish Pool," *Broadcast* (July 30, 1993).

23. "Spain: Only One Bidder for Hispasat," *Broadcast* (June 25, 1993).

24. See note 3, chapter 11.

25. "Spain: Media Revolution Takes Another Turn," *Media Week* (May 28, 1993): 21.

26. Ibid.

27. Ibid.

28. Burns, "Survey of Spain."

29. "Spain: Media Revolution Takes Another Turn," *Media Week.*

30. The national register of viewer attention for 1993 indicated that TVE-1 decreased its share to 31 percent (down one point from 1992) and TVE-2 decreased to 10.8 percent

(down almost four points). Antena-3 received 21.5 percent, followed by Telecinco's 20.3 percent. FORTA companies saw a slight reduction to 14.3 percent for 1993. Figures from *El País,* August 15, 1993.

31. "Spain: Media Revolution Takes Another Turn," *Media Week.* The strongest of the regionals, TV-3 of Catalonia, lost about 3 percent of its audience in 1992, although its new channel, Canal 33, increased viewership. The Catalan channels together continue to rank second in their electronic region. Topping the list are TVE-1 and Telecinco; at the bottom is Antena-3.

32. José María Villagrasa, "Spain: The Emergence of Commercial Television," 396. A French film, Sofres, controlled the ratings industry in Spain in 1994.

33. "Spain: Media Revolution Takes Another Turn," *Media Week.* In December 1993, the government finally adopted the EC directive; it was the last European government to do so.

34. Fickling, "Spain," 4.

35. The three big groups in 1991 were Riera, Fotofilm, and Madrid Films; others included Video Efecto, Zoom TV, Atanor, and Molinare (Spain). All of them expanded into video production facilities after private TV began in Spain. See *Broadcast* (April 19, 1991).

36. Ibid. Such is this spatial hierarchy that the postproduction firm K2000, which had a high-end Quantel Mirage effect unit, had to move from Bilbao to Madrid for want of jobs; ETB could not provide it with enough work.

37. *Broadcast* (April 16, 1993): 42.

38. Ibid.

39. Ibid.

40. OECD, *Economic Surveys,* 123.

41. Keith G. Salmon, *The Modern Spanish Economy: Transformation and Integration into Europe,* 150–57.

42. Ibid., 151. Banesto's largest foreign partner is J. P. Morgan, and it also invests with the Bank of America.

43. Because of accounting problems, it's not clear how much RTVE owes to creditors. Moreover, translating the figure to dollars is difficult given the increased value of the dollar against the peseta. The figure could be anywhere from 1.2 to 2.5 billion dollars after the 1993 budget for RTVE is spent.

44. One program is the Interterritorial Compensation Fund, a Spanish government project; the other is the European Regional Development Fund, created by the EC and administered by the central state.

45. OECD, *Economic Surveys,* 62–66.

46. Ibid., 76–77.

47. Ibid., 77–80.

48. See notes 23 and 24, chapter 12.

49. In 1991, 96.7 pesetas bought you one dollar; in 1993, you had to have 135 pesetas to get a buck.

50. Liabilities increased 130 percent in this period, while assets grew 85 percent. The comparative figure in 1991 was 24.5 billion pesetas in liabilities, 15.8 billion pesetas in assets. See OECD, *Economic Surveys,* 121.

51. Cf. Karle Nordenstreng and H. I. Schiller, eds., *Beyond National Sovereignty: International Communication in the 1990s.*

52. The disappearance of the coordinates has not guaranteed the end of cold war enmities, however. For a compelling critique of the conventional wisdom on this transfor-

mation, see Perry Anderson, *A Zone of Engagement,* 331–35; for a short review of the impact on communications, see Annabelle Sreberny-Mohammadi, "The Global and the Local in International Communications."

53. Cees Hamelink, *Cultural Autonomy in Global Communications.*

54. Armand Mattelart, *Advertising International: The Privatization of Public Space,* 37.

55. Ibid.; cf. John Tomlinson, *Cultural Imperialism.*

56. Armand Mattelart and Michèle Mattelart, *Rethinking Media Theory,* 134.

57. Hamelink, *Cultural Autonomy.*

58. Samir Amin, *Delinking.* For study on precedent and viability of delinking, see Dieter Senghaas, *Aprender de Europa: consideraciones sobre la historia del desarrollo;* D. Senghaas, "Self Reliance and Autocentric Development: Historical Experiences and Contemporary Challenges"; D. Senghaas, "Introduction," *Journal of Peace Research;* and D. Senghaas and U. Menzel, "Autocentric Development despite International Competence Differentials."

59. Aijaz Ahmad, *In Theory,* 11.

Bibliography

Aceves, J. B., E. C. Hansen, and G. Levitas, eds. *Economic Transformation and Steady State Values: Essays in the Ethnography of Spain.* Queens College Publications in Anthropology 2. Flushing, N.Y.: Queens College Publications, 1976.

Ahmad, A. "Jameson's Rhetoric of Otherness and the 'National Allegory.' " *Social Text* 16 (Fall 1987): 3–25.

———. *In Theory.* London: Verso, 1992.

Alcaide Inchausti, J. "Las cuatro Españas económicas y la solidaridad regional." *Economía regional: hechos y tendencias.* Papeles de Economía Española Series 34. Madrid: Fundación para la Investigación Económica y Social, 1988. 62–81.

Amin, S. *Delinking.* New York: Monthly Review Press, 1990.

Anderson, B. *Imagined Communities,* 2d ed. London: Verso, 1991.

Anderson, P. *A Zone of Engagement.* London: Verso, 1992.

Ang, I. "The Battle between Television and Its Audience." In P. Drummond and R. Patterson, eds., *Television in Transition.* London: BFI Publishing, 1986. 250–66.

———. "Culture and Communication: Towards an Ethnographic Critique of Media Consumption in the Transnational Media System." *European Journal of Communication* 5 (1990): 239–60.

———. *Desperately Seeking the Audience.* London: Routledge, 1991.

ANIEL (Asociación Nacional de Industrias Electrónicas). *Memoria 1986.* Madrid: ANIEL, 1987.

———. *Spanish Electronics.* Madrid: ANIEL, n.d.

Anuario estadístico del País Vasco. Vitoria: Gobierno Vasco, 1986.

Arrighi, G., ed. *Semiperipheral Development.* Beverly Hills: Sage Publications, 1985.

Bagdikian, B. *The Media Monopoly,* 4th ed. Boston: Beacon Press, 1992.

Banco de Bilbao. *Renta nacional de España y su distribución provincial 1985.* Madrid: Servicio de Estudios del Banco de Bilbao, 1988.

Bañón, R. "Spain in Transition." Lecture presented at the University of Wisconsin-Madison, October 23, 1985. Supplemental interview, October 23, 1985.

Bar Cendon, A. "¿Normalidad o excepcionalidad?: para una tipología del sistema de partidos en España, 1977–1982." *SISTEMA* 65 (March 1985).

Baran, P., and P. Sweezy. *Monopoly Capital*. New York: Modern Reader, 1966.

Barrasa, G. "Condicionamientos y posibilidades de la tecnología para la televisión." In E. Bustamante and J. Villafañe, eds., *La televisión en España mañana*. Madrid: Siglo XXI/RTVE, 1986. 283–310.

———, and A. López. "España: esfuerzos insuficientes e inconexos." *Telos* (Madrid) (April-June 1985): 80–93.

Bassets, L., ed. *De las ondas rojas a las radios libres*. Barcelona: Editorial Gustavo Gili, 1981.

Berger, J. "The Changing View of Man in the Portrait." *The Moment of Cubism and Other Essays*. London: Weidenfeld & Nicolson, 1969. 41–47.

Besas, P. "Some Clubs Hoist Pirates' Flag." *Variety* (May 9, 1984): 493.

Boletín Oficial del Estado. *Constitución Española*. Madrid: BOE, 1984.

Brand, J. "Andalusia: Nationalism as a Strategy for Autonomy." *Canadian Review of Studies in Nationalism* 15, no. 1–2 (1988).

Braudel, F. *The Perspective of the World: Civilization and Capitalism, 15th-18th Century*, vol. 3. Trans. Sian Reynolds. New York: Harper and Row, 1986.

Burns, T. "Survey of Spain." *London Financial Times* (April 2, 1993).

Bustamante, E. *Los amos de la información en España*. Madrid: Akal, 1982.

———. "Riesgos nacionales, retos internacionales." In E. Bustamante and J. Villafañe, eds., *La televisión en España mañana*. Madrid: Siglo XXI/RTVE, 1986. 251–81.

———. "TV and Public Service in Spain: A Difficult Encounter." *Media, Culture and Society* 11 (1989): 67–87.

Bustamante, E., and J. Villafañe. "La larga marcha de la televisión privada." *Liberación* (March 2, 1985): 2–4.

———, and ———, eds. *La televisión en España mañana: modelos televisivos y opciones ideológicas*. Madrid: Siglo XXI/RTVE, 1986.

Bustamante, E., and R. Zallo, coordinators. *Las industrias culturales en España: grupos multimedia y transnacionales*. Madrid: Akal, 1988.

Camiller, P. "Spanish Socialism in the Atlantic." *New Left Review* 156 (March/April 1986): 5–36.

Campo Urbano, S. J. [Salustiano del Campo], J. F. Tezanos, and W. Santin. "La elite política española y la transición a la Democracia." *SISTEMA* 48 (May 1981).

Carney, J., R. Hudson, and J. Lewis, eds. *Regions in Crisis: New Perspectives in European Regional Theory*. London: Croom Helm, 1980.

Carnoy, M. *The State and Political Theory*. Princeton, N.J.: Princeton University Press, 1984.

Carr, R. *Spain, 1808–1975*, 2d ed. Oxford: Clarendon Press, 1982.

———, and J. P. Fusi. *Spain: Dictatorship to Democracy*. London: Allen & Unwin Publishers, 1984.

Carreras i Verdaguer, C. *Geografía humana de Cataluña*. Barcelona: Oikos-tau, 1985.

Casanova, J. "The Modernization of Spain." *Telos* (United States) 53 (Fall 1982): 29–43.

Castells, M., ed. *High Technology, Space and Society*. Beverly Hills: Sage Publications, 1985.

———, A. Barrera, P. Casal, C. Castaño, P. Escario, J. Melero, and J. Nadal. *Nuevas tecnologías, economía, y sociedad en España*, vols. 1 and 2. Madrid: Gabinete de la Presidencia del Gobierno/Alianza Editorial, 1986.

Clark, R. P. *The Basques: The Franco Years and Beyond*. Reno: University of Nevada Press, 1979.

Compañía Telefónica Nacional de España (CTNE, or Telefónica). *Memoria 1984* (yearly report). Madrid: CTNE, 1985.

Connell, I., and L. Curti. "Popular Broadcasting in Italy and Britain: Some Issues and Problems." In P. Drummond and R. Peterson, eds., *Television in Transition*. London: BFI Publishing, 1986. 87–111.

Corbella, J. M. "Desarrollo socioeconómico y equipamiento de medios de comunicación." *Telos* (Madrid) 5 (January-March 1986): 134–44.

Córdoba y Ordóñez, J. *España autonómica*. Madrid: Editorial Magisterio Español, 1986.

Costa, P.-O. *La crisis de la televisión pública*. Barcelona: Ediciones Paidós, 1986.

Cuadrado Roura, J. R. "Tendencias económico-regionales antes y después de la crisis en España." *Economía regional: hechos y tendencias*. Papeles de Economía Española Series 34. Madrid: Fundación para la Investigación Económica y Social, 1988. 17–61.

——, V. Granados, and J. Aurioles. "Technological Dependency in a Mediterranean Economy: The Case of Spain." In A. Gillespie, ed., *Technological Change and Regional Development*. London: Pion Ltd., 1983. 118–31.

Curran, J. "Mass Media and Democracy: A Reappraisal." In J. Curran and M. Gurevitch, eds., *Mass Media and Society*. London: Edward Arnold, 1991. 82–117.

De Mateo, R., J. M. Corbella, and D. E. Jones. "Structure, Property and Control of Spanish Television (1956–1988)." Paper presented to the 1988 International Television Studies Conference, London, July 20–22, 1988.

Díaz López, C. "Centre-Periphery Structures in Spain: From Historical Conflict to Territorial-Consociational Accommodation?" In Y. Mény and V. Wright, eds., *Centre-Periphery Relations in Western Europe*. London: George Allen & Unwin, 1985. 236–72.

Díaz Mancisidor, A. *Historia de radio Bilbao: antecedentes y primeros años*. Bilbao: Banco de Bilbao, 1983.

Díez, A. "La oposición bloquea las 'mejoras' que el PSOE pretendía introducir en la ley de televisión privada." *El País* (December 11, 1987): 19.

Doglio, D. "El futuro de los servicios públicos radiotelevisivos." In G. Richeri, ed., *La televisión: entre servicio público y negocio*. Barcelona: Gustavo Gili, 1983. 148–63.

DuBoff, R. *Accumulation and Power: An Economic History of the United States*. New York: M. E. Sharpe, 1989.

Durán Herrera, J. J., and M. P. Sánchez Muñoz. *La internacionalización de la empresa española: inversiones españolas en el exterior*. Madrid: Ministerio de Economía y Comercio, 1981.

Dyson, K., and P. Humphreys. *Broadcasting and New Media Policies in Western Europe*. London: Routledge, 1988.

Eardley, S. "Spain: Increased Competition at Home Is Forcing Broadcasters to Rethink Their International Strategy." *Broadcast* (April 19, 1991): 25.

Economía regional: hechos y tendencias. Papeles de Economía Española Series 34. Madrid: Fundación para la Investigación Económica y Social, 1988.

Economía regional: ideas y políticas. Papeles de Economía Española Series 35. Madrid: Fundación para la Investigación Económica y Social, 1988.

Economist Intelligence Unit. *Country Profile: Spain, 1986–87*. London: The Economist Publications, 1986.

El País. Anuario 1985, Anuario 1986, Anuario 1988. Madrid: Prisa, 1986, 1987, 1989.

Elordi, C. "La televisión pronto llegará." *La Calle* 37 (December 5–11, 1978): 56–60.

Emery, W. B. *National and International Systems of Broadcasting*. East Lansing: Michigan State University, 1969.

Federación Española de Municipios y Provincias (FEMP) and Instituto de Estudios de Administración Local (IEAL). "Encuesta de servicios, equipos y producciones de video." *Autonomía local* 12 (February-March). Madrid: FEMP/IEAL, 1985. 33–34.

Fejes, F. "Media Imperialism: An Assessment." *Media, Culture and Society* 3, no. 3 (1981): 281–91.

———. "The United States in Third World Communications: Latin America, 1900–1945." *Journalism Monographs* 88 (November 1983).

Fickling, J. "Spain: From Broadcast Backwater to One of the Most Exciting Markets in Europe." *Broadcast* (April 19, 1991): 4.

"Finance: Torn beyond Repair?" [anon.]. *Economist* 324, no. 7778 (September 26, 1992): 89–90.

Fischer, K. "Spain: *Marketing Week* Report on Spain." *Marketing Week* (November 26, 1993): 4.

Fiske, J. *Television Culture*. London: Methuen, 1987.

Forbes, D. K., and P. J. Rimmer, eds. *Uneven Development and the Geographical Transfer of Value*. Australian National University Research School of Pacific Studies 16. Canberra: Australian National University, 1984.

Fregoso, R. L. "The PEIN in Spain: Telecommunications and Government Policy." *Journal of Communication* 38, no. 1 (Winter 1988): 85–95.

———. *The Information Society in Spain: The Confluence of Cultural and Economic Forces*. Unpublished Ph.D. dissertation, University of California at San Diego, 1988.

García Manrique, E., and C. Ocaña Ocaña. *Geografía humana de Andalucía*. Barcelona: Oikos-tau, 1986.

García San Miguel, L. *Teoría de la transición: un análisis del modelo español, 1973–1978*. Madrid: Editora Nacional, 1981.

Garitaonaindía, C. "La televisión y las comunidades autónomas." *Revista Vasca* 2 (January-April 1982): 143–65.

———, and J. V. Idoyaga. "La televisión en las regiones, nacionalidades, y naciones de Europa." *Jakin* (October 1985).

Garitaonaindía, C., A. Gurrea, J. V. Idoyaga, J. A. Mingolarra, R. Zallo, and S. Zunzunegui. "Estructura y política de comunicación en Euskadi." Paper presented to the 1988 Congress and General Assembly of the International Association for Mass Communication Research, Barcelona, July 25–29, 1988.

Garnham, N. *Capitalism and Communication: Global Culture and the Economics of Information*. Media, Culture and Society Series. London: Sage Publications, 1990.

Giddens, A. "Time, Space and Regionalisation." In D. Gregory and J. Urry, eds., *Social Relations and Spatial Structures*. London: Macmillan, 1985. 265–95.

———. *The Consequences of Modernity*. Stanford, Calif.: Stanford University Press, 1990.

———. *Modernity and Self-Identity*. London: Polity Press, 1991.

Giner, S. "Political Economy, Legitimation and the State in Southern Europe." In R. Hudson and J. Lewis, eds., *Uneven Development in Southern Europe: Studies in Accumulation, Class, Migration and the State*. London: Methuen, 1985. 309–50.

Gitlin, T. *Inside Prime Time*. New York: Pantheon, 1983.

Golding, P., and G. Murdock. "Privatizing Pleasure." *Marxism Today* (October 1983).

Gómez Piñeiro, F. J. *Geografía de Euskal Herria*. Barcelona: Oikos-tau, 1985.

Gore, C. *Regions in Question*. London: Methuen, 1984.

Gramsci, A. "Analysis of Situations, Relations of Force." In A. Mattelart and S. Siegelaub, eds., *Communication and Class Struggle*, vol. 1. New York: International General, 1979. 108–12.

Gregory, D., and J. Urry, eds. *Social Relations and Spatial Structures*. London: Macmillan, 1985.

Guback, T., and T. Varis. *Transnational Communication and Cultural Industries.* Paris: UNESCO, 1982.

Gubern, R. "Megacomunicación vs. mesocomunicación." *Telos* (Madrid) 3 (July-September, 1985): 6–7.

Gunder Frank, A. "No End to History! History to No End?" In K. Nordenstreng and H. I. Schiller, eds., *Beyond National Sovereignty: International Communication in the 1990s.* Norwood, N.J.: Ablex Publishing Corporation, 1993. 3–27.

Gunther, R. "Constitutional Change in Contemporary Spain." In K. G. Banting and R. Simeon, eds., *The Politics of Constitutional Change in Industrial Societies: Redesigning the State.* London: MacMillan, 1985. 42–70.

———. "The Spanish Socialist Party: From Clandestine Opposition to Party of Government." In S. Payne, ed., *The Politics of Democratic Spain.* Chicago: The Chicago Council on Foreign Relations, 1986. 8–49.

Hadjimichalis, C. *Uneven Development and Regionalism: State, Territory and Class in Southern Europe.* London: Croom Helm Ltd., 1987.

Hägerstrand, T. "Decentralization and Radio Broadcasting: On the 'Possibility Space' of a Communication Technology." *European Journal of Communication* 1, no. 1 (March 1986): 7–26.

Hall, S. "The Emergence of Cultural Studies and the Crisis of the Humanities." *October* 53 (1990): 11–23.

Hamelink, C. J., *Cultural Autonomy in Global Communications.* London: Longman, 1983.

———. "Is Information Technology Neutral?" In J. Becker, G. Hedebro, and L. Paldán, eds., *Communication and Domination.* Norwood, N.J.: Ablex Publishing Corporation, 1986. 16–24.

Harvey, D. *The Limits to Capital.* Chicago: University of Chicago Press, 1982.

Hedebro, G. *Communications and Social Change in Developing Nations.* Ames: Iowa State University Press, 1982.

Herman, E., and N. Chomsky. *Manufacturing Consent.* New York: Pantheon, 1988.

Hills, J. *Deregulating Telecomms: Competition and Control in the United States, Japan, and Britain.* Westport, Conn.: Quorum Books, 1986.

"Hispasat 1B Scoops the Spanish Pool" [anon.]. *Broadcast* (July 30, 1993).

Hobsbawm, E. J. *Nations and Nationalism since 1780: Programme, Myth, Reality,* 2d ed. Cambridge: Cambridge University Press, 1992.

Hooper, J. *The Spaniards: A Portrait of the New Spain.* London: Penguin, 1987.

Howkins, J. "Basques Use TV to Speak Their Own Language." *Intermedia* 11, no. 3 (1983) 20–25.

Hudson, R., and J. Lewis, eds. *Uneven Development in Southern Europe: Studies in Accumulation, Class, Migration and the State.* London: Methuen, 1985.

Huneeus, C. "Transition to Democracy in Spain. Unión de Centro Democrático as a 'Consociational Party': An Exploratory Analysis." In *European Consortium for Political Research.* Brussels, Joint Session of Workshops, April 17–21, 1979.

Idoyaga, J. V. *Televisiones regionales en Europa.* Unpublished thesis, University of the Basque Country, School of Information Sciences, 1983.

International TV and Video Almanac. New York: Quigley, 1993.

Iseppi, F. "Il sogno italo-americano delle televisioni private." In G. Richeri, ed., *Il video negli anni 80.* Bari: De Donato, 1981.

Izquierda Unida. *Programa Electoral de Izquierda Unida.* Madrid: IU, 1986. (Political program of the United Left Party of Spain).

J. Walter Thompson. *La inversión publicitaria en España 1987*. Madrid: J. Walter Thompson, 1988.

Jackson, G. "Socialists: Front and Center." *The Nation* (March 15, 1986): 854–56.

Jameson, F., "Third World Literature in the Era of Multinational Capital." *Social Text* 15 (Fall 1986): 65–88.

———. "Cognitive Mapping." In C. Nelson and L. Grossberg, eds., *Marxism and the Interpretation of Culture*. Urbana: Illinois University Press, 1988. 347–60.

Javaloys, J. G. *La autonomía regional*. Madrid: Ediciones ICE, 1978.

Jessop, B. "Corporatism, Parliamentarism and Social Democracy." In P. C. Schmitter and G. Lehmbruch, eds., *Trends Towards Corporatist Intermediation*. London: Sage Publishers, 1979. 185–212.

Kenwood, A. G., and A. L. Lougheed. *The Growth of the International Economy, 1820–1990*, 3d ed. London: Routledge, 1992.

Kuhn, R., ed. *Broadcasting and Politics in Western Europe*. London: Frank Cass & Co., 1985.

Lara, F., J. A. Pérez Millan, and P. Pérez Castro. "La imagen cinematográfica ante el reto de la imagen electrónica." In Raúl Rispa, ed., *Nuevas tecnologías en la vida cultural española*. Madrid: Fundesco, 1985. 175.

Lefebvre, H. "Reflections on the Politics of Space." Trans. M. J. Enders. *Antipode* 8, no. 2 (May 1976): 30–37.

Lessing, L. "The Electronics Era." *Fortune* (July 1951): 76 +.

Lipietz, A. *Mirages and Miracles: The Crisis of Global Fordism*. Trans. D. Macey. London: Verso, 1987.

López Aranguren, E. *La conciencia regional en el proceso autonómico español*. Madrid: Centros de Investigación Sociológicos, 1983.

López Escobar, E. "Spain Waits for Private TV." *Intermedia* 2, no. 6 (November 1983): 41–44.

———, and A. Faus Belau. "Broadcasting in Spain: A History of Heavy-handed State Control." In R. Kuhn, ed., *Broadcasting and Politics in Western Europe*. London: Frank Cass & Co., 1985. 122–36.

Mac Laughlin, J. "Reflections on Nations as 'Imagined Communities.'" *Journal of Multilingual and Multicultural Development* 9, no. 5 (1988): 449–57.

Maistre, G. *Geographie des mass-media*. Montreal: Les Presse de l'Universite du Quebec, 1976.

Mandel, E. "Dialectics of Class and Region in Belgium." *New Left Review* 20 (1963): 5–31.

———. "Capitalism and Regional Disparities." *Southeast Economy and Society* 1, no. 1 (1976): 41–47.

Maravall, J. M. *La política de la transición*. Madrid: Taurus, 1981.

Massey, D. *Spatial Divisions of Labor*. New York: Methuen, 1984.

Mattelart, A. "For a Class Analysis of Communication." In A. Mattelart and S. Siegelaub, eds., *Communication and Class Struggle*, vol. 1. New York: International General, 1979. 23–70.

———. "For a Class and Group Analysis of Popular Communication Practices." In A. Mattelart and S. Siegelaub, eds., *Communication and Class Struggle*, vol. 2. New York: International General, 1983. 17–67.

———. *Advertising International: The Privatization of Public Space*. Trans. Michael Chanan. London: Comedia/Routledge, 1991.

———, and M. Mattelart. *Rethinking Media Theory: Signposts and New Directions*. Trans. J. A. Cohen and M. Urquidi. Minneapolis: University of Minnesota Press, 1992.

Mattelart, A., X. Delcourt, and M. Mattelart. *International Image Markets*. London: Comedia, 1984.

Maxwell, R. "The Image Is Gold: Value, the Audience Commodity, and Fetishism." *Journal of Film and Video* (Spring-Summer 1991): 29–45.

Mény, Y., and V. Wright, eds. *Centre-Periphery Relations in Western Europe*. London: George Allen & Unwin, 1985.

Mercadé, F. "El marco ideológico de los nacionalismos en España." In C. Dupláa and G. Barnes, eds., *Las nacionalidades del Estado Español: una problemática cultural*. Minneapolis: Institute for the Study of Ideologies and Literature, 1986.

Miege, B. *The Capitalization of Cultural Production*. New York: International General, 1989.

Mimmi, F. "Continue la radicale metamorfosi del sistema televisivo a Madrid." *Il Sole 24 Ore* (July 16, 1993): 27.

Ministerio de Cultura (Spanish Ministry of Culture). *Encuesta de comportamiento cultural de los españoles*. Madrid: Secretaria General Técnica del Ministerio de Cultura, 1985.

———. *Hábitos culturales*. Análisis e Investigaciones Culturales 30. Madrid: Secretaria General Técnica del Ministerio de Cultura, 1987.

Ministerio de Industria y Energía (Spanish Ministry of Industry and Energy). *La inovación en la Comunidad Económica Europea: organismos y programas*. Madrid: Ministerio de Industria y Energía, 1986.

Mitxelena, K. *La lengua vasca*. Durango (Vizcaya): Leopoldo Zugaza, Editor, 1977.

Moragas i Spà, M. "Mass Communication and Political Change in Spain, 1975–1980." Trans. R. Astroff. In E. Wartella and D. C. Whitney, eds., *Mass Communication Review Yearbook*, vol. 4. Beverly Hills: Sage, 1983.

———, and M. C. Piulats. *Local Communication in Catalonia (1975–1988)*. Barcelona: Diputació de Barcelona, 1988.

Morley, D., and K. Robins. "Spaces of Identity: Communications Technologies and the Reconfiguration of Europe." *Screen* 30, no. 4 (Autumn 1989).

Morodo, R. *La transición política*. Madrid: Editorial TECNOS, 1984.

Mujal-León, E. "The Foreign Policy of the Spanish Government." In S. Payne, ed., *The Politics of Democratic Spain*. Chicago: The Chicago Council on Foreign Relations, 1986. 197–245.

Murdock, G. "Blindspots about Western Marxism: A Reply to Dallas Smythe." *Canadian Journal of Political and Social Theory* 2, no. 2 (1978): 109–19.

———. "The Role of Radio and Television in Shaping the Form and the Contents of Audience Cultures: Broadcasting and Cultural Diversity." *The State's Role vis-à-vis the Culture Industries*. Strasbourg: The Council of Europe, 1980. 121–30.

———. "Large Corporations and the Control of the Communications Industries." In M. Gurevitch et al., eds., *Culture, Society and the Media*. New York: Methuen, 1982. 118–50.

———. "Television and Citizenship: In Defense of Public Broadcasting." In A. Tomlinson, ed., *Consumption, Identity, and Style*. London: Routledge, 1990. 77–101.

Nadal, J. *El fracaso de la revolución industrial en España, 1814–1913*, 2d ed. Barcelona: Editorial Ariel, 1977.

Naylon, J. *Andalusia*. Problem Regions of Europe series. Oxford: Oxford University Press, 1975.

Nogueira, D. "Unrelated Diversity." *The Business of Film* (January/February 1991): 9.

Nordenstreng, K., and T. Varis. *Television Traffic — A One Way Street?* Paris: UNESCO, 1974.

Nordenstreng, K., and H. I. Schiller, eds. *Beyond National Sovereignty: International Communication in the 1990s*. Norwood, N.J.: Ablex Publishing Corporation, 1993.

ó Caollaí, M. "Cultural Domination in Europe: The Case of Ireland." In J. Becker, G. Hedebro, and L. Paldán, eds., *Communication and Domination*. Norwood, N.J.: Ablex Publishing Corporation, 1986. 104–13.

Offe, C. *Disorganized Capitalism*. Cambridge: MIT Press, 1985.

Organization for Economic Cooperation and Development (OECD). *Changing Market Structures in Telecommunications*. North Holland: Elsevier Science Publishers, 1984. 369–73.

———. *OECD Economic Surveys, Spain, 1993*. Paris: OECD, 1993.

Owen, B. M., J. H. Beebe, and W. G. Manning. *Television Economics*. Lexington, Mass.: D. C. Heath, 1974.

Parés i Maicas, M., L. Badia, and I. M. Araiko. *Spanish Bibliography on Mass Communication*. Bellaterra, Barcelona: Publicaciones de la Universitat Autònoma de Barcelona, 1988.

Pavolini, L. "Communicazioni di masa e democrazia: una nuova fase della reforma." In G. Vacca, ed., *Communicazioni di massa e democrazia*. Rome: Editori Riuniti, 1980.

Payne, S. "The Elections of June 1986." In S. Payne, ed., *The Politics of Democratic Spain*. Chicago: The Chicago Council on Foreign Relations, 1986. 246–55.

Pendakur, M. "Political Economy and Ethnography: Transformations in an Indian Village." In J. Wasko, V. Mosco, and M. Pendakur, eds., *Illuminating the Blindspots: Essays Honoring Dallas W. Smythe*. Norwood, N.J.: Ablex Publishing Corporation, 1993. 82–108.

Pérez Ornia, J. R. "El video: de la producción al consumo." *Autonomía local* 12 (February-March). Madrid: FEMP/IEAL, 1985. 23–24.

Piemme, J. M. *La televisión: un medio en cuestión*. Barcelona: Editorial Fontanella, 1980.

Poulantzas, N. *La Crise des Dictatures: Portugal, Grèce, Espagne*. Paris: Maspéro, 1975.

Prado Pico, E. "El movimiento por la libertad de emisión en España." In L. Bassets, ed., *De las ondas rojas a las radios libres*. Barcelona: Editorial Gustavo Gili, 1981. 237–55.

———. "La radio privada a Catalunya." *Arrel* 3 (special issue, April-September 1982): 49–53.

———. "La televisión comunitaria en Cataluña." *Telos* (Madrid) 2 (April/June 1985): 53–58.

Preston, P. *The Triumph of Democracy in Spain*. London: Methuen, 1986.

Radiotelevisión Española. *Plan Integral de Mecanización e Informatización* (PIMI). Madrid: RTVE, Gabinete de Planificación, November 1983.

———. *Anuario 1984, Anuario 1985*. Madrid: RTVE, 1985, 1986.

"Regionals Play Wildcard" [anon.]. *Television Business International* (December/January 1990–91): 46.

Richeri, G. "Television from Service to Business: European Tendencies and the Italian Case." In P. Drummond and R. Paterson, eds., *Television in Transition*. London: BFI Publishing, 1985–86. 21–35.

———. "Crisis de televisión pública y nuevas tendencias en los sistemas europeos." In E. Bustamante and J. Villafañe, eds., *La televisión en España mañana: modelos televisivos y opciones ideológicas*. Madrid: Siglo XXI/RTVE, 1986. 23–38.

———, ed. *La televisión: entre servicio público y negocio*. Barcelona: Editorial Gustavo Gili, 1983.

Robins, K., "Reimagined Communities? European Image Spaces, beyond Fordism." *Cultural Studies* 3, no. 2 (May 1989): 145–65.

———. "Global Times." *Marxism Today* (December 1989): 20–27.

Rodriguez, C. "Media for Participation and Social Change: Local Television in Catalonia." *ComDev News* (Fall 1990/Winter 1991): 4+.

Roncagliolo, R. "Transnational Communication and Culture." In R. Atwood and E. McAnany, eds., *Communications and Latin American Society.* Madison: University of Wisconsin Press, 1986. 79–88.

Rossant, J. "One Day Panic, Next Day Sales." *Business Week* (October 26, 1992): 49–50.

Rowland, W. D. "The Illusion of Fulfillment: The Broadcast Reform Movement." *Journalism Monographs* 79 (December 1982).

Salmon, K. G. *The Modern Spanish Economy: Transformation and Integration into Europe.* London: Pinter Publishers, 1991.

Sánchez Muñoz, P. *Dependencia tecnológica española.* Madrid: Ministerio de Economía y Hacienda, Secretaria de Estado de Comercio, 1984.

Santamaría, J., ed. *Transición a la democracia en el sur de Europa y América Latina.* Madrid: Centro de Investigaciones Sociológicas, 1981.

Scannell, P. "Public Service Broadcasting: The History of a Concept." In A. Goodwin and G. Whannel, eds., *Understanding Television.* London: Routledge, 1990. 11–29.

Schiller, D. *Telematics and Government.* Norwood, N.J.: Ablex Publishing Corporation, 1982.

——. "How to Think about Information." In V. Mosco and J. Wasko, eds., *The Political Economy of Information.* Madison: University of Wisconsin Press, 1988. 44–75.

Schiller, H. I. *Mass Communication and American Empire.* New York: Augustus M. Kelley, 1969.

——. *Communication and Cultural Domination.* New York: International Arts & Sciences Press, 1976.

——. *Who Knows: Information in the Age of the Fortune 500.* Norwood, N.J.: Ablex Publishing Corporation, 1981.

——. *Information and the Crisis Economy.* Norwood, N.J.: Ablex Publishing Corporation, 1984.

——. *Culture Inc.* New York: Oxford University Press, 1989.

Schlesinger, P. "On National Identity: Some Conceptions and Misconceptions Criticized." *Social Science Information* 26, no. 2 (June 1987): 219–64.

Schulte, H. F. *The Spanish Press, 1470–1966: Print, Power, Politics.* Urbana: University of Illinois Press, 1968.

Seers, D., and K. Öström, eds. *The Crisis of the European Regions.* London: Macmillan, 1983.

Senghaas, D. "Introduction." *Journal of Peace Research* 4, no. 12 (1975): 249–56.

——. "Self Reliance and Autocentric Development: Historical Experiences and Contemporary Challenges." *Bulletin of Peace Proposals* 1 (1980): 44–51.

——. *Aprender de Europa: consideraciones sobre la historia del desarrollo.* Trans. C. Santiago. Barcelona: Editorial Alfa, 1985.

——, and U. Menzel. "Autocentric Development despite International Competence Differentials." *Economics* 21 (1980): 7–35.

Shabad, G. "After Autonomy: The Dynamics of Regionalism in Spain." In S. Payne, ed., *The Politics of Democratic Spain.* Chicago: The Chicago Council on Foreign Relations, 1986. 111–80.

Sinova, J. *La gran mentira.* Madrid: Planeta, 1983.

Smith, A. *The Shadow in the Cave.* Urbana: University of Illinois Press, 1973.

Smythe, D. "Communications: Blindspot of Western Marxism." *Canadian Journal of Political and Social Theory* 1, no. 3 (1977): 1–27.

———. *Dependency Road: Communications, Capitalism, Consciousness and Canada.* Norwood, N.J.: Ablex Publishing Corporation, 1981.

"Spain: Columbia Tristar Renews Licensing Deal with FORTA" [anon.]. *Broadcast* (March 12, 1993): 16.

"Spain: Media Revolution Takes Another Turn" [anon.]. *Media Week* (May 28, 1993): 21.

"Spain: Only One Bidder for Hispasat" [anon.]. *Broadcast* (June 25, 1993): 13.

"Spain: TV Channels Consider Rate Hikes" [anon.]. *Advertising Age* (January 17, 1994).

Sreberny-Mohammadi, A. "The Global and the Local in International Communications." In J. Curran and M. Gurevitch, eds., *Mass Media and Society*. London: Edward Arnold, 1991. 118–38.

Steinberg, V. "La revolución del video: ver lo que uno quiere cuando uno quiere." *Cambio 16* (June 9, 1986): 148–54.

Stevenson, R. W. "Spain and Portugal in Devaluations." *New York Times* (May 14, 1993): D2.

Sussman, G., and J. A. Lent, eds. *Transnational Communications: Wiring the Third World.* Newbury Park, Calif.: Sage Publications, 1991.

Tamames, R., and T. Clegg. "Spain: Regional Autonomy and the Democratic Transition." In *Regionalization in France, Italy and Spain*. London: London School of Economics, International Centre for Economics and Related Disciplines, 1984.

Tecnos. *Legislación básica de derecho de la información*. Madrid: Editorial Tecnos, 1985.

Televisió de Catalunya. *Publicación Informativa 1986*. Barcelona: TV-3, 1987.

Thomas, T. "Spain Joins the World." *Economist* (March 30, 1986): 3–30.

Tomlinson, J. *Cultural Imperialism*. London: Pinter Publishers, 1991.

Torrents, N. "Cinema and the Media after the Death of Franco." In C. Abel and N. Torrents, eds., *Spain: Conditional Democracy*. London: Croom Helm Ltd., 1984.

Tucker, I. "Spain: Fierce Competition Forces Change." *Banking World* 9, no. 5 (May 1991): 36–37.

U.S. Department of Commerce. "The Spanish Industrial Reconversion and Development Program." Washington, D.C.: International Trade Administration, October 1985.

Van Dinh, T., and R. Porter. "Is the Concept of National Sovereignty Outdated?" In J. Becker, G. Hedebro, and L. Paldán, eds., *Communication and Domination*. Norwood, N.J.: Ablex Publishing Corporation, 1986. 120–28.

Varis, T. *Flow of Television Programmes in Western Europe.* Series no. 14. Tampere, Finland: TAPRI/University of Tampere, 1984.

———. "Patterns of Television Program Flow in International Relations." In J. Becker, G. Hedebro, and L. Paldán, eds., *Communication and Domination*. Norwood, N.J.: Ablex Publishing Corporation, 1986. 55–65.

Vázquez Barquero, A., and M. Hebbert. "Spain: Economy and State in Transition." In R. Hudson and J. Lewis, eds., *Uneven Development in Southern Europe: Studies in Accumulation, Class, Migration and the State*. London: Methuen, 1985. 284–308.

Vázquez Montalbán, M. *La penetración americana en España*. Madrid: Editorial Cuadernos para el Diálogo, 1974.

———. *Crónica sentimental de la transición*. Barcelona: Planeta, 1985.

———. "Año de consolidaciones." *El País Anuario 1986*. Madrid: Prisa, 1987. 64.

Vicens Vives, J. *An Economic History of Spain*. Princeton: Princeton University Press, 1969.

Vilar, P. *Spain: A Brief History*. Oxford: Pergamon Press, 1967.

Villafañe, J. "Decentralización y servicio público." In E. Bustamante and J. Villafañe, eds., *La televisión en España mañana: modelos televisivos y opciones ideológicas*. Madrid: Siglo XXI/RTVE, 1986. 185–207.

Villagrasa, J. M. "Spain: The Emergence of Commercial Television." In A. Silj, ed., *The New Television in Europe*. London: John Libbey, 1992. 337–426.

Virseda, F. "Los argumentos jurídicos de la Ley del Tercer Canal." In E. Bustamante and J. Villafañe, eds., *La televisión en España mañana: modelos televisivos y opciones ideológicas*. Madrid: Siglo XXI/RTVE, 1986. 244–47.

Wallerstein, I. *The Modern World System*. New York: Academic Press, 1974.

——. *Historical Capitalism*. London: Verso, 1983.

Warner, A. "Down, but Not Out." *Banker* 143, no. 803 (January 1993): 18.

Wasko, J., V. Mosco, and M. Pendakur, eds. *Illuminating the Blindspots: Essays Honoring Dallas W. Smythe*. Norwood, N.J.: Ablex Publishing Corporation, 1993.

Webster, F. "The Politics of New Technology." *Socialist Register 1985/86*. London: Merlin Press, 1986. 385–413.

Webster, J. "Kuwait Investment: Spanish Inquisition." *International Management* 47, no. 9 (October 1992): 60–62.

——. "Eye on Europe: Spain-Hispasat Hitch Puts TV Project on Hold." *International Management* 48, no. 3 (April 1993): 26.

West, C. "The New Cultural Politics of Difference." *October* 53 (1990): 93–109.

Williams, A., ed. *Southern Europe Transformed*. London: Harper Row Publishers, 1984.

Williams, R. *Television: Technology and Cultural Form*. New York: Schocken, 1974.

"World Television: The Inexorable Spread" [anon.]. *Screen Digest* (February 1991): 33–40.

Interviews

Autonomous University of Barcelona
Toni Estupiñá, Center for Documentation and Research, School of Information Sciences
Miquel de Moragas i Spá, professor, School of Information Sciences
Emili Prado Pico, director, Department of Audiovisual Communication

Basque government
José Antonio Mingolarra, Department of Culture

Basque Radio and Television Corporation (EITB)
Julián Pérez Delgado, acting managing director

Canal Sur (Andalusian TV Corporation)
Juan Luis Manfredi, head of program acquisition

Catalan government
Agustí Gallart Teixidó, chief, Cabinet of Radio-Television

Catalan Corporation of Radio and Television (CCRTV)
Lluís Ferrando, program acquisitions
Lluís Grau i Bruni, engineer, production and transmission
Jaume Pérez i Sants, administrative director

Estudio General de Medios, Audience Measurement
Juan Luis Méndez Rodríguez, managing director

Fundesco (Foundation for the Advancement of Social Communication)
Enrique Bustamante, professor and researcher

Galician Radio and Television Corporation (CRTVG)
    Antonio Posse Peña, director of engineering
    Jaime Souza Porto, director, business administration

Spanish government (executive)
    Francisco Virseda Barca, director general of social communication

Spanish Television (TVE)
    Virgilio Liras Muro, subdirector, technical management

Telemadrid (Madrid TV Corporation)
    Arsenio Muñoz González, acting managing director

Valencian Radio and Television Corporation (CRTVV)
    Amadeu Fabregat, director general
    Hortensia Moriones i Almaraz, head, Technical Council

Index

ABC, 44, 57
abortion, 41
advertising, 23–24, 27–28; as percentage of GNP, 171 n. 6; and regional inequality, 124–31; regionalization of, 123–24; revenues, 123, 171 n. 5; and violations of law, 143
AEG-Telefunken, 27, 73
Ahmad, Aijaz, 153, 158 n. 48
Alcaide Inchausti, Julio, 20, 128–29
Alcázar, El, 44
Alfonso XIII, 18
Alianza Popular, xxv, 35, 59–60, 69–70, 83–84, 141. *See also* Manuel Fraga
American Cable, 77
American Telephone and Telegraph (AT&T), xxxiv, 27, 29, 85
Anaya, 93, 138
Andalusia, xxiii, 14–15, 19, 21–22, 43, 98, 106, 148, 159 n. 14
Andalusian Television (Canal Sur) of Radiotelevisión de Andalucía (RTVA), 110, 129–30, 134; conflict with Catalan Television, 130–31; and foreign programming, 173 n. 26
Ang, Ien, xxxii–xxxiii
ANIEL, 73
Antena-3: radio, 52–53, 57; television, 92–94, 138, 140–43, 146, 167 n. 3, 173 n. 6; television program

production, 144; television ratings, xxiv, 174 n. 30
anticommunism, 18–19
Anticorruption Committee, 36
Aragón, 14–15, 118–19, 121; agreement with Antena-3, 140
Arana Goiri, Sabino, 14
Arias Salgado, Gabriel, 105
Aribau, Carles, 16
Arrighi, Giovanni, 19
Asensio, Antonio, 138, 141, 173 n. 6. *See also* Antena-3; Grupo Zeta
Association of European Journalists, 68
Asturias, 14–15, 106, 118–19
audience, xxii; commodity exchange of, 126–31; commodity form of, 122; maximization of, 120, 125; measurements of, xxiv, 140, 171 n. 8, 172 n. 9, 174 n. 30; space, 126; war of audiences, 123–24. *See also* electronic regions
autonomy, xxx, xxxvii, 15; official, 12–13, 17–18, 21–22
Avui, 110

Balearic Islands, 14–15, 76, 121
Banca March, 80, 92, 174 n. 12; partnership with National Westminster Bank, 146
Banco Central Hispano, 138

Richard Maxwell teaches international communication and political economy of media and culture in the Department of Radio-TV-Film at Northwestern University.